Discourse Markers and Modal Particles

Pragmatics & Beyond New Series (P&BNS)

Pragmatics & Beyond New Series is a continuation of Pragmatics & Beyond and its Companion Series. The New Series offers a selection of high quality work covering the full richness of Pragmatics as an interdisciplinary field, within language sciences.

For an overview of all books published in this series, please see
http://benjamins.com/catalog/pbns

Volume 234

Discourse Markers and Modal Particles. Categorization and description
Edited by Liesbeth Degand, Bert Cornillie and Paola Pietrandrea

Discourse Markers and Modal Particles

Categorization and description

Edited by

Liesbeth Degand
Université catholique de Louvain

Bert Cornillie
University of Leuven

Paola Pietrandrea
Université de Tours & LLL CNRS

John Benjamins Publishing Company
Amsterdam / Philadelphia

The paper used in this publication meets the minimum requirements of the American National Standard for Information Sciences – Permanence of Paper for Printed Library Materials, ANSI Z39.48-1984.

Library of Congress Cataloging-in-Publication Data

Discourse Markers and Modal Particles : Categorization and description / Edited by
     Liesbeth Degand, Bert Cornillie and Paola Pietrandrea.
p. cm. (Pragmatics & Beyond New Series, ISSN 0922-842X ; v. 234)
Includes bibliographical references and index.
1. Discourse markers. 2. Grammar, Comparative and general--Particles. 3. Pragmatics.
     I. Degand, Liesbeth. II. Cornillie, Bert, 1975- III. Pietrandrea, Paola.
P302.35.D58   2013
401'.41--dc23
                                        2013028947
ISBN 978 90 272 5639 3 (Hb ; alk. paper)
ISBN 978 90 272 7122 8 (Eb)

John Benjamins Publishing Co. · P.O. Box 36224 · 1020 ME Amsterdam · The Netherlands
John Benjamins North America · P.O. Box 27519 · Philadelphia PA 19118-0519 · USA

Table of contents

Modal particles and discourse markers: Two sides of the same coin?
Introduction   1
Liesbeth Degand, Bert Cornillie and Paola Pietrandrea

"Same same but different" – Modal particles, discourse markers
and the art (and purpose) of categorization   19
Gabriele Diewald

A radical construction grammar perspective on the modal
particle-discourse particle distinction   47
Kerstin Fischer and Maria Alm

Analyzing modal adverbs as modal particles and discourse markers   89
Karin Aijmer

Modal particles, discourse markers, and adverbs with *lt*-suffix in Estonian   107
Annika Valdmets

Modal particles: Problems in defining a category   133
Steven Schoonjans

From TAM to discourse: The role of information status
in North-Western Italian *già* 'already'   163
Mario Squartini

The fuzzy boundaries between discourse marking and modal marking   191
Maria Josep Cuenca

From discourse markers to modal/final particles: What the position
reveals about the continuum   217
Katsunobu Izutsu and Mitsuko Narita Izutsu

Index   237

Modal particles and discourse markers: Two sides of the same coin?

Introduction

Liesbeth Degand, Bert Cornillie and Paola Pietrandrea
Université catholique de Louvain, University of Leuven
and Université de Tours & LLL CNRS

In this introductory chapter, we situate the investigation of the intersection between modal particles (MP) and discourse markers (DM) within the wider context of categorization work in linguistics. We examine the definitions provided in the literature for DMs and MPs, and review different reasons for the possible confusion between the two classes, among which their functional proximity and diachronic relation. The overview of the contributions to the volume shows that it is nevertheless possible to precise whether and to what extent DMs and MPs constitute one single class. According to the parameters taken into account, authors will tend to group them into a single (pragmatic) class or into two distinct classes.

1. Aims

The aim of the present volume is to investigate the intersection between modal particles (MP) and discourse markers (DM), and to discuss whether or not it is possible to draw a line between these two types of linguistic expressions. The authors contributing to this volume have been asked to be explicit about how they categorize DMs and MPs. This common question has been addressed throughout all chapters and is hence the red thread of this book.

Over recent years, DMs and MPs have received quite some attention in the linguistic literature, but mostly independently from one another (but see e.g. Hartmann 1986; Traugott 2007; Haselow 2011). The chapters in this book all go beyond the statement that DM/MP are a fuzzy category that is difficult to describe, and explicitly address the complexity of categorizing multifunctional expressions. Indeed, as we will see, the authors hold the opinion that the analysis of the distributional constraints imposed on specific markers (in given languages) allows for the description of those features determining the uses of MPs and DMs. This should bring us closer to consistent criteria for a refined categorization of both types of linguistic expressions.

2.   On categorization and linguistic categories

The central question in this book concerns the categorization of linguistic expressions: are MPs and DMs separate linguistic categories, or not? Are MPs a subtype of DMs, or should both be seen as subcategories of the more encompassing class of pragmatic markers (Fraser 1996) or discourse particles, as they both share a general indexical function (Fischer 2006)? If the latter is the case, what is it that distinguishes DMs from MPs? And, what makes it so difficult to tell them apart?

Before entering into the details of the categorization options for DMs and MPs, we would like to situate this research within the wider context of categorization work in linguistics. In his book with the telling title *Linguistic categorization*, Taylor (2003, 4) aims to uncover the "double role of categorization in the study of language", thus referring to "the process by which people, in using language, are categorizing their experience of the world", but also to "the categories of language itself", which appear to be structured much along the same lines as the non-linguistic ones. As to the principles for the formation of categories (be they linguistic or not), Eleanor Rosch (1978) in her seminal study "Principles of categorization" proposes two general ones: the principle of "cognitive economy" and the principle of "perceived world structure". "The first has to do with the function of category systems and asserts that the task of category systems is to provide maximum information with the least cognitive effort." (Rosch 1978, 28). The second principle states that the perceived world comes as structured information rather than as arbitrary or unpredictable attributes. Thus maximum information with least cognitive effort is achieved if categories map the perceived world structure as closely as possible. This condition can be achieved either by the mapping of categories to given attribute structures or by the definition or redefinition of attributes to render a given set of categories appropriately structured.

These principles lie at the basis of the notion of 'prototype categories' as defined within cognitive linguistics. Typical of this approach is the notion of 'fuzzy boundaries', since it is often the case that categories have no clear boundaries. There may be borderline cases, where clear, unambiguous categorization is not possible. Thus, "an entity may be a marginal example of more than one category, but a good example of none" (Taylor 2003, 6).

The same applies to grammatical categories. Thus, determining whether a linguistic expression belongs to one grammatical class or another is not always straightforward. The topic of study of this book, i.e. DMs and MPs, is a case in point. Analysing whether they belong to the same grammatical category, or not, amounts to determining whether they display the morphological, distributional and semantic properties of that category. The most prototypical members will display all of these properties, while other members will be less typical (less focal) "and yet others are situated in the borderline area of the category, exhibiting grammatical properties of two or more categories." (Company 2002, 201). Croft (2000, 2001) advocates a 'constructionalist' definition of categories (see also Fischer and Alm in this volume), where "the constructions are the primitive elements of syntactic representation; categories are derived from constructions" (Croft 2000, 84). He formulates the following hypothesis: "[t]he internal category structure (e.g. prototype and extensions) of a grammatical category is provided by the universal theory of grammar, while its boundaries are provided by the particular language grammar" (Croft 2000, 91).

The contributions in this volume regarding the categorization of DMs and MPs in several (typologically distinct languages) seem to offer evidence for this hypothesis in that some particular languages (German, Swedish, Estonian) seem to display a clear boundary between MPs and DMs, while others do so less (Catalan, French, Italian, Japanese).

3. On the categorization of modal particles and discourse markers

Both DMs and MPs are multifunctional linguistic expressions "functioning in cognitive, expressive, social, and textual domains" (Schiffrin 2001, 54). But MPs have often been described in a more restricted sense, i.e. as specifying "the relationship between speaker and hearer" (Hansen 1998, 42) or "to signal one's understanding of what the situation is all about with respect to the argumentative relations built up in the current situation" (Fischer 2007, 47), or as referring back to a communicately given propositional or illocutionary entity (Diewald 2006, this volume). On the other hand, DMs too "are related to the speech situation [and] (...) express attitudes and emotions" (Bazzanella 2006, 449). "The study of discourse markers is therefore a part of the study of modal and metatextual comment" (Lewis 2006, 43). Distinctions between MPs and DMs thus become hard to maintain, especially on purely functional grounds. As noted by Traugott (2007, 141):

> "[o]ne approach is to distinguish sharply between discourse markers and modal particles on both formal and discourse functional grounds (...). Another is to make no difference between the terms, apparently on discourse pragmatic grounds, while recognizing that "formally" clause-internal position is the modal particle position".

In the first contribution of this book with the telling title *"Same same but different"* – *Modal particles, discourse markers and the art (and purpose) of categorization*, Diewald observes that "modal particles and discourse markers have been a major testing ground for linguistic categorization". She furthermore draws our attention to the fact that we cannot answer the question whether MPs and DMs should be treated as one category, as two distinct categories, or as two subclasses of one more abstract category without deciding upon some preliminary issues first, which she formulates as follows:

1. Are DMs and MPs seen as cross-linguistically relevant – universal – categories or as language specific ones?
2. What are the essential characteristics evoked for a definition or classification? Are they functional or formal? Should they be approached onomasiologically or semasiologically?
3. Are these criteria used equally for both classes? Or is there a difference in the classificational bases between MPs and DMs?

While not all authors in this volume address these three questions as explicitly as Diewald does, all theoretical concepts and research lines presented in the chapters involve the issue of categorization, focusing on those criteria which are deemed crucial in determining whether MPs and DMs belong to the same or different (lexical or grammatical) classes. First of all, the cross-linguistic dimension present in this volume, with studies covering languages as diverse as German, Catalan, French, Japanese, Estonian, Italian, Swedish and English, offers a solid ground towards an exploration of the cross-linguistic validity of the distinction between MPs and DMs. Secondly, all authors of the papers explicitly provide both a formal and a functional definition of MPs and DMs and address the question whether there are paradigms of MPs and DMs. Thirdly, a general meta-theoretical discussion of the definitions provided is at the heart of each article. It should also be added that the theoretical discussions included in this volume are based on examing empirical data, mostly authentic corpus data, very often belonging to interactional contexts, which are used to support the different classification proposals.

Closely related to the question of categorization is the one of the semantic description of these (complex) linguistic expressions: which features are prominent in the semantics of DMs/MPs? Which of these semantic components may account for the extensions from DMs to MPs and the other way around? There seems to be agreement on the multifunctionality of these linguistic expressions, i.e. that there is no one-to-one mapping between an expression and its meaning and function. Depending on their context of use some meaning components of an expression may become prominent or not. This gives rise to the inevitable question of whether these linguistic expressions should receive a monosemic or a polysemic account (cf. Fischer 2006).

3.1   On discourse markers

It has become standard in any overview article or chapter on DMs to state that reaching agreement on what makes a DM is as good as impossible, be it alone on terminological matters (cf. Aijmer and Simon-Vandenbergen 2011; Degand and Simon-Vandenbergen 2011; Dér 2010; Fischer 2006; Fraser 1999; Lewis 2011; Norrick 2009; Schourup 1999; to name but a few). A great deal of the disagreement can be put on the account of the fact that DMs are multifunctional linguistic expressions and that they do not form a recognized (closed) word class. Indeed, there is "little consensus on whether they are a syntactic or a pragmatic category, on which types of expressions the category includes, on the relationship of discourse markers to other posited categories such as connectives, interjections, modal particles, speaker-oriented sentence adverbials, and on the term "discourse marker" as opposed to alternatives such as "discourse connective" or "pragmatic marker" or "pragmatic particle"" (Lewis 2011, 419–20). Among the many functions that DMs may fulfill in different "domains" (Schiffrin 1987, 2006), there are "the sequential structure of the dialogue, the turn-taking system, speech management, interpersonal management, the topic structure, and participation frameworks" (Fischer 2006, 9). This large variety of functions DMs may fulfill is, in our view, an important challenge for the attempt to define one overall category of DMs, and it calls for further sub-classification, e.g. response signals, segmentation signals, hesitation markers, discourse connectives, evidential markers, conversational management markers, etc. (Diewald this volume; Fraser 2006).

Schiffrin (1987, 328) presents a number of "tentative suggestions" for an expression to be used as a DM:

a. "it has to be syntactically detachable from a sentence
b. it has to be commonly used in initial position of an utterance
c. it has to have a range of prosodic contours (e.g. tonic stress and followed by a pause, phonological reduction)
d. it has to be able to operate at both local and global levels of discourse, and on different planes of discourse this means that it either has to have no meaning, a vague meaning, or to be reflexive (of the language, of the speaker)"

Sankoff and colleagues (1997) distinguish three major types of DMs: discourse coordinators, interaction markers, and punctors. They tend to have the following properties:

1. They do not enter into the construction syntactically with other elements of the sentence. This property excludes sentence adverbs and conjunctions used with their original semantics.
2. The propositional meaning of the sentence does not depend on their presence.
3. They are subject to semantic bleaching as compared with their source forms.
4. They undergo greater phonological reduction than their source forms.
5. They are articulated as part of smoothly following speech production. This property excludes hesitation markers.

Of course, as soon as one kind of operationalization is given, counterexamples can be found of linguistic expressions that are used as DMs in spite of obeying to one of the above mentioned properties (cf. also Heine and Kaltenböck 2012).

A number of authors suggest restricting the category of DMs to "linguistic items of variable scope, and whose primary function is connective. (...) they do not contribute to the propositional content of their host units (...) and they function as instructions from the speaker to the hearer on how to integrate the host unit into a coherent mental representation of the discourse" (Hansen 1997, 160–161). Fraser shares a similar view when he states that DMs "impose a relationship between some aspects of the discourse segment they are a part of, call it S2, and some aspect of a prior discourse segment, call it S1. In other words they function like a two-place relation, one argument lying in the segment they introduce, the other lying in the prior discourse" (Fraser 1999, 938). By doing so, these definitions seem to abandon the idea of a macro category of DMs to the detriment of non-connective DMs. These definitions have in common that they focus on the text connecting function of DMs, where the coherence of the text results from its coherent mental representation (to which DMs may contribute) (see also Knott and Dale 1994; Louwerse and Mitchell 2003). This is what Diewald (this volume) refers to as text connective markers, belonging to "school 1". Basing herself on Fischer's (2006b) introduction to the volume *Approaches to Discourse Particles*, she further defines "school 2" where

> "discourse markers are defined as indexical elements relating items of discourse to other items of discourse. Their indigenous functional domain is the expression of those types of connections and interrelations that are essential to and distinctive of spoken dialogic communication: They point to organizational and structural features, as well as to chunks of the non-linguistic situation and environment; they take care of the thematic structure, and they control the turn-taking system and other aspects of speech management". (Diewald, this volume).

3.2   On modal particles

The situation is slightly different for the class of MPs, which are generally recognized as a specific word class, at least in Germanic (and Scandinavian) languages (see e.g. Abraham 1988, 2000; Aijmer 1996; Braber 2010; Diewald 2006, this volume). As for the defining features of this language-specific word category, most authors agree that they are not inflected, are most often unstressed, cannot form an utterance by themselves and have no referential meaning. MPs are furthermore mutually combinable, restricted to a specific distributional position (generally the middle field in Germanic languages), and they have scope over the utterance (Hansen 1998; Waltereit and Detges 2007; the chapters by Diewald, Cuenca, Schoonjans in this volume). We would like to suggest here that the focus on the affective, attitudinal, opinionating, illocutionary meanings and uses of this class of particles[1] (Hartman 1986; Izutsu and Izutsu, this volume; Weydt 1969) might be one of the sources for the "fuzzy boundaries" between MPs, on the one hand, and DMs, on the other (Cuenca, this volume). Such meanings can of course also be expressed in languages that lack this specific MP class. In Waltereit's (2001, 1392) words, "it seems difficult to conceive of the *function* of modal particles as being restricted to particular languages". Thus, Romance languages or English, which lack for such particles, must have "other means for expressing the same thing" (*ibid.*). Waltereit (2001) indeed shows that there are other modalization forms carrying out a function analogous to MPs. Interestingly, Fischer (2000: 27) mentions that English tag questions have been found to be used as translation equivalents for German MPs (Kohler 1978; Fillmore 1981; Nehls 1989). In Spanish complex grammatical constructions such as the duplication of the infinitive serve as equivalents of MPs (e.g. *fumar fumar no fuma* 'he doesn't really smoke'. Cf. Valenzuela, Hilferty and Garachana 2005; Gras 2011).

3.3   On the fuzzy boundaries between DMs and MPs

Attractive as it is from a typological point of view, the meaning-based approach detracts from morpho-syntactic (formal) criteria, with the risk that we lose our grip on the categorization exercise. It appears indeed that quite a number of linguistic expressions that have been described as DMs share meanings that can be qualified as attitudinal, expressive, or speech-act bound. Fairbanks (2009, 59), for instance, when trying to define DMs as one encompassing category, describes them as "operat[ing] on different planes of discourse (i.e. serv[ing] some discourse function), contributing to either textual coherence or interpersonal/epistemic meanings, or both simultaneously". Liu (2009) adds that "they have textual and/or

---

1.   Cf. "Mit ihrer Hilfe kann der Sprecher Gewißheit, Annahme, Distanzierung, gefühlsmäßige Einstellung oder rationale und qualitative Bewertung signalisieren". (Helbig & Helbig 1990, back cover page) [With their help, the speaker can indicate certainty, supposition, distancing, emotional adjustment or indicate rational and qualitative assessment.]

interpersonal functions", and according to Heine and Kaltenböck (2012) "[t]he main function of DMs is to relate an utterance to the situation of discourse, more specifically to speaker-hearer interaction, speaker attitudes, and/or the organization of texts", while Brinton (2008, 18) refers to their "interpersonal functions" among which she counts "subjective functions such as expressing responses, reactions, attitudes, understanding, tentativeness, or continued attention, as well as interactive functions such as expressing intimacy, cooperation, shared knowledge, deference, or face-saving (politeness)". Clearly, some of these meanings can be expressed by MPs too.

Another source for the possible confusion between the categories of MPs and DMs is the diachronic link that can be established between the two. Cuenca (this volume) refers to the studies by Fitzmaurice (2004), Traugott (2007), and Waltereit and Detges (2007), who have highlighted the diachronic relationship between MPs and DMs. To this literature we can add the chapters in this volume by Izutsu and Izutsu and by Valdmets and the diachronic case studies of German MPs in Molnár (2002). The different case studies do not seem to suggest cross-linguistically attested directionality from either MPs to DMs or from DMs to MPs.

Finally, one of the probably most obvious reasons for the difficulty of defining the class of DMs, leading to potential conflicts with other categories of 'linguistic expressions functioning at the discourse level', lies in their loose, and non-restrictive definitions, of the type "discourse markers (...) mark discourse. They instruct discourse participants about how to consider an upcoming utterance, providing a path toward the integration of different components of language use into one coherent discourse (...)." (Louwerse and Mitchell 2003, 202); they are "sequentially dependent elements that bracket units of talk" (Schiffrin 1987, 31); "defined as linguistic items, with no syntactic function at the sentence level, which serve, according to their morphosyntactic, semantic and pragmatic properties, as a guide for the interpretation of utterances." (Trujillo Saez 2003), etc. Such general definitions are very hard to translate into operational criteria for identifying DMs in actual data.

4. Overview of the volume

The contributors in this volume approach the issue of categorizing DMs from a different perspective, namely focusing on one potential subclass: MPs. According to a number of authors (Diewald, Squartini, Valdmets), MPs are a clearly distinct grammatical category functioning on a different level; according to others, MPs and DMs share a remarkable number of functional features that lead to a fuzzy boundary between the two categories, which are however viewed as distinct (Cuenca; Izutsu and Izutsu; Fischer and Alm). From a broader epistemological point of view, Schoonjans suggests on the basis of the concept of vertical granularity that it is justified to put together several categories in one superordinate category (hence also MPs as subtype of DMs), if similarities are more important than differences.

As already mentioned, the contributions in this volume describe the distributional behavior and the functional properties of DMs and MPs in a variety of languages. The relation between DMs and MPs can strongly differ from language to language. The first chapters of the book are devoted to the analysis of DMs and MPs in languages that allow for a disentanglement of the functions of MPs and DMs because they show a clear formal distinction between these two groups of linguistic expressions. These are the Germanic languages (Diewald; Fischer and Alm; Aijmer), but also Estonian (Valdmets), a Finno-Ugric language. The following chapters examine the distinction between MPs and DMs in Romance languages. Romance languages do not have a topological utterance structure that is as well defined as in German; still some distributional constraints are recognizable especially in French (Schoonjans) and Northern Italian (Squartini), less in Catalan (Cuenca). This areal situation allows for a study of the distribution and functions of MPs and DMs in a perspective of typological syntax. The volume ends with the contrastive chapter by Izutsu and Izutsu on the comparison between Japanese and French DMs and MPs.

Gabriele Diewald's chapter, which has already been mentioned above, thus takes the lead by making explicit the issues involved in the categorization problem of DMs and MPs. In her view, the two types of linguistic expressions work on different layers of linguistic structure and therefore are non-comparable. In her terms "the guiding question of this volume, i.e. whether MPs and DMs are two sides of the same coin, is slightly misleading: DM and MP are coins belonging to different currencies. As such they may be exchanged against each other but they cannot be integrated into one valuta system". In her article, she then undertakes to disentangle the two notions for German, a language displaying DMs as well as MPs, and proposes two, or rather three, distinct (language-specific) classifications. In German, MPs form a proper word class that is distinct from and can be viewed as a missing link between "two much less clearly delimited, only universally specified groups (DMs and TCMs [Text Connective Markers])". Referring to prior work (Diewald 2006, 408), she considers MPs to "cover an intermediate domain between the functions of text-connecting elements such as conjunctions and conjunctional adverbs on the one hand, and discourse-structuring elements such as turn signals, hesitation markers, etc. on the other". TCMs, then, fulfill "strictly textual functions" (*ibid.*), while DMs fulfill "strictly discourse-relational functions" (*ibid.*). Thus, while all three classes share an indexical function, in that they connect the linguistic host they occur in with some element beyond, the elements of these classes operate on different levels: MPs have scope over propositions or speech-acts; DMs have scope over non-propositional discourse elements (which need not be linguistically expressed); and TCMs connect textually encoded (propositional) elements.

The second chapter is co-authored by Kerstin Fischer and Maria Alm, and is titled *A radical construction grammar perspective on the modal particle-discourse particle distinction*. In this contribution, the authors – who prefer the term *discourse particle* to *discourse marker* – propose to make use of a construction grammar approach to "shed light on the discourse particle – MP distinction on the basis of two particles, German *also* and Swedish *alltså*". These two particles can indeed function in both ways, thus allowing for a direct comparison of the functions of discourse particles and MPs. In line with Diewald's contribution, Fischer and Alm note that the lexemes themselves "are unspecified for the functions they are going to fulfill in interaction, as well as for the word class to which they belong". Rather, it is their use in a specific grammatical construction that determines their function, and this may differ according to the language in question, even for languages as close as Swedish and German. Interestingly, Fischer and Alm observe that there is concordance between the interpretations that *also* and *alltså* receive when used within a certain construction and other items in the same construction. In other words, the functional components identified for uses of *also/alltså* belong to the construction and not to the item within the construction. In our view, these findings strengthen Izutsu and Izutsu's cross-linguistic model (although the theoretical framework diverges), where a given sentential position allows for the development of certain meanings. Broadly speaking, following prior work by Diewald and Fischer (1998), Diewald (2006) and Fischer (2007), Fischer and Alm distinguish three main communicative tasks that have to be fulfilled in interaction: "a) the reporting of events, i.e. what is talked about, b) the anchoring of the current utterance in the argumentative structure of the discourse, i.e. it concerns why something is said and defines the participants' attitude towards it, and c) the contingencies of the current interaction, including the management of the communicative event itself". In this context of division of tasks, specific constructions are tuned towards specific communicative functions. In particular, MP constructions refer to the rhetorical or argumentative domain while discourse particle constructions refer to aspects of the communicative background frame. In sum, not the linguistic items themselves are specified for word class, it is the constructions that make a linguistic expression a discourse or a MP. In conclusion, the authors state that "within a language the definition of the two classes of discourse particles and MPs has to be construction-based and thus language-specific".

Karin Aijmer presents her view on the problem in question in her chapter *Analysing modal adverbs as modal particles and discourse markers.* On the basis of a case study of *of course*, Aijmer argues for a functional split between adverbial, DM and MP uses of a certain form; the modal adverb use being differentiated both from DMs and MPs. The latter two uses are distinguished primarily on functional grounds on the basis of a translation corpus. A first observation concerns the discourse-marking functions of *of course*, which are observed when *of course* expresses contrast or concession, or when it shows up in combination with adversative markers such as *but* and with additive markers such as *and*. The DM status of these *of course* uses follows from their emphatic role in the discourse organization. As for the syntactic surrounding of *of course* as a DM, it is usually placed in sentence-initial position (followed by a comma) but also shows up after a conjunction. The MP uses of *of course*, by contrast, are syntactically integrated in the clause and do not appear in sentence-initial position. Functionally speaking, the MP uses of *of course* are closely associated with common ground and context-adjustment. The MP *of course* is most often used for marking consensus and consolidating a harmonious relationship with the hearer. This interactional feature leads Karin Aijmer to conclude that "there is nothing obviously modal about modal particles".

In her chapter on *Modal particles, discourse markers, and adverbs with lt-suffix (Eng. '-ly') in Estonian*, Annika Valdmets addresses the question of the developmental paths of four Estonian MPs/DMs/adverbs with *lt*-suffix, namely *loomulikult* 'naturally; of course', *ilmselt* 'visibly; apparently', *tegelikult* 'in reality; actually' and *lihtsalt* 'simply; just'. She shows that the adverbs under examination all have the tendency to evolve into pragmatic markers. The group of pragmatic markers is divided into two: MPs and DMs. On the basis of corpus data, Valdmets clearly distinguishes between MP and DM uses of the same forms. All of those items have their initial/dictionary function as an adverb. However, over the course of time they come to be used more and more as MPs or DMs. As adverbs, they are content words that have all of the characteristics of a typical adverb: primarily the analysis shows that the item has grammatical relations with the clause and it carries a concrete meaning. As a MP or a DM, the adverbial forms have omitted their previous function and they are now semantically abstract items that have only marginal grammatical relations with the clause.

As for the relation between MPs and DMs, Valdmets shows that the scope of MPs is smaller than that of DMs. MPs function on a clausal level while DMs have scope over the discourse or at least over larger chunks of text. DMs are connective units between two sentences. DMs are placed at the beginning of a sentence, whereas MPs are usually in the middle field, although the left or right periphery is not rigidly held apart in Estonian. Estonian MPs and DMs also have features in common. They may be considered (inter)subjective procedural items which add a speaker-oriented dimension to what is being said. Finally, the question of the directionality of the change is also addressed for the Estonian markers. The corpus analysis suggests that MPs and DMs both evolve from adverbs.

In his chapter on *Modal particles: problems in defining a category*, Steven Schoonjans elaborates further on the flexibility of categorization. From a meta point of view, he discusses the problems of the current delineations of the class of MPs in German, thus countering the idea that in German MPs form a well-defined word class. He first shows that the established criteria for defining MPs cannot be considered necessary conditions, because of the existence of quite a few "exceptions". He also points out that whether an expression is a member of the class or not is also a matter of discussion. Only eight particles seem to be described consistently as MPs, whereas more than ten other particles appear in only some of the literature. It is also shown that there is no agreement on whether MPs can be a specific word class. This should not be a problem according to Schoonjans, who argues that the category of MPs has a prototypical structure with fuzzy boundaries and shows overlap with other categories. Interestingly, "each particular type is to a higher or lower degree a prototypical member of this category, and can at the same time be a prototypical member of different categories" (Schoonjans this volume). Schoonjans argues for interpreting prototypicality in terms of granularity and conceptualization. Whether a form is a MP depends, according to him, on "the level of horizontal granularity, i.e. on the amount of variation the prototype may show and to the extent a form may deviate from the prototype and still be a (non-prototypical) member of the category". Conceptualization then is concerned with the idea that "how the category is conceived partly determines which features are thought to be more important or more salient". Hence, via their conceptualization analysts and speakers have an impact on the structure of the prototype and the level of horizontal granularity chosen. Finally, after having discussed German examples, he also presents a comparison with French data, which confirm that the weight that scholars give to certain features determines the linguistic categorization.

In his chapter entitled *From TAM to discourse via information structure: North-Western Italian* già *'already' and its French cognate* déjà, Mario Squartini argues that DMs and MPs can be considered two sides of the same coin. On the basis of an in-depth analysis of *già* he reveals that both types of markers share the information status feature of 'given' information. Yet, this feature has different functions according to the different uses of *già*: in interrogative/MP uses *già* is involved in 'backchecking', whereas the use of *già* as an interjection/ DM refers to 'confirmativity'. On the other hand, the case of *già* also shows that formal properties including morphosyntactic and scopal behaviour "keep the two coins mutually exclusive". The MP uses of *già* confirm that MPs are integrated within the utterance, whereas the DM uses, which derive from a more independent, interjectional use of *già*, have extrasentential scope allowing them to regulate and connect discourse chunks. The DM use of *già* can also be observed in combinations such as *ah già*, *eh già* and *oh già*. The latter expression is a conclusive marker in regional Italian playing a role in turn alternations, which is undoubtedly a prototypical function of DMs.

Mario Squartini discusses North-Western Italian *già* in relation to French, Spanish and Central Italian. The comparison of the four Romance varieties illustrates that only North-Western Italian combines both MP and DM uses. Spanish and Central Italian only have DM uses, whereas French has a MP use, and hence, does not witness any overlap with DM uses. Interestingly, according to Squartini, the MP use in French is currently undergoing an extension of the back-checking function towards more general illocutionary domains. This extension process is in line with other processes involving semantic change such as pragmaticalization and intersubjectification.

Studying frequent discourse phenomena in oral Catalan, Maria Josep Cuenca confronts us with linguistic expressions that exhibit features typically associated with both modal markers and DMs. In her chapter on *The fuzzy limits between discourse marking and modal marking*, she sets out to describe "focal category behaviors in a cline from discourse to modal marking" which makes it possible "to account for 'anomalous' items that challenge any attempt of classification, and (...) to define category boundaries assuming a dynamic and fuzzy model of categorization". Cuenca identifies several reasons for the existence of these fuzzy boundaries between linguistic categories. In the first place, identifying the word classes implementing discourse marking and modal marking functions is far from trivial a task because both DMs and modal markers have been recognized as a set of expressions that include different word classes. Noteworthy here is that Cuenca introduces the term *modal marker* (MM), of which MPs are just one word class among others on the 'modal' side of her cline. Other reasons to end up with fuzzy category boundaries include the lack of necessary and sufficient conditions to classify a linguistic expression as a modal marker or a DM; the multifunctionality of the linguistic expressions under scrutiny, where some linguistic forms may have both modal and discourse marking functions; and the contextual dependence of the items where "the same form, even as a particle, can develop various pragmatic functions according to factors such as its position, the units in which it occurs (type, modality, etc.) or intonation". Within her gradient view of categorization of the two classes, Cuenca identifies conjunctions and parenthetical connectives as prototypical DMs, since they make explicit the relationship between two content units, i.e. they bracket unit of talks and function as two position operators. On the other end of the cline, she identifies modal adverbs, interjections and MPs as prototypical MMs that typically modify the illocution of an utterance and act as one position operators. In the middle of this cline, i.e. occupying the intersection between modal and DMs, we find pragmatic connectives, and to some extent also interjections and MPs. To support this gradient classification model, Cuenca provides evidence from the modal and connective functions of a number of (oral) Catalan expressions, namely *home/dona, (és) clar* and *és que*, that appear to present a hybrid character.

In the final chapter of this volume, Katsunobu Izutsu and Mitsuko Izutsu pursue a definitely cross-linguistic endeavor in their chapter *From Discourse Markers to Modal/Final Particles: What the Position Reveals about the Continuum*. Within the theoretical framework of grammaticalization, the authors propose a cross-linguistic model for the development of modal/final particles from DMs. DMs and MPs are thus linked in sofar that the former are viewed as the source form for the development of the latter. More precisely, they argue that some DMs in "German, French, and Japanese have come to serve as modal particles by developing (inter) subjective meanings in a limited sentential position: the middle field in German and the final or internal position in French, and the final position in Japanese". The autors observe "striking similarities" between some German MPs and their "equivalents" in French and Japanese, which makes it necessary "to devise a broader perspective of modal particles and a cross-linguistic framework or model for their analysis". The central idea of this model is that the development of (inter)subjective meanings in DMs in (language-specific) restricted sentential positions gives rise to the emergence of MPs. According to Izutsu and Izutsu, MPs are thus typical (inter)subjective markers in that they indicate the speaker's (positive or negative) assumptions, including emotive or affective meanings, related to the content expressed. Such meanings have long been recognized to be typical of right peripheral position in final particle languages such as Japanese. Izutsu and Izutsu suggest interpreting such final particles as peripheral members of the MP category.

5. Conclusions

The articles collected in this volume help us to provide an answer to the question asked in the title of this introduction: are DMs and MPs two sides of the same coin? The most straightforward, but probably not most satisfying, answer is: it depends on the approach adopted for the categorization task. If DMs and MPs are defined in pragmatic terms, the answer is yes, MPs and DMs are linguistic elements encoding two aspects of a general indexical function. Both relate the utterance in their scope to the context: DMs relate the utterance in their scope to the linguistic context; MPs relate the utterance in their scope to the situational context.

If DMs and MPs are defined in formal terms, the answer is clearly no, they are not two sides of the same coin. MPs are a clearly defined word class in German and some other Germanic (and Finno-Ugric) languages, characterized by their middle field position in the topological structure of utterances, whereas DMs are a much more heterogeneous collection of linguistic expressions fulfilling various indexical functions and not characterized by precise distributional constraints.

It should be said though that, by combining the two approaches, viz., by taking into account at the same time formal and functional properties of DMs and MPs, and by adopting a broad cross-linguistic perspective, the precise distinction between the two classes of linguistic elements becomes clearer.

Formal approaches to MPs help us to identify the functional specificity of MPs: some languages have a class of distributionally constrained words dedicated to semantically qualify the speech act with regard to the pragmatic presupposed context. This very particular indexical function appears to be 'grammaticalized', at least in Germanic languages. Other languages do not show exactly the same constraints, nevertheless, the same semantic function can be fulfilled by a group of pragmatic markers characterized by distributional properties distinguishing them from other DMs.

All in all, the articles gathered in the present volume show that DMs and MPs are two subclasses of the general class of pragmatic markers. They both have an indexical function. DMs relate items of discourse to other items of discourse, whereas MPs qualify speech acts with regards to a pragmatic presupposed context. MPs as a well defined word class are mainly present in German and other Germanic languages, but the pragmatic function of MPs is encoded in many languages by more or less grammaticalized sub-classes of pragmatic markers, clearly distinct from DMs.

Acknowledgements

We would like to thank the participants to the panel at the IPRA conference in Manchester (July 2011) which gave rise to this volume, more in particular Elizabeth Traugott (Stanford University) who accepted to be a discussant during that panel. We also would like to thank the contributors to this volume and the Series editor for the very nice collaboration while working on this volume. We are most grateful to two anonymous reviewers from the Pragmatics and Beyond New Series for their very thoughtfull comments and suggestions that helped improve the present introduction and the chapters hereafter.

References

Abraham, Werner. 1988. "Vorbemerkungen zur Modalpartikelsyntax im Deutschen." *Linguistische Berichte* 118: 443–465.

Abraham, Werner. 2000. "Modal Particles in German: Word Classification and Legacy beyond Grammaticalisation." In *Approaches to the Typology of Word Classes*, ed. by Petra Maria Vogel, and Bernard Comrie, 321–350. Berlin/New York: Mouton de Gruyter.

Aijmer, Karin. 1996. "Swedish Modal Particles in a Contrastive Perspective." *Language Sciences* 18 (1–2): 393–427.

Aijmer, Karin. 2002. *English Discourse Particles: Evidence from a Corpus*. Amsterdam: John Benjamins Publishing Company.

Bazzanella, Carla. 2006. "Discourse Markers in Italian: Towards a Compositional Meaning." In *Approaches to Discourse Particles*, ed. by Kerstin Fischer, 449–464. Amsterdam: Elsevier.

Braber, Nathalie. 2006. "Emotional and Emotive Language: Modal Particles and Tags in Unified Berlin." *Journal of Pragmatics* 38 (9): 1487–1503.

Brinton, Laurel J. 2008. The Comment Clause in English: Syntactic Origins and Pragmatic Development. 1st ed. Cambridge: Cambridge University Press.

Company Company, Concepción. 2002. "Grammaticalization and Category Weakness." In *New Reflections on Grammaticalization*, ed. by Ilse Wischer, and Gabriele Diewald, 201–215. Amsterdam/Philadelphia: John Benjamins.

Croft, William. 2000. "Parts of Speech as Language Universals and as Language-Particular Categories." In *Approaches to the Typology of Word Classes*, ed. by Petra Maria Vogel, and Bernard Comrie, 65–102. Berlin/New York: Mouton de Gruyter.

Croft, William. 2001. *Radical Construction Grammar: Syntactic Theory in Typological Perspective*. Oxford: Oxford University Press.

Cuenca, Maria Josep. [this volume]. "The Fuzzy Boundaries Between Discourse Marking and Modal Marking."

Diewald, Gabriele. 2006. "Discourse Particles and Modal Particles as Grammatical Elements." In *Approaches to Discourse Particles*, ed. by Kerstin Fischer, 403–425. Amsterdam: Elsevier.

Diewald, Gabriele. [this volume]. ""*Same same but different*" – Modal Particles, Discourse Markers and the Art (and Purpose) of Categorization."

Diewald, Gabriele, and Kerstin Fischer. 1998. "Zur diskursiven und modalen Funktion der Partikeln *aber, auch, doch* und *ja* in Instruktionsdialogen." *Linguistica* 38: 75–99.

Fairbanks, Brendan. 2009. *Ojibwe Discourse Markers*. Doctoral Dissertation. University of Minnesota.

Fillmore, Charles J. 1981. "Pragmatics and the Description of Discourse." In *Radical Pragmatics*, ed. by Peter Cole, 143–166. New York: Academic Press.

Fischer, Kerstin. 2000. *From Cognitive Semantics to Lexical Pragmatics. The Functional Polysemy of Discourse Particles*. Berlin/New York: Mouton de Gruyter.

Fischer, Kerstin. 2007. "Grounding and Common Ground: Modal Particles and their Translation Equivalents." In *Lexical Markers of Common Grounds*, ed. by Anita Fetzer, and Kerstin Fischer, 47–65. Amsterdam: Elsevier.

Fischer, Kerstin (ed.). 2006. *Approaches to Discourse Particles*, [Studies in Pragmatics 1]. Amsterdam: Elsevier.

Fraser, Bruce (2006). "Towards a Theory of Discourse Markers." In *Approaches to Discourse Particles*, Kerstin Fischer (ed.), 189–204. Amsterdam: Elsevier.

Fischer, Kerstin and Alm, Maria. [this volume]. A Radical Construction Grammar Perspective on the Modal Particle-Discourse Particle Distinction.

Fraser, Bruce 1999. "What are discourse markers?" *Journal of Pragmatics* 31 (7). 931–952.

Gras, Pedro. 2011. *Gramática de Construcciones en Interacción. Propuesta de un modelo y aplicación al análisis de estructuras independientes con marcas de subordinación.* Doctoral dissertation. Universitat de Barcelona.

Hansen, Maj-Britt Mosegaard. 1998. "The Semantic Status of Discourse Markers." *Lingua* 104 (3–4); 235–260.

Hartmann, Dietrich. 1986. "Context Analysis or Analysis of Sentence Meaning? On Modal Particles in German." *Journal of Pragmatics* 10 (5): 543–557.

Haselow, Alexander. 2011. "Discourse Marker and Modal Particle: The Functions of Utterance-Final *then* in Spoken English." *Journal of Pragmatics* 43 (14): 3603–3623.

Helbig, Gerhard, and Helbig, Agnes. 1990. "*Lexikon deutscher Modalwörter.*" Leipzig: Verlag Enzyklopädie.

Heine, Bernd, and Günther Kaltenböck (2012). On Discourse Markers: Grammaticalization, Pragmaticalization, or Something Else? Ms. University of Köln.

Izutsu, Katsunobu & Izutsu, Mitsuko Narita. [this volume]. "From Discourse Markers to Modal/Final Particles: What the Position Reveals about the Continuum."

Knott, Alistair, and Robert Dale. 1994. "Using Linguistic Phenomena to Motivate a Set of Coherence Relations." *Discourse Processes* 18: 35–62.

Kohler, Klaus. 1978. "Englische "Question Tags" und ihre deutschen Entsprechungen." *Arbeitsberichte des Instituts für Phonetik der Universität Kiel* 10: 61–77.

Lewis, Diana. 2006. "Discourse Markers in English: A Discourse-Pragmatic View." In *Approaches to Discourse Particles*, ed. by Kerstin Fischer, 43–59. Amsterdam: Elsevier.

Lewis, Diana. 2011. "A Discourse-Constructional Approach to the Emergence of Discourse Markers in English." *Linguistics* 49 (2): 415–443.

Liu, Binmei. 2009. "Chinese Discourse Markers in Oral Speech of Mainland Mandarin Speakers". *Proceedings of the 21st North American Conference on Chinese Linguistics* (NACCL-21). Vol 2. ed. by Yun Xiao, 358–374. Smithfield, Rhode Island: Bryant University.

Louwerse, Max M. and Heather Hite Mitchell. 2003. "Toward a Taxonomy of a Set of Discourse Markers in Dialog: A Theoretical and Computational Linguistic Account." *Discourse Processes* 35 (3): 199–239.

Matras, Yaron. 2000. "Fusion and the Cognitive Basis for Bilingual Discourse Markers." *International Journal of Bilingualism* 4 (4): 505–528.

Molnár, Anna. 2002. Die Grammatikalisierung deutscher Modalpartikeln: Fallstudien. Frankfurt am Main: Peter Lang.

Nehls, Dietrich. 1989. "German Modal Particles Rendered by English Auxiliary Verbs." In *Sprechen mit Partikeln*, ed. by Harald Weydt, 282–292. Berlin/New York: de Gruyter.

Rosch, Eleanor. 1978. "Principles of Categorization." In *Cognition and Categorization*, ed. by Eleanor Rosch, and Barbara L. Lloyd, 27–48. Hillsdale, NJ: Lawrence Erlbaum.

Sankoff, Gillian, Pierrette Thibault, Naomi Nagy, Helene Blondeau, Marie-Odile Fonollosa, and Lucie Gagnon. 1997. "Variation in the Use of Discourse Markers in a Language Contact Situation." *Language Variation and Change* 9 (2): 191–217.

Schiffrin, Deborah. 1987. *Discourse Markers*. Cambridge: Cambridge University Press.

Schiffrin, Deborah. 2001. "Discourse Markers, Meaning, and Context." In *The Handbook of Discourse Analysis*, ed. by Deborah Schiffrin, Deborah Tannen, and Heidi E. Hamilton, 54–75. [Blackwell Handbooks in Linguistics]. Oxford/Maldon, MA: Blackwell.

Schiffrin, Deborah. 2006. *In Other Words. Variation in reference and narrative.* Cambridge: Cambridge University Press.

Schoonjans, Steven. [this volume]. "Modal Particles: Problems in Defining a Category."

Taylor, John R. 2003. *Linguistic Categorization.* Oxford: Oxford University Press.

Traugott, Elizabeth Closs. 2007. "Discourse Markers, Modal Particles, and Contrastive Analysis, Synchronic and Diachronic." *Catalan Journal of Linguistics* 6: 139–157.

Trujillo Saez, Fernando. 2003. "Culture in Writing: Discourse Markers in English and Spanish Student Writing." In *Tadea seu liber de Amicitia*, ed. by Departamento de Didactica de la Lengua y la Literatura, 345–364. Granada, Imprenta Generalife.

Valdmets, Annika. [this volume]. "Modal Particles, Discourse Markers, and Adverbs with *lt*-suffix (Eng. '-ly') in Estonian."

Valenzuela, Javier, Joseph Hilferty, and Mar Garachana. 2005. "On the Reality of Constructions. The Spanish Reduplicative-Topic Construction." *Annual Review of Cognitive Linguistics* 3: 201–215.

Waltereit, Richard, and Ulrich Detges. 2007. "Different Functions, Different Histories. Modal Particles and Discourse Markers from a Diachronic Point of View." *Catalan Journal of Linguistics* 6: 61–80.

Waltereit, Richard. 2001. "Modal Particles and their Functional Equivalents: A Speech-Act-Theoretic Approach." *Journal of Pragmatics* 33 (9), 1391–1417.

Weydt, Harald. 1969. *Abtönungspartikel. Die deutschen Modalpartikeln und ihre französischen Entsprechungen.* Bad Hamburg v.d.H.

"Same same but different" – Modal particles, discourse markers and the art (and purpose) of categorization*

Gabriele Diewald
Leibniz Universität Hannover

The term "Discourse Marker" (DM) tends to be defined via onomasiological – functional and universal – criteria, while the term "Modal Particle" (MP) usually refers to a semasiologically defined language-specific word class. Thus, both terms belong to different layers of linguistic description and may not be juxtaposed in direct comparison. Starting from this problem in current efforts of classification and using data from German, the paper proposes a definition of these terms which takes into account their different status. It is suggested that the broad functional domain of DM be set off against and contrasted with a newly established sister domain called "Text-Connective Marker" (= TCM), while the term MP be reserved for a language-specific word class with clearly specifiable formal and functional features.

1. Introduction

Like other grammatical categories and/or semantic domains such as, for example, modality and evidentiality, or aspect and tense, modal particles and discourse markers have been a major testing ground for linguistic categorization. As the title of this volume *Discourse markers and modal particles: two sides of the same coin?* explicitly spells out, the question is whether and on which criteria modal particles (MPs) and discourse markers (DMs) should be treated as one category, as two distinct categories, or as two subclasses (with possibly different hierarchical status) of one more abstract category. In order to solve these problems concerning the categorial relationship between DMs and MPs some preliminary issues have to be decided upon first. These are:

---

* The motto in the title is inspired by the film *Same same but different* directed by Detlev Buck in 2009.

1.   Are DMs and MPs seen as cross-linguistically relevant – universal – categories or as language-specific ones?
2.   What are the essential characteristics evoked for a definition or classification? Functional or formal? Onomasiological or semiasiological?
3.   Are these criteria used equally for both classes? Or is there a difference in the classificational bases between MPs and DMs?

Taking into account prior research, the first part of this paper is devoted to these issues. It will become obvious that DM and MP are labels for linguistic phenomena which refer to different layers of linguistic structure and therefore are non-comparable: The term DM tends to be defined via universally relevant functional (i.e. onomasiological) criteria, the term MP usually refers to a language-specific word class which is typically defined via formal, i.e. semasiological, as well as functional characteristics. Seen from this angle, the guiding question of this volume, i.e. whether MPs and DMs are two sides of the same coin, is slightly misleading: DM and MP are coins belonging to different currencies. As such they may be exchanged against each other but they cannot be integrated into one valuta system.

Nevertheless, as German is a language displaying DMs as well as MPs, the paper undertakes the task of disentangling these items for German, and suggests a language-specific classification which, however, may pave the way for cross-linguistic categorization. While this task is undertaken in the second half of this contribution (see Sections 3 to 5), a quick glance at some German data (typical oral utterances overheard in joint activity siutations like constructing wood toys together) is in place here for orientation.

(1)   *Es soll <u>halt</u> schwimmen.*
      It is meant HALT to swim.
      '*The thing is*, it is meant to swim.'

(2)   *und dann kommt der große Balken, <u>gell</u>?*
      and then comes the large beam,   GELL?
      'and then comes the large beam, *am I right*?'

It is common knowledge that while *halt* in (1) is used as a modal particle, *gell* in (2) is an instance of a discourse marker (for definitions see next sections). Furthermore, there is agreement that many items functioning as MPs or DMs in German display polyfunctionality and/or heterosemy, i.e. they change their function and their word class membership depending on context and distribution. Thus, the type *ja*, which appears three times in sentence (3), is an instance of this polyfunctionality and heterosemy as it is used in different functions and/or with different word class membership in each of its three tokens. The first token shows *ja* as a DM, more precisely a turn-taking signal (speaker signal), the second token represents the modal particle *ja*, and the third token again is a DM, this time a turn-final signal.

(3) *ja, und dann kommt ja der große Balken, ja?*
    JA, and then comes JA the large beam, JA?
    'Okay, and then – *we know that* – comes the large beam, *right?*'

Thus, we witness a complex situation in German. On one hand, as *halt* and *gell* in (1) and (2) show, German has clear-cut, prototypical examples of each class which do not have heterosemes (i.e which are lexicalized/inventarized only as MP or DM respectively). This is a fact that strongly supports the claim for two distinct categories in the language. On the other hand, there are various intermediate, polyfunctional and heteroseme cases (see *ja* in 3), which call for a concept of flexible categorization. Moreover, in addition to synchronic complexity, the diachronic data of the items in question display a strong tendency towards grammaticalization, and thus we are confronted with all the accompanying phenomena of trans- and intercategoriality.[1] While Sections 3 and 4 are devoted to the features of German MPs as a distinct word class and grammatical category with a language-specific correlation of functional and formal characteristics, Section 5 will briefly discuss data on intercategoriality. Taken together, this discussion leads on to suggesting language-specific flexible categorization founded on cross-linguistic categories. This plea will be supported by more general reflections on the art and purpose of linguistic categorization in the final Section 6.

2. Discourse markers – definitions and earlier research

An important first step towards clarifying the notions of discourse markers and – to a lesser extent – modal particles is made in the collective volume edited by Fischer in 2006.[2] Fischer herself states that "there is surprisingly litte overlap in the different definitions" (Fischer 2006, 2) and an enormous "diversity of views regarding which items should be considered, how they should be labelled, which functions they fulfil, and which units they act upon" (p. 7). She specifies this observation as follows:

> Moreover, the studies available so far are hardly comparable; the approaches vary with respect to very many different aspects: the language(s) under consideration, the items taken into account, the terminology used, the functions considered, the problems focussed on, and the methodologies employed. (Fischer 2006, 1)

---

1.   For the diachronic development of modal particles, which is not discussed here, see Diewald 2006, 2008; Diewald and Ferraresi 2008; Diewald, Kresic and Smirnova 2009.

2.   For recent discussion also cf. Degand and Vandenbergen (eds) 2011.

As the topic of the present volume shows, this situation has not changed substantially since then. Therefore, it is necessary to briefly discuss earlier definitions and to indicate which one is chosen here. As discourse markers are more widely disputed than modal particles, it is useful to start with the former. Following Fischer, we may discern two broad "schools" in the field: One school restricts the term "discourse marker" to items with a text-connective function that are syntactically integrated, i.e. "hosted" by a sentential matrix. The second school regards discourse markers as non-integrated material, independent of syntactic structure, but bound to utterance structure.[3] Their defining function is discourse management, i.e. they connect non-propositional components of communicative situations.[4]

Fraser, a proponent of the first position, defines discourse markers as follows:

> To summarize, I have defined DMs as a pragmatic class, lexical expressions drawn from the syntactic classes of conjunctions, adverbials, and prepositional phrases. With certain exceptions, they signal a relationship between the segment they introduce, S2, and the prior segment, S1. They have a core meaning which is procedural, not conceptual, and their more specific interpretation is 'negotiated' by the context, both linguistic and conceptual. There are two types: those that relate aspects of the explicit message conveyed by S2 with aspects of a message, direct or indirect, associated with S1; and those that relate the topic of S2 to that of S1. (Fraser 1999, 950)

This view, which explicitly confines DMs to *anaphoric items, i.e. to items pointing backward in the text*, is affirmed by Fraser (2006, 191). [5] In the present volume, Cuenca follows this definition:[6]

---

3.   The criterion of syntactic or topological integration is a complex one as it depends on language-specific features as well as on the syntactic theory adhered to. Anticipating explanations in the rest of this paper, it may be stated that – as far as German is concerned – modal particles are topologically and syntactically integrated into the sentence (cf. Section 3), whereas there are no comparable positional restrictions for discourse markers. For a detailed discussion of this issue see also Fischer and Alm (this volume).

4.   Cf. Fischer (2006, 8): "[...] on the one hand, there are those items that constitute parts of utterances, such as connectives; on the other, there are completely unintegrated items that may constitute independent utterances such as feedback signals or interjections."

5.   For diverging positions see also Fischer and Alm (this volume), Squartini (this volume), Aijmer (this volume) and Valdmets (this volume).

6.   A similar, though not identical position is held by Lewis 2006 who lists items like *well, I mean, so, in fact, though, of course, anyway, actually, on the other hand* as members of the group of discourse markers (2006, 43). Her definition, which is language-specific for English, is as follows: "English discourse marker in the approach described here is a label for an expression that combines the semantics of discourse-relational predications with syntactic dependency on a clausal host and low informational salience. Discourse markers are defined by these discourse-semantic, syntactic, and information-structural parameters" (Lewis 2006, 44).

It is hardly controversial that conjunctions (e.g. *and, or, but*) are discourse markers. Conjunctions are linking words that indicate grammatical relationship (subordination and coordination) and propositional meanings (addition, disjunction, contrast, concession, cause, consequence, condition, purpose, comparison, time, place, manner). They typically introduce clauses in compound sentences. (Cuenca, this volume)

According to this approach *so* in the following example, which is uttered in the context of scheduling a business meeting, is classified as a typical discourse marker:

(4)   <u>mdmr_3_06</u>: *yes; I'm free two to five on Wednesday, <u>so</u> how 'bout meeting three to five?*   (quoted from Fischer 2006, 8)

As in this view discourse markers appear as syntactically integrated text connectives of propositionally relevant entities, the modal particles of German, which share this property (see Section 3), must be regarded as a sub-group of DMs in the sense of school 1, i.e. on a par with conjunctions, connective adverbials, and other text-connective devices,[7] whereas items with discourse-organizational functions (which are defined as discourse markers by the second school) are excluded. As a label for a super-ordinate category, incorporating both text-connective and discourse-organizational items (i.e. DMs as defined by school 1 and DMs as defined by school 2), Fraser (2006, 189) suggests the term "pragmatic markers".

The alternative solution offered by school 2 takes the term "discourse" to refer to dialogic interaction, and thus defines discourse markers as linguistic elements that fulfill discourse-organizational functions, i.e. the managenment of conversation. DMs are seen as elements that "relate items of discourse to other items of discourse" (Diewald 2006, 406). Squartini (this volume), who shares this view and links it to the notion of "conclusivity", speaks of discourse markers "strictu sensu".[8]

Diewald (2006, 408) goes on to expound that discourse markers "relate non-propositional discourse elements which are not textually expressed, [and which are] syntactically non-integrated, i.e., [have] no syntactically fixed position [and thus] no constituent value". In other words, DMs are prosodically, syntactically, and semantically independent. A similar view on the functions of discourse

---

7.   In Section 4 it will be expounded that the type of backward pointing achieved by MPs is different from that of truly anaphorical devices insofar as MPs point back to non-expressed propositional and illocutionary entities which are assumed as given, can be interpolated, and are variants of the proposition or speech act containing the MP.

8.   He continues with the observation that the definition given by Diewald 2006 is "rephrased by Detges and Waltereit (2009, 44) with their characterization of discourse markers as elements denoting a 'two-place relationship'".

markers is expressed in Hansen.[9] As this quote is very illuminating, it is given in full length:

> Like many others working in this area, I define discourse markers in primarily functional-pragmatic, rather than formal-syntactic terms. According to my definition, the role played by linguistic items functioning as discourse markers is nonpropositional and metadiscoursive, and their functional scope is in general quite variable. The role of markers is, in my view, to provide instructions to the hearer on how to integrate their host utterance into a developing mental model of the discourse in such a way as to make that utterance appear optimally coherent. This means that markers have connectivity (in a wide sense) as at least part of their meaning. Importantly, however, connectivity is not limited to relations between neighbouring utterances or utterance parts, and the notion of a 'developing mental model of the discourse' is not constituted by language only – the context (situational and cognitive) is an essential part of it, and the connective role of discourse markers may therefore pertain to relations between the host utterance and its context in this wider, nonlinguistic sense. (Hansen 2006, 25)

This description is highly compatible with the approach suggested here. It should be noted that Hansen uses the criterion of syntactic (non-)integratedness in a general way as she speaks of integration of DM into their *host utterance*, which in not a syntactic but a discourse pragmatic type of segment.

As to the connective function pragmatic markers in general are acknowledged to share, it is referred to in the present paper as *indexical or relational function*. It is a pointing relation between an origo (a starting point), and a target, i.e. the entity pointed to. As such – as an indexical relation – it always is *a two-place relation* no matter whether the target is expressed in the linguistic string or not.

DMs "strictu sensu" as defined by school 2 are independent of syntactic structure; their scope is not the sentence, not the clause, and not (only) the speech act, but the utterance. They may appear utterance initial, utterance final, utterance internal, or independently of any utterance. Examples for discourse markers in this sense are *gell* in (5), which repeats example (2), *obwohl* in (6), and *aber* in (7):

(5)   *und dann kommt der große Balken, gell?*
      and then comes the large beam, GELL?
      'and then comes the large beam, *am I right?*'

---

9.   See also Fischer, who points out that the various functions fulfilled by DMs in this reading of the term "concern domains such as the sequential structure of the dialogue, the turn-taking system, speech management, interpersonal management, the topic structure, and participation frameworks" (Fischer 2006, 9); cf. also Schiffrin 2006.

(6) *Glaubst du, daß er das Spiel gewinnen wird?* <u>*Obwohl*</u> *– mir kann's ja egal sein.*

Do you think he'll win the game? OBWOHL – I don't care.

'Do you think he'll win the game? *Well, anyway* – I don't care.'

(Zifonun, Hoffmann and Strecker 1997, 2316)

(7) K: *und das wird dann da so seitlich draufgeschraubt oder?*

'and that's going to be screwed there to the side this way, isn't it?'

   I: *ja genau,* <u>*aber*</u> *mach das erstmal so.*

yes exactly, ABER do it this way first.

'yes exactly, *but* do it this way first.'

(Sagerer et al. 1994, quoted from Diewald and Fischer 1998)

The turn-final DM *gell* in (5), an instance for the sub-group of turn-taking signals, asks for agreement and initiates the transition of the turn from the present speaker to the hearer. The correction signal *obwohl* in (6) has the function of withdrawing the illocutionary force of the previous utterance and introducing the following segment as a justification for this withdrawal. The domain of *aber* in (7), finally, is the thematic plane of discourse. The first line renders the first interlocutor's (K) question concerning the next step in the common interaction (constructing a toy airplane), the second interlocutor (I) responds to that, and in using *aber* relates his or her utterance to the preceding utterance of the partner, simultaneously indicating that he or she wants to change the topic (cf. Diewald and Fischer 1998, 87). Finally, (8) gives an example for a DM that has utterance status itself, thus displaying the limiting case of zero realization of a host.

(8) A: *hast Du?*
   B: <u>*ja.*</u>
   A: 'got it?'
   B: 'yes.'

The large variety of functions of DMs provides criteria for establishing sub-groups like response signals, segmentation signals, hesitation markers, etc. As to their morphological shape, discourse markers are very variable, including non-lexicalized material (like interjections), particles, and syntactic strings (like *I think*) of various size. In German, among the most frequent discourse markers are item such as *ach, äh, ähm, also, gut, hm, ja, nee, nein, oh* and *okay* (Fischer and Johanntokrax 1995; Diewald and Fischer 1998).

Summarizing the position of the second school, discourse markers are defined as indexical elements relating items of discourse to other items of discourse. Their indigenous functional domain is the expression of those types of connections and interrelations that are essential to and distinctive of spoken dialogic communication. They point to organizational and structural features as well as to chunks of the non-linguistic situation and environment; they take care of the thematic structure, and they control the turn-taking system and other aspects of speech management.

The definition of school 2 has the advantage of taking the notion of *discourse* literally and of using it to set off the group of markers operating on the interactional dialogic plane from markers for text-connective (ana- and cataphoric) functions. The definition of DM according to school 2 calls for a further terminological convention that will be followed in the rest of the paper. While DMs are discourse relational items as defined by school 2, the group of items and functions called DM by school 1 is called *text-connective markers (TCM)*. I refrain from inventing a cover term for both classes ("pragmatic markers" may do, though it carries misleading associations).

It should have become obvious that the functional commonalities of all elements discussed here – DM as seen by school 1, and DM as seen by school 2 – are their indexical or relational potential. This is the feature shared by both groups. It is the criterion by which they are *the same*. They may be distinguished, though, by the domains to which this indexical potential is applied. For one group, this is the textual, propositional, conceptual domain, and for the other group, it is the communicative, dialogic, non-propositional domain. It is this feature by which they are *different*.

As the definitions of both groups rely on the functional, onomasiological feature of indexicality, they have to be judged as universal labels that do not make any claim as to language-specific realization and categorization. The functions of communication management as well as textual coherence may be fulfilled by a vast number of linguistic categories and constructions. Consequently, the extension of each class of DM – no matter whether it is defined according to school 1 or to school 2 – encompasses linguistic items of all types of formal appearance (from individual word classes via multi word constructions to non-lexical material).

The formal criterion of syntactic integratedness – though being semasiological – is universal, too. It correlates with the functional criterion, and supplies an additional means of discerning both classes.

This provides us with a first stable dividing line between (a) syntactically non-integrated items with discourse connective (non-propositional) functions, and (b) syntactically integrated items with connective functions on the propositional, textual plane.

Now, how about modal particles? They are syntactically integrated and point to propositional entities (see next section), i.e. they obviously – at least at first sight

– belong among group 2 (TCMs). This means that we are not able to set up a direct, immediate opposition between MPs and DM, as MPs are a sub-class of TCM.

Furthermore, as mentioned in the introduction, MPs typically are defined as a language-specific word class (for its features, again, see next section), while DMs as well as TCMs are defined by universal criteria (be they functional or formal). Thus, we are dealing with classes on completely different theoretical levels. We are dealing with different valuta, which, per definition, cannot be subject to one homogeneous classification. Due to this, we also do not yet have a criterion to single out MPs from the class of TCM, and make them visible against the other classes united in the universal class of TCM. The next section is devoted to exactly this task. It provides evidence for establishing a language-specific (German) class of MPs in contrast to other language-specific classes of non-inflecting word categories like conjunctions, connective adverbials, scalar particles etc., which are all on duty for specific functions in the universal domains of TCM as well as DM.

3. The modal particles of German as a word class

The MPs of German have been of heightened interest to linguists in recent decades. In present-day German, there are about 40 items which are generally acknowledged to belong to the class of MPs either as core members or as peripheral members. The core group consists of the following 15 extremely frequent items: *aber, auch, bloß, denn, doch, eben, eigentlich, etwa, halt, ja, mal, nur, schon, vielleicht, wohl* (Gelhaus 1998, 379; Helbig and Buscha 2002, 421ff.).[10] Peripheral members are more numerous and – due to ongoing grammaticalization – typically do not (yet) display all features and functions found in the prototpyical members of the category (Diewald 2007, 118). The following items are frequently mentioned as participants of this group: *fein, ganz, gerade, glatt, gleich, einfach, erst, ruhig, wieder.* Membership of a peripheral candidate in the class of MPs can be tested via its replaceability by core items.

In the present volume, a number of articles deal with modal particles in languages other than German, e.g. in Catalan (Cuenca), in Italian and French (Squartini), in Swedish (Aijmer; Fischer and Alm), in Dutch, Danish and Norwegian (all three treated in Aijmer). It is worth noting that the majority of

---

10. A similar list, without *eigentlich* and *wohl,* is given in Helbig and Buscha (2002, 421ff.). Weydt and Hentschel (1983, 4) refer to the core group by the label "Abtönungspartikeln im engeren Sinne", and exclude *einfach, erst* and *ruhig.* Zifonun, Hoffmann, Strecker [et al.] (1997, 59) count the regionally used particle *man* among the core group.

them refer to the research tradition on German modal particles, and most prominently so when the class of modal particles is defined explicitly and with some rigor. In the light of the results produced by this strong tradition of research (see below) we may assert that there is a broad and substantial understanding concerning the core features of this class as well as its core members. Peripheral members of the class, which are in the process of grammaticalization, i.e. of developing towards a particular grammatical function, by necessity display intercategorial behaviour, and it is not surprising that there exist different judgements on the degree of development of single items by different researchers (cf. e.g. Schoonjans (this volume) for a discussion of gradience and instances of non-complete realization of prototypical features).

Thus, it is useful to take a closer look at the classification of modal particles in German, embedded into a quick survey of non-inflecting word classes. As is generally known "[a]mong non-inflecting linguistic items, membership in a specific word class is primarily defined via functional criteria, with concomitant morphosyntactic features providing additional criteria" (Diewald 2006, 406). A fine-grained classification of non-inflected, particle-like words in German is suggested in Zifonun, Hoffmann, Strecker [et al.] (1997, 66ff.) with alternative terminology given in the first column (my translation; see also Diewald 2007, 119).

Table 1. Classification of particle items according to Zifonun, Hoffmann, Strecker [et al.] (1997, 66f.) [my translation]

Category label (alternative label)	Central feature	Examples
Abtönungspartikel (Modalpartikel)	erwartungs-/wissensbezogen 'refers to knowledge and expectations'	*eben, vielleicht, ja*
Gradpartikel (Fokuspartikel)	Gesagtes gradierend 'grades what is being expressed'	*ausgerechnet, bereits, sogar, vor allem*
Intensitätspartikel (Steigerungspartikel)	Eigenschaft spezifizierend 'specifies characteristic feature'	*recht, sehr, ungemein, weitaus*
Konnektivpartikel (Rangierpartikel)	relationale Integration von Satz/K[ommunikativer] M[inimaleinheit] 'relational integration of sentence/communicative basic unit'	*erstens, allerdings, dennoch, indessen, sonst, zwar*
Modalpartikel (Modalwort)	Sachverhaltsgeltung spezifizierend 'specifies degree of factuality of proposition'	*bedauerlicherweise, sicherlich, vielleicht*
Negationspartikel	Sachverhaltsgeltung negierend 'negates proposition'	*nicht, gar nicht*

Though group membership is not always easy to decide upon, the classification provides us with an indispensible grid for investigating these elements further. Most grammars of German take into account that among the class of particles the so-called modal particles form a distinct subclass. It is not possible here to fully discuss the criteria for singling out the other classes of particles, but it is worth devoting some space to the *standard criteria for defining modal particles*, which typically are given as a list containing the following, widely acknowledged features (cf. Helbig and Buscha 2002, 421ff.; Helbig 1994; Weydt and Hentschel 1993; Hentschel and Weydt 2002; Zifonun, Hoffman, Strecker [et al.] 1997, 59; König 1997, 58; Möllering 2004, 21–39):

a. Modal particles are non-inflecting. Lexemes functioning as modal particles do not inflect even if their heterosemes do. This is a feature modal particles share with all other particles of German.
b. Modal particles have heterosemes in other word classes. This applies to all modal particles of German (with the exception of *halt*). Among the word classes modal particles are heterosemes of are conjunctions, focus and scalar particles, so-called modal words (Modalwörter), adverbs and adjectives. Thus *aber* in (9) is a modal particle, *aber* in (10) is a conjunction; *schon* in (11) is a particle, while in (12) it is a temporal adverb (Helbig and Buscha 2002, 425ff.):

> (9) *Das ist aber   eine Überraschung.*
> That is ABER a   surprise
> 'That is a surprise, *isn't it.*'

> (10) *Ich würde gerne kommen, aber ich habe Grippe und kann nicht aus dem Haus.*
> 'I would love to come, *but* I have got the flu and cannot leave the house.'

> (11) *Das ist schon   eine   Gemeinheit.*
> That is SCHON a dirty trick.
> 'That is a dirty trick, *to be sure.*'

> (12) *Schon sind wir fertig.*
> 'We are done *already.*'

c. Modal particles are obligatorily unstressed. Most authors (see however Meibauer 1994) hold that modal particles per definition are unstressed, and consequently classify stressed items as heterosemes to modal particles (i.e. as adverbs, focus particles etc.; cf. Helbig 1994, Thurmair 1989). This discussion will not be taken up here.

d. Modal particles do not have constituent value or phrasal value. They can nei-
    ther be used as sentential equivalents, nor can they appear in the first position
    of a German V-2 sentence. They cannot be coordinated or questioned. These
    features separate them from neighboring non-inflecting classes like adverbs
    and modal words.
e. Modal particles are combinable. Though they cannot be coordinated, they
    may be serialized, whereby complex rules of combination and order apply
    (Thurmair 1989). In these combinations, the item more to the left always has
    scope over the item(s) to the right. An example is given below:

(13) *Hast du denn vielleicht   mal die   Suppe probiert?*
                                  (Zifonun, Hoffma, Strecker [et al.] 1997, 59)
      Have you DENN VIELLEICHT MAL tasted the   soup?
      '*Do you happen to just for once* have tasted the soup?'

f. Modal particles are restricted to the middle field of the German sentence
    (Thurmair 1989, 25–32, Abraham 1990), that is to the right of the finite verb
    in V-2 position and to the left of the right sentence bracket (see Fischer and
    Alm (this volume) for further details). Within the middle field, they may ap-
    pear in various slots, as illustrated in the following sentence, where each po-
    tential MP-slot is indicated by bracketed *ja*.

(14) *Mit einem Karateschlag hat (ja) Frau Müller (ja) gestern (ja) im Büro (ja)*
      den Schreibtisch des Abteilungsleiters (ja) in zwei Hälften zerlegt.
      With a carate blow has (JA) Mrs Müller (JA) yesterday (JA) at the office
      (JA) the desk of the department head (JA) into two parts knocked.
      '*As we all/both know*, Mrs Müller knocked the desk of the department
      head into two parts yesterday at the office.'

While numerous studies work towards an explanation of this fact, there is still no
satisfactory final solution.[11] It is important to note, though, that the middle field
criterion is a robust and testable criterion for class membership as it separates MPs
from all other non-inflecting word classes, i.e. from conjunctions, adverbs, discourse marking particles, modal adverbs etc. None of the latter ones are subject to
the same restrictions: All other non-inflecting items either are non-restricted to a
particular field, or may appear in any constituent position (adverbs), or do have
other restrictions (e.g. conjunctions), or are syntactically non-integrated to begin
with (DM, see Section 2). Thus, the restriction to the middle field is an essential

---

11. Cf. Abraham 1991; Thurmair (1989, 29ff.); Brandt [et al.] (1992, 73ff.); König (1997, 58);
Möllering 2004.

criterion, and all items looking like an MP, but being located outside the middle field, are to be treated as heterosemes of that MP.

g. Modal particles very often display an affinity with a particular sentence type, i.e. either with structural types, or with illocutionary types, or with complex constructions, called *Satzmodi* (sentential moods). For example, the MP *aber* is restricted to sentences with exclamative and directive functions; *eben, halt* and *ja* are confined to statements, *schon* to statements and directives; *denn, eigentlich* and *wohl* show affinity with questions, and *bloß, nur* and *vielleicht* are restricted to wishes and exclamations; *doch*, on the other hand, is very volatile and only excluded from genuine questions (cf. Gelhaus 1998, 380; Thurmair 1989).

h. Modal particles do not have referential meaning. Very often, this feature sets them in sharp contrast to their heterosemes in the class of adjectives or adverbs, e.g. *bloß, eben* or *ruhig*. If these items are used as adjectives, they display lexical content, if used as modal particles, they encode few abstract semantic features. (15) and (16) illustrate this difference. (15) shows the adjective usage of *ruhig* ('calm'), in which it can be replaced by other adjectives with a similar meaning, like *still* or *gelassen*. (16) is an example of its modal particle usage, where *ruhig* is not substitutable by those adjectives, but by other modal particles, e.g. *doch* or *schon*.

(15) *Den ganzen Tag blieb er <u>ruhig</u> (still/gelassen).*
  'All day long, he stayed *calm*.'

(16) *Da darf es <u>ruhig</u> (doch/schon) (*still/*gelassen) ein bißchen später, so zwischen 4 und 5 Uhr, sein.*   (Keil 1990, 45)
  Then it may RUHIG get a bit later, say between 4 and 5 o' clock.
  'It may get a bit later, *as far as I am concerned*, say between 4 and 5 o'clock.'

i. Modal particles have *sentential* scope or *utterance* scope (illocutionary scope), i.e. they have the widest scope of all sententially integrated particles. Therefore, they cannot function as the reference point of a negation particle (Zifonun, Hoffmann, Strecker [et al.] 1997, 59). Their wide scope separates them from scalar particles like *sehr* in (17) and focus particles like *sogar* in (18), which grade or focus individual constituents (Gelhaus 1998, 377ff.; for the distinction of MPs and "scalar particles" s. Abraham 1991, 243ff.):

(17) *Über die Einladung habe ich mich <u>sehr</u> gefreut.*
  'I am *very* glad about the invitation.'

(18) *<u>Sogar</u> meine Schwester ist pünktlich gekommen.*
  '*Even* my sister came in time.'

As mentioned, this cluster of features is generally acknowledged (with continued discussion about single problematic points) as relevant and sufficient for identifying MPs. Still, it is obvious that most of these criteria are negative ones, i.e. they specify what MPs are *not*. The next section lays out the positive distinctive feature of the class of MPs in German, which is a functional one.

4.   The class-constitutive function of modal particles in German

Traditionally, modal particles are assumed to have a variety of only vaguely describable pragmatic functions, and researchers very often do not even think of looking for a class-constitutive common function, which would be similar, say, to the function of conjunctions. This predominating general attitude is summarized in the following quote:

> Die Funktion der Abtönungspartikeln läßt sich (beim derzeitigen Forschungsstand) nur grob bestimmen. Sie tragen zur Einpassung der kommunikativen Minimaleinheit in den jeweiligen Handlungszusammenhang bei, indem sie auf den Erwartungen und Einstellungen des Sprechers und Adressaten operieren. (Zifonun, Hoffmann, Strecker [et al.] 1997: 59)
>
> The function of modal particles can be circumscribed but roughly (given the actual state of the art in particle research). They contribute to the fitting of the communicative minimal unit [i.e. the sentence] into the relevant interactional context, by operating on the expectations and attitudes of the speaker and recipient. [my translation].

In a number of studies, I have argued against this quasi agnostic position, and have shown that the modal particles form a clear-cut grammatical category with a well-defined categorial function and distinctive oppositions between the core members of the category (Diewald 2006, 2007, 2011; Diewald and Fischer 1998; Diewald and Ferraresi 2008, 79f.). As this is important in the present context, the central points of the argumentation are summarized in the following paragraphs.

The distinctive function of MPs is best illustrated by minimal pairs contrasting an utterance with MP and the same utterance without an MP, e.g. *eben* in (19a) versus the same string without *eben* in (19b). It should be kept in mind that *mutatis mutandis* – i.e. abstracting from the specifics of the MP lexeme *eben* – these explanations hold for all MPs, and that they address the constitutive function of the whole class:

(19)   a.   *Deutsch ist eben schwer.*
                German is EBEN difficult
                '*And yes*, German is difficult.'

b.   *Deutsch ist schwer.*
'German is difficult.'

In contrast to an unmodalized statement like *Deutsch ist schwer* ('German is diffi-cult') in (19b), which does not refer to any linguistic or non-linguistic entity, the MP *eben* in (19a) provides an indexical relation to a particular proposition. As Foolen (1989, 312f.) rightly points out this presupposed proposition is always a "logical variant of the explicitly expressed proposition".[12] In the case of our sen-tence (19a) this variant is 'Deutsch ist schwer'. Thus, by using *eben* in *Deutsch ist eben schwer,* the speaker indicates that the proposition 'Deutsch ist schwer' to him or her counts as known information (which, of course, may be a mere imputation), and that he or she affirms that statement. A paraphrase for this complex meaning of utterance (19a) might be: 'The statement *Deutsch ist schwer* [= given proposi-tion *p*] has been expressed by many people, including myself, before. You and I know that. I iterate this statement indicating its giveness, and therefore say: *Deutsch ist eben schwer* [= modalized variant of given proposition: *eben p*].'

In short: By using a modal particle the speaker marks the very proposition it is used in as given, as communicatively presupposed, as a particular type of prag-matic presupposition.

In earlier work, I have called this pragmatically given unit the "pragmatic pre-text" of an utterance with a MP, in order to indicate three important characteristics of this type of givenness: i. it is *propositional content* (sometimes together with il-locutionary information) as opposed to discourse pragmatic chunks of informa-tion, ii. it is *pragmatically given* in the communicative situation, i.e. it is typically not expressed in the linguistic medium itself, and iii. – notwithstanding ii. – it is *potential text*, i.e. it can be made explicit via a linguistically encoded proposition.

Thus, MPs are a convenient and subtle way of introducing all kinds of implica-tions, assumptions, allusions, without being explicit about that, and this potential is the reason for the wealth of specific communicative and rhetoric functions for which MPs in German are renowned and which have lead to long listings of func-tions attributed to them (cf. Zifonun, Hoffmann, Strecker [et al.] 1997, 904 with the relevant bibliographical notes). Without belittling these functions, it has to be stated that all of them can be derived from the basic function of pragmatic back-ward pointing described in the last paragraphs, the essence of which in turn can be summarized and expanded to its discourse pragmatic relevance as follows: In

---

12.   Foolen is one of the few linguists having argued for a substantial class constitutive function of the MPs as early as in the late 80s of the last century. The relevant quote is: "[als] Klassenbedeutung für Modalpartikeln gilt, daß sie immer auf eine implizite, im Kontext rele-vante Proposition hinweisen. Diese implizite Proposition ist immer eine logische Variante der explizit ausgedrückten Proposition" Foolen(1989, 312f.).

referring back to a propositional or illocutionary entity that is treated as communicatively given, though unexpressed, *the MP marks its utterance as a non-initial utterance, i.e. as a second, reactive turn in a dialogic structure* (which need not be enacted in reality but which is presupposed as communicative background).

In addition to this indexical meaning, which is constitutive of the class of MPs, each modal particle has a diachronically motivated, lexeme-specific semantic feature. The specific semantic content of *aber* is adversative ('*p* in contrast to the pragmatically given unit -*p*'), that of *ja* is affirmative ('*p* identical with the pragmatically given unit *p*'), that of *auch* augmentative ('*p* confirming and enriching the pragmatically given unit *p*'), and that of *schon* concessive ('*p* inspite of low relevance of pragmatically given unit *p*'). This produces paradigmatic oppositions as in (20) (cf. Diewald and Ferraresi 2008, 79f.), which can be explicated by full accounts of their systematic backward pointing structure (for reasons of space, however, the particle meanings are given as very rough glosses only in the paraphrase):

(20)   *Deutsch ist eben/aber/ja/auch/schon schwer.*
       'German is difficult – I iterate this/in contrast to the opposite assumption/ we all know/this and other things hold/admittedly.'

The combination of a class meaning and relatively abstract distinctive meanings between items belonging to the class is one of the essential characteristics of a grammatical paradigm (others being the degree of obligatoriness and the type of relational meaning). Diewald 2011 has shown in detail that the German MPs form a grammatical paradigm in the strict sense such as, for example, the paradigm of determiners. For reasons of space this discussion is not taken up here at any length.

As shown in Sections 1 and 2, MPs are members of the broad domain of pragmatic markers which contains DMs and TCMs, sharing as a common feature an indexical function. On the other hand, MPs differ from typical DMs as well as from typical TCMs: They occupy a place between discourse markers like turn taking signals on one hand and text-connective markers like conjunctions on the other (cf. Diewald 2006). The difference between them lies in the type of the target item of the pointing process, i.e. the domain addressed by the pointing relation. Unlike DMs, MPs apply to propositions and speech-act alternatives (they have propositional or speech-act scope), while DMs point to non-propositional elements of discourse, i.e. they have scope over non-propositional discourse elements of various sizes (cf. Section 2 for examples).

The distinction between MPs and TCMs in the strict sense can be pinned down to the fact that MPs refer to non-expressed but supposedly given propositional elements, while conjunctions (and other TCMs in the strict sense) connect textually encoded (typically propositional) conjuncts; cf. the conjunction *obwohl* in the following example:

(21) <u>*Obwohl*</u> *es schon spät war, machte sie sich zu einem Spaziergang auf.*
'*Although* it was already late, she set out for a walk.'

Furthermore, there is a marked difference in the topological restrictions applying to conjunctions on one hand, and to MPs on the other: Conjunctions have a fixed position at the left periphery (of one or both conjuncts), MPs have a fixed position in the middle field.

Using the combination of the universal functional and formal criteria and the specific discourse structuring function of MPs introduced in this and the preceding sections, we are able to complete our classification for DMs, TCP and MPs in German and set up the following distinctions (cf. Diewald 2006, 408):

DMs relate non-propositional discourse elements which are not textually expressed, which are syntactically non-integrated (i.e. have no syntactically fixed position) and which do not have constituent value. DMs are found in a variety of formal realizations. The latter is also true for TCM, which, however, in contrast to DMs are syntactically integrated, and have functions on the propositional and conceptual level. DMs as well as TCMs are *not* specific word classes (neither in German or any other language).

MPs, on the other hand, are one of the acknowledged word classes of German. They are characterized by a cluster of features (high syntactic integration, topological restriction to the middle field, no constituent value, morphological particle etc.). Their function is indexical as is the function of DMs and TCMs, but it is specific insofar as it points to propositions and speech-act alternatives which are not textually expressed but treated as 'given'. Thus, German is a language that is equipped with an array of fine-grained grammatical devices for indicating relational pragmatic functions. It has numerous language-specific word classes acting in the broad universal domains of DMs and TCMs. The most familiar ones are discourse relevant items like *ne, ja, gell* etc., on one hand, and conjunctions, pronominal adverbs, modal words etc., on the other. And, in addition to these, there is the class of MPs. Diewald 2006 comments on their specific function as follows:

> [...] MPs, which are an important grammatical device of contemporary spoken discourse, cover an intermediate domain between the functions of text-connecting elements such as conjunctions and conjunctional adverbs on the one hand, and discourse-structuring elements such as turn signals, hesitation markers, etc. on the other. That is to say, modal particles are treated here as the link between strictly textual functions and strictly discourse-relational functions. Taking into account that languages like English, which have been the object of extensive research concerning their discourse marking devices, do not have a functional class comparable to MPs in German, the latter might even be called the 'missing link' to deepen our understanding of the interrelations between 'text-connecting' and 'discourse-marking' elements. (Diewald 2006, 408f.)

In short, German has a proper word class as a missing link between two much less clearly delimited, only universally specified groups (DMs and TCMs).

One further issue deserves attention here. The fact that the function of MPs is a grammatical function in German, of course, does not mean that it must be realized as a grammatical function in other languages, or that this function must be expressed by a separate set of items in a language at all. Therefore, the following consideration by Cuenca [this volume] is not a counter-argument against the class of MPs as a truly grammatical category of German.

> [...] discourse markers are a set of expressions that include different word classes. The same can be said of modal markers and, among them, of modal particles. Waltereit (2001), for instance, convincingly argues that the functions of German modal particles can be equivalent to the effects created by lexical and morphological devices in English or Romance languages, which lack for such particles.[13]

Thus, we may conclude this section as follows: MPs are a separate word class in German, and therefore not comparable to DM or TCM. In particular, we cannot integrate the notions MP and DM properly into one level of classification. DM is a label on a different theoretical level than MP. The answer to the question raised in this volume whether they are two sides of the same coin is clearly: No, they are not.

- MPs are different from DMs concerning their hierarchical level as well as their specific function.
- MPs are different from TCMs concerning their hierarchical level as well as their specific function.
- They are the "same" only in so far as they share a broad indexical function.

Having made these decisions, we need to take a look at the indeterminacy, gradiences and intercategoriality of the class of MPs in German.

5.   Intercategoriality

Class membership cannot be reliably attributed to particular linguistic items *per se* (whether lexical or not), i.e. it is not determinable on the basis of isolated segmental units, but has to take into account contextual and functional features. This

---

13.   Cuenca continues as follows: "The basic difference between both classes can be determined by considering that discourse markers, at least in their more traditional definition as connective elements or items bracketing units of talk, are two position operators, i.e. units typically linking two content segments, whereas modal markers are one position operators modifying the illocution of an utterance". As should have become clear, this definition and classification is not supported here.

problem of fundamental intercategoriality is illustrated by linguistic elements of German which do have functions as MPs, but also fulfill functions typical of other word classes. Two phenomena are of interest here:

1. Heterosemes: One item has several functions and word class affiliations in complementary contexts (isolating contexts).
2. Ambiguity: An item allows two distinct readings in one usage.

Ad 1: Heterosemes. As discussed in Section 3, modal particles have heterosemes in other word classes, ranging from major lexical word classes like adjectives and adverbs to so-called function words like conjunctions, focus particles and discourse markers of a variety of types. As several examples have already been given in Sections 1 and 3 (cf. the use of *ja* in 3 and 8, the uses of *aber* and *schon* in 9 to 12, and the use of *ruhig* in 15 and 16), it is sufficient here to add just a few further examples.

Doch has adverbial (22) and modal particle (23) usages:

(22) *Ich habe es echt mehrmals probiert, aber dann habe ich es doch falsch eingelegt.*
      'I did try several times, but then I inserted it in the wrong way *nevertheless*.'

(23) *Das ist doch ein Klacks für Dich.*
      This is DOCH very easy for you.
      'This is very easy for you – *I am convinced of it after deliberating about whether it is or whether it is not*.'

The adverbial usage in (22) can be translated by e.g. *nevertheless* in English. The MP usage of *doch* refers to a given pragmatic pre-text which consists of a deliberate choice between two alternative propositions, contrasted by their polarity (p1: 'Das ist ein Klacks für dich' – p2: 'Das ist kein Klacks for dich'). The utterance with *doch* points to this choice, and confirms the first alternative as a result of deliberating upon the two (p1 & MP: *Das ist doch ein Klacks für dich*). Similarly, *aber* and *auch,* and a number of further MPs of the core group have conjunctional, adverbial and modal particle usages.

Not only core members, but also peripheral members of the class of MPs show heterosemes and complementary, i.e. isolating contexts. *Ruhig*, for example, can be used as an attributive adjective (24), a predicative adjective and/or verb phrase adverb (25), as a modal particle (26, identical with example 16), and as a – newly developing – discourse marker (27).

(24) *Er ist ein ruhiger Mensch.*
      'He is a *calm* person.'

(25) *Sie kommen ruhig herein.*
      'They enter *quietly*.'/'They enter *in a composed state of mind*.'

(26) *Da darf es <u>ruhig</u> ein bißchen später, so zwischen 4 und 5 Uhr, sein*
                                                                    (Keil 1990, 45)
     Then, it may get RUHIG a bit later, say between 4 and 5 o'clock.
     'It may get a bit later, *as far as I am concerned,* say between 4 and 5 o'clock.'

(27) *und ich darf das <u>ruhig</u> einmal sagen ohne als sentimental zu gelten*
                                                            (IDS-DSAV, FR 182_50)
     and I may RUHIG say that for once without counting as sentimental.
     'and I may – *aptly* – say that for once without counting as sentimental.'

The function of *ruhig* as MP is much less known than that of core members of the class. Therefore, a short description is appropriate. As laid out in Diewald (2008, 227f.), the MP *ruhig* is known to be restricted to particular types of directive speech acts, namely to various types of permissions (including advice and general suggestions). An act of permission can be defined as "a directive speech act the recipient has asked for", i.e. as incorporating a reactive semantic component. This reactive meaning is explicitly emphasized by the MP *ruhig*, and can be summarized as suggested in the following quote:

> It [the MP *ruhig*] indicates a contrast between the expected attitude of the speaker and the actual attitude of the speaker concerning the imminent action. By using *ruhig* the speaker says: 'in contrast to your/somebody's expectation (irrelevant reservations), I do not have objections'. (Diewald 2008, 227f.)

Thus, utterance (26) with *ruhig* as MP may be paraphrased as:

(28) 'In contrast to your presupposition that I might object to it being later, I say that it may be later, about between 4 and 5 o'clock.'

In (26) the combination of the formal subject *es* and the stative predicate excludes the interpretation of *ruhig* as an adjective, i.e. neither the predicative nor the adverbial reading are possible here. The interpretation of *ruhig* as a modal particle is the only one available in this context, i.e. we have an isolating context for the MP-reading here.

     Usages like the one in (27), which display the first step of *ruhig* towards the development of a discourse marker (a floor keeping signal), are restricted to first person subjects and declarative sentences. They are a 20th century innovation (discussed in Diewald 2008). Though further research is needed here, this usage supports the assumption that discourse markers develop from connective devices like conjunctions, connective adverbials and modal particles (cf. Haselow 2011; Barth and Couper-Kuhlen 2002; Günthner 1999). That is, we may assume that transcategorial linguistic change from MPs to turn-organizational DMs is a common phenomenon.

Summing up the remarks on heterosemes: Due to language change (mostly, but not necessarily grammaticalization) and lexical split, we have multiple heterosemy in German in the field of non-inflecting word classes including MPs. For each heteroseme, there are isolating contexts bringing out their distinctive, class-constitutive features.

The fact that linguistic items participate in different word classes in one synchronic layer is an instance of intercategoriality of particular lexemes, which is the result of transcategorial language change.

Ad 2: Ambiguity. The second point to be discussed, functional ambiguity, is closely connected to the dynamic forces of language change as well. Functional ambiguity is intercategoriality in its narrow sense. It is relevant in those cases, where class membership of a particular item cannot be determined on unequivocally, although there is one given linguistic context. As modal particles are restricted to the middle field, this phenomenon, too, is observable only in this topological position. Among the most common cases is the ambiguity between modal particle (with features like non-referential, non-constituent etc., see Section 3) and adverbial (with features like referential meaning, constituent value etc., see Section 3), as in the following example:

(29) *Ich gehe eben zur Post.*
       I go EBEN to the post office

Eben can be interpreted either as a temporal adverb meaning 'just now' as in the paraphrase (30) or as a modal particle as paraphrased in (31):

(30) 'I am on my way to the post office *just now*.'
(31) 'I am *just* on my way to the post office.'

An analogous and also very common case is the ambiguity between a predicative (or adverbial) function and a modal particle function, which may arise in instances like the following (cf. also example 25):

(32) *Kommen Sie ruhig herein!*
       Come RUHIG in!

Ruhig can be interpreted as an adjective used predicatively or adverbially ('Come in in a calm state of mind', 'Come in quietly') on one hand, or as a modal particle on the other ('Come in – I don't object'). This ambiguity arises in all instances of directives containing *ruhig* in the middle field together with a modal verb, an infinitive of an action verb, and an animate subject.

Most interesting of course are instances of intercategoriality between the modal particle function and a discourse marking function. Again – due to the topological restriction of the class of MPs – these are only possible in the middle field; e.g. in the following examples (which were produced in group discussions):

(33)   *sagen wir ruhig die Reaktionäre*   (IDS-DSAV FR200_54)
       say-SUBJI-1PL we RUHIG the reactionaries

(34)   *gehn wir ruhig mal kriminalistisch vor*   (IDS-DSAV FR212_60)
       go-SUBJI-1PL we RUHIG once criminologically ahead

Quite obviously, these are instances with a particular constructional make-up: They display a V1-pattern with the verb in the subjunctive I, followed by the first person plural subjects (*wir*) and the item *ruhig*. This construction shows an ambiguity between the reading of *ruhig* as MP, and another reading as a kind of DM. The MP reading for (33) can be paraphrased as follows:

(35)   'Though you might think we object to saying "die Reaktionäre", we do not object to it.'

However, this construction no longer expresses a true permission, but a hortative construction (i.e. a "permission" of the first person to a first person plural subject). Therefore, the illocutive function of permission changes into a kind of encouragement including the speaker, whereby the dialogic and reactive component is reduced as compared to the prototypical MP-usages. Thus, the use of the MP *ruhig* in this new construction also marks the rise of a new discourse function. A paraphrase of *ruhig* in this use might take the following wording:

(36)   'I suggest (we do) *proposition* although we have refrained from (doing) *proposition* before.'

Data like these suggest the existence of a continuum leading from MP to DM, i.e. from partly implicit textual relations (relation to pragmatic pre-text) to (non-textual) discourse relations. It is assumed here that these changes are grammaticalization processes leading to further differentiation in the domain of pragmatic functions, and that modal particles in German do in fact constitute a distinct category, which however is part of a continuum of several word classes in the neighboring domains of DMs and TCMs. A language-specific categorization like the one to be found in German systematizes these continua between DMs and TCMs and makes them manageable. However, as linguistic entities shade into each other in their usage, categorization has to take into account intercategoriality as a widespread and natural phenomenon.

6. Same same but different – a plea for flexible categorization

This final section takes up the issue of flexible categorization, i.e. the problem of "the complexity of categorizing multifunctional expressions" as observed by Degand et al. in the conception of this volume. We have seen that classes of linguistic items situated on different hierarchical levels of linguistic structure and on different planes of the communicative context cannot be compared directly, nor subsumed together under one classificatory system. This is particularly true when universal categories are confronted with language-specific categories. Thus, MPs, which are language-specific items defined according to the formal and functional criteria of the language in question, cannot be directly compared to or jointly categorized with universal functional categories, like DMs or TCMs. Or briefly put: MPs and DMs are coins of different currencies.

Nevertheless, the function that is fulfilled by the word class of MP in German can be fulfilled by other means of any degree of grammaticalization or lexicalization in any language. Thus, it is appropriate to look for functional equivalence and to compare the respective linguistic exponents of that function in different languages. For example, German MPs are known to be rendered by tag questions in English very often, and – to add an example from a more distant area of grammar – the English continuous form (e.g. *The children are playing in the garden*) is known to be rendered by adverbials like *gerade* (*Die Kinder spielen gerade im Garten*) or the construction with the verb 'to be' (*sein*) and a prepositional phrase with *am* and the nominalized main verb (*Die Kinder sind am Spielen*) in German. Still, in the latter case, nobody would claim that German has a grammatical category of aspect and, in the former case, nobody would claim that English has a grammatical category of MPs.

Analogously, observing that the functions fulfilled by MPs may be fulfilled by other discernible items in another languages (e.g. in Romance languages as discussed in Cuenca, this volume), does not *per se* lead to the conclusion that these items are modal particles.

In German, on the other hand, all relevant tests show that MPs have a specific and distinctive function and constitute a grammatical category and word class. As such (i.e as a language-specific class) they can be set off from the broad functional domains of DMs and TCMs. In order to tackle these facts, it is necessary to apply a concept of flexible categorization. The notion of flexible categorization does not mean arbitrary classification. Instead, it refers to the fact that different perspectives and intentions will lead to different ways of priorizing particular features. Flexible categorization answers the need to reconcile universal functional categories with language-specific classes as well as the need to provide for intercategoriality on a language-specific level. In the argumentation presented in this paper, it has become evident that i. linguistic categories are language-specific, insofar as their realization is subject to and integrated into the semasiological distinctions and paradigmatic oppositions of that particular language, that, therefore, ii. if generalization across languages is aimed at, the items and features to be compared must be sufficiently abstract and typically defined in functional terms, and that iii. the findings and tenets of grammaticalization studies concerning clines and non-discrete boundaries in linguistic categories are fundamental for any attempt at classifying linguistic items (independently of whether the issue of grammaticalization is explicitly addressed).

Widening the view to a more general perspective, we may conclude with the following list of general considerations concerning the art and purpose of linguistic categorization:

- Linguistic categories – such as word classes or functional/grammatical categories – are not ontologically given items. Depending on the respective language, they are subject to the specific conditions and restrictions that are operative in that language, and thus, any two particular languages may realize equivalent functions deploying very different formal and structural techniques on different layers of the linguistic system (e.g. morphological marker versus intonational contour).
- The relevant features constituting a category and their internal hierarchies vary between languages.
- Classifications in linguistic research are set up in accordance with the epistemological layout of the research to be undertaken.
- Linguistic categories are working hypotheses. They are not set up once and for all, but may be modified when new research questions arise or new results are achieved.
- There may be different categorizations for different purposes at the same time.
- Correspondences between different categorizational choices as well as their mutual (in-)translatability and (non-)compatibilities should be made as explicit as possible.

Though seemingly trivial, the neglect of these considerations lies at the bottom of many misunderstandings and misguided attempts at finding final solutions for classificatory questions. The present paper is meant as a step towards overcoming these deadlocks.

References:

Abraham, Werner. 1990. "Zur heterogenen Entfaltung der Modalpartikel im Ahd. und Mhd." In *Neuere Forschungen zur historischen Syntax des Deutschen: Referate der Internationalen Fachkonferenz Eichstätt 1989*, ed. by Anne Betten, 124–138. Tübingen: Niemeyer.

Abraham, Werner, 1991. "Discourse Particles in German: How Does their Illocutionary Force Come About?" In *Discourse Particles: Descriptive and Theoretical Investigations on the Logical, Syntactic, and Pragmatic Properties of Discourse Particles in German*, ed. by Werner Abraham, 203–252. Amsterdam: Benjamins.

Aijmer, Karin [this volume]. "Analysing Modal Adverbs as Modal Particles and Discourse Markers."

Auer, Peter, and Susanne Günthner. 2005. "Die Entstehung von Diskursmarkern im Deutschen – ein Fall von Grammatikalisierung?" In *Grammatikalisierung im Deutschen*, ed. by Thorsten Leuschner, and Tanja Mortelmans, 335–362. Berlin: de Gruyter.

Autenrieth, Tanja. 2002. *Heterosemie und Grammatikalisierung bei Modalpartikeln. Eine synchrone und diachrone Studie anhand von eben, halt, e(cher)t, einfach, schlicht und glatt.* Tübingen: Niemeyer.

Barth-Weingarten, Dagmar, and Elizabeth Couper-Kuhlen. 2002. "On the Development of Final *though*: A Case of Grammaticalization?" In *New reflections on grammaticalization*, ed. by Ilse Wischer, and Gabriele Diewald, 345–361. Amsterdam/Philadelphia: Benjamins.

Brandt, Margareta, Marga Reis, Inger Rosengren, and Ilse Zimmermann. 1992. "Satztyp, Satzmodus und Illokution." In *Satz und Illokution*, Bd. 1, ed. by Inger Rosengren, 1–90. Tübingen: Niemeyer.

Cuenca, Maria Josep [this volume]. "The Fuzzy Limits between Discourse Marking and Modal Marking."

Degand, Liesbeth, and Anne-Marie Simon-Vandenbergen (eds). 2011. *Grammaticalization, Pragmaticalization and/or (Inter)Subjectification: Methodological issues for the study of discourse markers* [Thematic issue: Linguistics 49,2]. Berlin/New York: de Gruyter.

Detges, Ulrich, and Richard Waltereit. 2009. "Diachronic pathways and pragmatic strategies: different types of pragmatic particles from a diachronic point of view." In *Current Trends in Diachronic Semantics and Pragmatics*, ed. by Maj-Britt Mosegaard Hansen, and Jacqueline Visconti, 43- 61. Bingley: Emerald.

Diewald, Gabriele, Kerstin Fischer. 1998. "Zur diskursiven und modalen Funktion der Partikeln *aber, auch, doch* und *ja* in Instruktionsdialogen." *Linguistica* 38: 75–99.

Diewald, Gabriele. 1999. "Die dialogische Bedeutungskomponente von Modalpartikeln." In *Dialogue Analysis and the Mass Media. Proceedings of the International Conference, Erlangen, April 2-3, 1998*, ed. by Bernd Naumann, 187–199.Tübingen: Niemeyer.

Diewald, Gabriele. 2006. "Discourse Particles and Modal Particles as Grammatical Elements." In *Approaches to Discourse Particles*, ed. by Kerstin Fischer, 403–425. Amsterdam: Elsevier.

Diewald, Gabriele. 2007. "Abtönungspartikel." In *Handbuch der deutschen Wortarten*, ed. by Ludger Hoffmann, 117–142. Berlin/New York: de Gruyter.

Diewald, Gabriele. 2008. "The Catalytic Function of Constructional Restrictions in Grammaticalization." In *Studies on Grammaticalization*, ed. by Elisabeth Verhoeven, Stavros Skopeteas, Yong-Min Shin, Yoko Nishina, and Johannes Helmbrecht, 219–240. Berlin: de Gruyter.

Diewald, Gabriele. 2011. "Pragmaticalization (defined) as Grammaticalization of Discourse Functions." *Linguistics* 49 (2): 365–390.

Diewald, Gabriele, and Gisella Ferraresi. 2008. "Semantic, Syntactic and Constructional Restrictions in the Diachronic Rise of Modal Particles in German: A Corpus-based Study on the Formation of a Grammaticalization Channel." In *Theoretical and Empirical Issues in Grammaticalization*, ed. by Elena Seoane, and María José López-Couso, 77–110. Amsterdam/Philadelphia: Benjamins.

Diewald, Gabriele, Marijana Kresic, and Elena Smirnova. 2009. "The Grammaticalization Channels of Evidentials and Modal Particles in German: Integration in Textual Structures as a Common Feature." In *Diachronic Semantics and Pragmatics*, ed. by Maj-Britt Mosegaard Hansen, and Jacqueline Visconti, 193–213. Bingley: Emerald.

Foolen, Ad. 1989. "Beschreibungsebenen für Modalpartikelbedeutungen." In *Sprechen mit Partikeln,* ed. by Harald Weydt, 305–317. Berlin/New York: de Gruyter.

Fraser, Bruce. 1999. "What are Discourse Markers?" *Journal of Pragmatics*, 31: 931–952.

Fraser, Bruce. 2006. "Towards a Theory of Discourse Markers." In *Approaches to Discourse Particles*, ed. by Kerstin Fischer, 189–204. Amsterdam: Elsevier.

Fischer, Kerstin. 2006. "Towards an Understanding of the Spectrum of Approaches to Discourse Particles: Introduction to the Volume." In *Approaches to Discourse Particles*, ed. by Kerstin Fischer, 1–20. Amsterdam: Elsevier.

Fischer, Kerstin (ed.). 2006. *Approaches to Discourse Particles* [Studies in Pragmatics 1]. Amsterdam: Elsevier.

Fischer, Kerstin, and Maria Alm. [this volume]. "A Radical Construction Grammar Perspective on the Modal Particle-Discourse Particle Distinction."

Fischer, Kerstin, and Michaela Johanntokrax. 1995. Ein linguistisches Merkmalsmodell für die Lexikalisierung von diskurssteuernden Partikeln. SFB 360 *Situierte künstliche Kommunikatoren*, Report 18.

Gelhaus, Herrmann. 1998. "Die Wortarten." In *Duden: Grammatik der deutschen Gegenwartssprache*, 6. Aufl., 85–407. Mannheim: Dudenverlag,

Günthner, Susanne. 1999. "Entwickelt sich der Konzessivkonnektor *obwohl* zum Diskursmarker? Grammatikalisierungstendenzen im gesprochenen Deutsch." *Linguistische Berichte* 180: 409–446.

Hansen, Maj-Britt Mosegaard. 2006. "A Dynamic Polysemy Approach to the Lexical Semantics of Discourse Markers (with an exemplary analysis of French *toujours*)." In *Approaches to Discourse Particles*, ed. by Kerstin Fischer, 21–41. Amsterdam: Elsevier.

Hansen Maj-Britt Mosegaard, and Jacqueline Visconti (eds). 2009. *Current Trends in Diachronic Semantics and Pragmatics*. [Studies in Pragmatics 7]. Bingley: Emerald.

Haselow, Alexander. 2011. "Discourse Marker and Modal Particle: The Functions of Sentence-final *then* in Spoken English." *Journal of Pragmatics* 43 (14): 3603–3623.

Helbig, Gerhard. 1994. *Lexikon deutscher Partikeln*. 3. durchges. Auflage. Leizig [etc.]: Langenscheidt, Verlag Enzyklopädie.

Helbig, Gerhard, and Joachim Buscha. 2002. *Deutsche Grammatik. Ein Handbuch für den Ausländerunterricht*. Berlin/München: Langenscheidt.

Hentschel, Elke, and Harald Weydt. 2002. "Die Wortart ,Partikel'." In *Lexikologie. Internationales Handbuch zur Natur und Struktur von Wörtern und Wortschätzen*. 1. Halbband, ed. by A. D. Cruse, F. Hundsnurscher, M. Job, and P. R. Lutzeier, P.R., 646–653. Berlin, New York: de Gruyter.

IDS-Korpora, Freiburger Korpus = EDV-verfügbares Textkorpus des Instituts für deutsche Sprache, Mannheim, Freiburger Korpus gesprochener deutscher Standardsprache.

IDS_DSAV, "Datenbank Gesprochenes Deutsch", EDV-verfügbares Textkorpus des Instituts für deutsche Sprache, Mannheim.

Keil, Martina. 1990. *Analyse von Partikeln für ein sprachverstehendes System – am Beispiel telefonischer Zugauskunftsdialoge.* Magisterarbeit in der Philosophischen Fakultät II (Sprach- und Literaturwissenschaften) der Universität Erlangen. [typoscript].

König, Ekkehard. 1997. "Zur Bedeutung von Modalpartikeln im Deutschen." In *Aspekte der Modalität im Deutschen – auch in kontrastiver Sicht*, ed. by Friedhelm Debus, and Oddleif Leirbukt, 57–75. Hildesheim: Olms.

Lewis, Diana M. 2006. "Discourse Markers in English: A Discourse-pragmatic View." In *Approaches to Discourse Particles*, ed. by Kerstin Fischer, 43–59. Amsterdam: Elsevier.

Meibauer, Joachim. 1994. *Modaler Kontrast und konzeptuelle Verschiebung. Studien zur Syntax und Semantik deutscher Modalpartikeln.* Tübingen: Niemeyer.

Möllering, Martina. 2004. *The Acquisition of German Modal particles. A Corpus-Based Approach.* Bern [etc.]: Peter Lang.

Sagerer, Gerhard, Hans-Jürgen Eikmeyer, and Gert Rickheit. 1994. "Wir bauen jetzt ein Flugzeug. Konstruieren im Dialog. Arbeitsmaterialien." Tech. Report, SFB 360 Situierte künstliche Kommunikatoren, University of Bielefeld.

Schiffrin, Deborah. 2006. "Discourse Marker Research and Theory: Revisting *and*." In *Approaches to Discourse Particles*, ed. by Kerstin Fischer, 315–338. Amsterdam: Elsevier.

Schoonjans, Steven [this volume]. "Modal Particles: Problems in Defining a Category."

Squartini, Mario [this volume]. "From TAM to Discourse via Information Structure: North-Western Italian *già* 'already' and its Fench Cognate *déjà*."

Thurmair, Maria. 1989. *Modalpartikeln und ihre Kombinationen.* Tübingen: Niemeyer.

Valdmets, Annika [this volume]. "Modal Particles, Discourse markers, and Adverbs with *lt*-suffix in Estonian."

Weydt, Harald, and Elke Hentschel. 1983. "Kleines Abtönungswörterbuch." In *Partikeln und Interaktion*, ed. by Harald Weydt, 3–24. Tübingen: Niemeyer.

Zifonun, Gisela, Ludger Hoffmann, and Bruno Strecker[et al.]. 1997. *Grammatik der deutschen Sprache.* 3 vol. Berlin, New York: de Gruyter.

A radical construction grammar perspective on the modal particle-discourse particle distinction

Kerstin Fischer and Maria Alm
University of Southern Denmark and University of Southern Denmark

In this paper, we suggest to approach issues of definitions of discourse and modal particles by taking a construction grammatical perspective and thus to study the formal and functional properties of these items as form-meaning pairings, i.e. as constructions. We furthermore propose to distinguish between the contributions of lexical and grammatical constructions. In accordance with Croft's (2001) Radical Construction Grammar approach, cross-linguistic comparison is then carried out on the basis of the conceptual space, which comprises the language specific sets of functions discourse and modal particles fulfill cross-linguistically. We illustrate the model proposed on a contrastive analysis of German *also* and Swedish *alltså*, which function both as discourse and modal particles.

1. Introduction: The approach taken

The definition of both discourse particles (e.g. Schourup 1999) and modal particles (cf., for instance, Diewald 2006) is a notorious problem. Definition is usually one of the core tasks a scholar studying the items under consideration has to fulfill, and there is still no agreement on how the classes can be appropriately characterized (cf. Fischer 2006a). Attempts at defining each class make use of both functional and formal criteria, yet there is no unanimous agreement on either, especially not cross-linguistically, as the discussion in the current volume illustrates. The proposal we are making here is therefore to study form and function components in terms of pairings, i.e. as constructions, and on the background of a conceptual space against which language specific constructions can be compared.

A construction grammar approach combines form and function naturally; construction grammar takes a language system to be an inventory of linguistic signs, so-called constructions, i.e. pairs of form and meaning components.

Taking a construction grammar perspective thus means to explore the co-occurrence relationships between functional and formal characteristics. The units considered in construction grammar may vary in size; construction grammar treats morphemes, lexemes, phrases, clauses and even exchanges equally as constructions and thus provides a single, unified framework for their description. Consequently, the natural habitats of discourse particles and modal particles are directly part of the description, which allows us to look at the contribution of the respective lexical item,[1] of the construction in which it occurs and of the word class function, if there is any, separately. We therefore argue that the characteristics of construction grammar are particularly useful to deal with a question such as the current one, namely how two word classes, such as discourse particles and modal particles, can be defined. Most importantly, a construction grammar approach enables us to disentangle the factors that contribute to the definition of, and delimitation between, the two classes. It does so by differentiating between the items under consideration and their contextually determined uses and by stating form-related and functional characteristics explicitly. Furthermore, construction grammar provides an explicit model for typological comparison. A construction grammatical perspective may thus eventually lead to a cross-linguistically valid definition of discourse particles and modal particles, and in any case it contributes to systematizing the discussion and to putting it on a solid methodological basis.

2.   Construction grammar and the description of spoken interaction

Construction grammar is increasingly used to describe not only the grammar of sentences, but also phenomena of spoken language interaction (cf. for instance, Fried and Östman 2005; Deppermann 2007; Fischer 2010). Construction grammar is particularly attractive for conversation analysts, but also for pragmaticians from other theoretical backgrounds, because the conversation analytic notion of structural context is in principle highly compatible with the sign-based nature of construction grammar. That is, the context in which an item occurs and which determines its functions and formal properties may be described as a construction. For instance, Heritage (1984) distinguishes numerous such contexts that determine the interpretation of the interjection *oh* in interaction; construction

---

1.   In Construction Grammar, lexical items are in fact also regarded to be constructions; however, in order to increase readability, we distinguish here between the lexical items functioning as discourse and modal particles and the larger, schematic structures, the constructions, in which they occur.

grammar allows here the description of the features that conversation analysts like Heritage use to describe the 'structural contexts' in which a particle like *oh* may occur (see Fischer forthcoming).

Furthermore, the fact that construction grammar is generally open concerning the size of the units considered has recently lead to the investigation of units also beyond the sentence (Fischer 2010; Antonodopoulo and Nikiforidou 2011). Construction grammar has thus moved from the description of phrasal or sentential units to the description of interaction (e.g. Couper-Kuhlen and Selting 2001; Imo and Günthner 2007; Deppermann 2007; Couper-Kuhlen and Thompson 2008). In addition, construction grammar has been extremely open with respect to the meaning-side of constructions, which may comprise cognitive, presuppositional, speech act, discourse structuring, information structural and other pragmatic information (cf. Fillmore, Kay and O'Connor 1988; Kay 1995, 2003; Kay and Michaelis 2012).

Besides its increasing use in the description of spoken interaction, construction grammar has been shown to be a powerful framework for the understanding of language acquisition (Tomasello 2003), a useful tool for cross-linguistic comparison (Croft 2001), and an excellent model to describe language change (Traugott 2008; Diewald 2008, 2011). In many respects, it has become a promising approach to linguistic theory and description, even though many aspects of the model are not fully worked out yet.

3.   Disentangling the contributions of lexemes and constructions

A construction grammatical approach to discourse and modal particles, which distinguishes between the contributions of the particle lexemes and constructions, is particularly useful to define discourse and modal particles since the particles themselves, while carrying some meaning, do not inform the hearer whether they are discourse particles or modal particles.[2] Thus, the lexemes themselves are unspecified for the functions they are going to fulfill in interaction, as well as for the word class to which they belong (see Diewald, this volume, for a similar point). The word class is thus not defined by the lexemes but is a matter of their use in context, in particular, in a grammatical construction.[3] The structural contexts in

---

2.   When we speak of lexemes here, we really mean lexical constructions; in Construction Grammar, lexical items are regarded to be constructions as well. However, for the sake of clarity, we speak of lexemes and constructions here in order to highlight their different contributions to the interpretation of individual discourse and modal particle occurrences.

3.   This simple observation has also been made in non-construction grammatical works (e.g. Lindström 2008).

which the particles under consideration occur have been found to determine, at least partly, the interpretations the particles have in conversation. That is, the contexts themselves carry meaning aspects. This is illustrated by the following examples of the English particle *yeah*:

(1)[4] fmjm_3_03: okay, the third sounds good (...) sounds like a date, how 'bout you, is that good?
        mdrd_3_04: **yeah**, it's excellent.

(2)   fsma_7_03: well, Wednesday I'm busy all days, Tuesday the only time I would have would be at three in the afternoon.
        fmmm_7_04: **yeah**, I'll be busy on Tuesday from two to four thirty, so maybe we should make it for next week sometime?

(3)   mdkr_5_01: **yeah**, Cindy, there's a couple of more things I'd like to discuss with you. um can we get together for a couple of hours this week or next?

Here, *yeah* functions in the first example as an answer signal, agreeing to the proposal made by the partner. However, in the second example, the speaker does in fact not agree to the proposal but merely signals to the partner that she has heard and understood her partner's utterance and that she is relating relevantly to it, yet it does not signal agreement. In the third example, *yeah* does not relate to anything that has happened before since it is the first turn in this appointment scheduling dialog. Here, *yeah* rather serves as a framing signal.

Our proposal is therefore to distinguish between the contribution of the lexical item (*yeah* in this case) from the construction in which it occurs.

Besides accounting for an individual particle's polyfunctionality, a construction grammar approach to discourse particles and modal particles accounts naturally for the fact that every item used within a certain construction receives interpretations similar to those of other items in the same construction. To demonstrate that this is the case, one needs to take several particles into consideration; below are a few examples that illustrate that it is the construction that carries many of the functional components identified for uses of *yeah* above;[5] this shows that these aspects of meaning actually belong to the construction and not to the lexical item within the construction. To illustrate this point, consider the three examples of *mm* below, which exhibit a very similar set of functions as those identified for *yeah* above:

---

4.   A list of the corpora used can be found in the appendix.

5.   In several studies, the impact of constructional meanings on the interpretations of discourse particles and modal particles could be demonstrated (see Fischer 2000a; 2006b; 2010; forthcoming).

(4) Liz: Who's talking to A:rnold. (1.6) tomorrow.=
    Mel: =(E-) (.) I: am.
    Liz: Are you?
    Mel: **Mm.**=
    Liz: =Oh; =that's good.   (Gardner 2001, 95)

In this example, *mm* functions as an answer particle, whereas in the following example, it does not indicate acceptance but instead only signals that the previous
turn was perceived and understood and that the current utterance is a relevant
contribution continuing on the same topic:

(5) Gar: Wuhyih wan me t'go mix y'a drink?
    Cur: Sh[it
    Car: **Mm** [I already got one.   (Gardner 2001, 90)

Finally, like *yeah* in example (3), *mm* functions here as a discourse framer, concluding the previous topic before opening up a new one:

(6) Bob: I said I'm quite prepared to talk to ya, about anything an' ev'rything,
           if you're stone cold so:ber. (7.8 seconds)
    Ann: **Mm:::** .hh well you handd'n eventful day, didn you .hh
                                                               (Gardner 2001, 70)

The similarities between *yeah* and *mm* result from their use in similar structural
contexts, that is, within the same grammatical constructions.

    In the following, we address to what extent the constructions in which parti-
cles can occur are cross-linguistically valid. In order to do that, we investigate in
detail two very similar particles in two very similar languages. From there, we
develop our model of how the distinction between discourse and modal particles
can be addressed cross-linguistically.

4. The case study: German *also* versus Swedish *alltså*

In this study, we demonstrate how a construction grammar approach can shed
light on the discourse particle – modal particle distinction on the basis of two
particles, German *also* and Swedish *alltså*. These two particles can function both
as a discourse particle and as a modal particle, which allows us to compare the
functions of discourse particles and modal particles in the two languages directly.
Both particles have a conclusive meaning which is stable irrespective of the context
in which the particles are used. German *also* and Swedish *alltså* are furthermore

highly frequent and relatively unrestricted with respect to situations of use so that data collection is not a problem.

We take a cross-linguistic perspective in order to uncover how a construction grammar approach can deal with language-specific constraints, and how a separation of different perspectives on the definition of the two classes (for instance, by items, by function, by syntactic position) can prove useful in order to develop definitions of discourse particles and modal particles, to distinguish between the two classes and to identify the language-specific properties of the classes.

4.1   Introduction: *Also* and *alltså*

The traditional analysis of *also* and *alltså* in grammatical descriptions of German and Swedish (e.g. Duden 2006; Teleman 1999) classifies them as conjunctional adverbs.[6] In traditional grammar descriptions, they are taken to fulfill the same function with respect to their host unit, which usually is the declarative sentence, regardless of their position.

Both the German and the Swedish main clause structure can be described with reference to the discontinuous verbal positions: Before the first verbal position there is a sentence-integrated position which we will call the front field.[7] In declarative main clauses, it is obligatory to fill this position. The first verbal position then holds the finite verb. The second verbal position holds all the non-finite parts of the predicate, if there are any present. Between the two verbal positions, there is another constituent position, which we will call the middle field. After the second verbal position, there is a third constituent position, which we will call the end field.[8]

---

6.   In the German literature, the term *connective particle* is also used for words like *also*. In our discussion, we will ignore the slight differences in terminology and definition. In the Swedish literature, only the term *conjunctional adverb* is used.

7.   In the Swedish literature, there are several suggestions what to call this position. In our discussion, we will use only the term *front field* in order to make the comparison between the languages easier.

8.   In modern German grammar description, this positon is usully called the *Nachfeld* (e.g. Duden 2006), which literally corresponds to "post field". However, in the Swedish literature the term *efterfält* "post field" is used to refer to the non-sentence-integrated final position (Lindström 2008: 70; Teleman 1999: 23ff.), whereas *slutfält*"end field" refers to the sentence--integrated position(s) at the end of the sentence (Teleman 1999: 3ff.; Lindström 2008: 69). To avoid confusion, we will use the term *end field* to refer to the sentence-integrated constituent position(s) after the second verb position in German and Swedish.

In addition, outside the narrow bounds of the clause structure there are non-sentence-integrated positions, in particular clause initial and clause final. In the grammar books these positions are defined as prefield[9] and post field respectively.[10] However, the non-integrated positions *prefield* and *post field* are not restricted to declarative clauses. They appear in combination with any syntactic phrasal type, which is important when analyzing spoken interaction, where the turn-constructional units often do not correspond syntactically to declarative sentences. Table 1 presents a schematic representation of the sentence structure of the German and Swedish declarative clause and the terminology used to describe it. The schematic representation also demonstrates the fact that the prefield and post field can be combined with other types of syntactic host units than sentences in spoken interaction.

In German, the front field, the middle field and the end field count as sentence-integrated positions. Sometimes the prefield is also included into the assembly of possible positions where conjunctional adverbs like *also* function as completely ordinary conjunctional adverbs (Duden 2006, 591; Konerding 2004; Pasch et al. 2003, 504; Zifonun et al. 1997: 59f., 1637f.), even though this is not really a sentence-integrated position (Auer 1996).

In Swedish, the front field, the middle field and the end field are the normal positions to hold sentence constituents. For an adverbial with sentence scope, the uncontroversial positions are the front field and the middle field, but *alltså* may also occur in the sentence-peripheral prefield and post field. In most Swedish grammar descriptions, the exact syntactic position of *alltså* is not considered to be of great importance for its classification as a conjunctional adverb, nor is the

Table 1. Schematic representation of German and Swedish sentence structure

Prefield	Positions of the inner clause of a declarative clause						Post field
	Front field	1st verbal position	Middle field	2nd verbal position	End field		
optional	obligatory	finite verb	optional	non-finite parts of the predicate	optional		optional

Any other syntactic host-unit type, including non-sentential units:
single words, phrases, other main clauses or sub clauses

---

9.   In English texts, this position is sometimes also called the pre-front field, a literal translation of the German term *Vor-Vorfeld*. In Teleman (1999: 23) and Lindström (2008: 70) this position is called *prefield*, and so we use this term.

10.   This term is taken from the Swedish literature. It is not to be mixed up with the German term *Nachfeld* "post field", see footnote 8 above.

syntactic shape of its host unit: "Conclusive adverbial elements occur in different kinds of main clauses and in not clause-formed sentences" (Teleman 1999, 143; translation M.A.) (cf. also Hultman 2003, 277; Teleman 1999, 122ff.; Jörgensen and Svensson 1996, 37). Only Lindström (2008) emphasizes the importance of the position of *alltså* for its interpretation: "Adverbs that clearly function as discourse markers position themselves in the pre- or post field of the sentence/.../" (Lindström 2008, 106; translation M.A.).

The category of conjunctional adverbs owes its name to two observations: First, these items are considered to have the same connective meaning/function as a coordinative conjunction even though their syntactic-distributional properties differ: Conjunctions occur at the beginning of their host units and do not cause subject inversion. Subject inversion means that the subject will have to be placed after the finite verb, i.e. in the middle field, when the front field is filled by another clause element. Second, conjunctional adverbs can occupy any position available to adverbials, and when they occupy the front field, they do cause subject inversion.

It is therefore not surprising that *alltså/also* are sometimes classified as coordinating conjunctions in those cases in which the prefield occurrences of *also/alltså* are unstressed and prosodically integrated into the following host-unit (Konerding 2004; Teleman 1999, 144), but as we shall see, this analysis is unsatisfactory as it does not consider all the functions *also/alltså* can fulfill in the syntactically initial-peripheral position. Correspondingly, researchers hesitate to analyze German *also* as a conjunction as soon as it carries an accent of its own and/or its meaning becomes opaque (Konerding 2002; 2004) and analyze it rather as a conjunctional adverb or as a discourse marker, both syntactic categories that can carry stress. Swedish interactional researchers rather discuss *alltså* as a discourse particle based on its sentence-peripheral initial or final position (Lindström 2008; Nilsson 2005; Kotsinas 1994).

Traditionally, the meaning and function of German *also* and Swedish *alltså* as conjunctional adverbs is suggested to be that their host unit – a sentence or a clear case of sentence ellipsis – is a conclusion drawn by the speaker. The conclusion presented by the speaker/writer in the host unit is based on evidence from the previous textual segments or on easily observable premises in the contextual situation in which the conversation takes place. Aijmer (2007) provides a good authentic example of *alltså* from written language where the particle marks the writer's use of the host unit to present a conclusion based on previous textually communicated propositions. In such cases, *also* and *alltså* can be paraphrased by "so" or "consequently":

(7) Polisen i Norrköping utgick från att Säpo slagit rikslarm. Säpo ansåg inte att rikslarm var en åtgärd som åvilade säkerhetstjänsten. **Alltså** hade ingen ens slagit larm.

The police in Norrköping assumed that Säpo had put out a nationwide alert. Säpo did not regard a nationwide alert as a measure within its scope. **So** no one put out an alert.   (Aijmer 2007, 40)

However, it has been observed in the literature that *also/alltså* cannot always be replaced by explicit paraphrases such as "so" or "consequently". Sometimes it is very hard to specify on what grounds a conclusion is supposed to be drawn. The difficulty in describing the meaning of German *also* has led researchers to suggest to classify prefield occurrences of *also* as modal particles (Helbig and Helbig 1995, 20) since modal particles are also known for their elusive meanings, even though the initial-peripheral position contradicts the usual criterion in German that modal particles appear sentence-medially (e.g. Thurmair 1989; Meibauer 1994).

We claim that the meaning of *also* and *alltså* is always conclusive, but it is not always used for signaling that its host-unit presents a conclusion based on textually or contextually conveyed premises. Instead, the conclusive relationship can also refer to non-textual aspects of discourse that are not necessarily expressed in the form of propositions (i.e. they are not textual elements) (Fischer 2000a; Diewald and Fischer 1998), such as the organization of the turn-taking system or the rhetorical development of the conversation (see below and Fischer 2000b, 2006).

4.2 German *also* and Swedish *alltså*: Their positions and functions

Since we are dealing with all kinds of syntactic host units for *also* and *alltså*, we prefer syntactic terms that are not based on the sentence structure to describe the position of *also/alltså*. We will include the prefield occurrences in the description of the *initial* (syntactically nonintegrated) *position* and the post field occurrences into the description of the *final* (syntactically nonintegrated) *position*. Table 2 provides an overview of the different positions in which the two particles can be found in interaction.

With respect to their position in the *turn*, we distinguish between turn-initial, turn-medial and turn-final occurrences since discourse particles fulfill different functions in these positions. Thus, in the following, we describe the functions *also* and *alltså* can fulfill in their positions with respect to turn and clause.

We will now compare some common uses of *also* (pronounced *also, allo* or *azo*) and *alltså* (pronounced *alltså, allså* and *asså*) in spoken German and Swedish.

Table 2. Overview of the discussed positions of *also/alltså*

Prefield	Front field	1st verbal position	Middle field	2nd verbal position	End field	Post field	Function
	Positions of the inner clause of a declarative clause						
also/ alltså	Declarative clauses & any other syntactic unit-types						uptake (cf. 4.2.1) framer (cf. 4.2.2) reformulation marker (cf. 4.2.2.)
	also/ alltså						conjunctional adverb (cf. 4.2.3)
			also/ alltså				modal particle (cf. 4.2.4)
					also²	*also²/ alltså*	functions of final *also/alltså* (cf. 4.2.5)
	Declarative clauses & any other syntactic unit-types						
↑	↑	↑	↑	↑	↑	↑	hesitation marker repair marker (cf. 4.2.6)

In the function as hesitation or repair marker, *also* and *alltså* can occur anywhere in a syntactic structure without being syntactically integrated.

Table 3. Schematic representation of turn initial, prefield *also/alltså*

new speaker:	Prefield *also/alltså* unintegrated	Front field	1st verbal position	Middle field	2nd verbal position	End field
		Positions of the inner clause of a declarative clause				
		Any other host-unit type, including non-sentential units: single words, phrases, other main clauses or sub clauses				

4.2.1 *Turn-initial prefield position*

Also and *alltså* can occur as the first word of a new turn, at the beginning of any kind of syntactic unit.

In example (8), the conversation partners discuss the right way to engage in order to help developing countries, and by means of German *also*, Thomas is trying to get the turn:

(8) Gisela: ((...)) .h aber irgendwie hätt ich ooch 'nen
                              SCHLE[CHtes gewissen,]
     Barbara: [((lacht auf))   ]

Gisela: [wenn man da] so GAR nichts macht.=
Thomas: [**also:**,] =**also:** uns- unsre: /
FREUNde drüben, die HA ben sich da schon engaGIERt äh /
so mit / drittwelt- -lä::den-, ((...)) (BR006B)
Gisela: ((...)) .h but somehow I would have a [bad conscience,]
Barbara: [((laughs))]
Gisela: [if you do] absolutely nothing.=
Thomas: [**PRT**,] =**PRT** our / friends over there, they have got them-
selves involved eh / like with / third world import stores, ((...))

In example (9), the conversation partners are discussing classification, and conversation partner J starts his turn with Swedish *alltså*:

(9) R: ((...)) å de e svårt att säja om de där e om man ska liksom sff föra allt
de ((laughing:)) allt de där ihop i en ((gesture)) kategori / m
J: **alltså** om vi börjar med den intuitionen då ord som man använder /
för att förklara andra ord / ((...)) (V4670011)
R: ((...)) and it is difficult to say if that is if you should kind of lump all of
it ((laughing:)) of that together into one ((gesture)) category / m
J: **PRT** if we start with that intuition then words that you use / to explain
other words / ((...))

In examples (8) and (9), *also* and *alltså* are used by the speakers to gain their interlocutors' attention and to claim the turn. In spoken language, the attention-getting and turn-claiming functions are easily detectable and have regularly been reported on in the literature (e.g. for German Alm 2007; 100ff.; Duden 2006, 601; Konerding 2004, 203, 214; Konerding 2002, 231; Zifonun et al. 1997, 481; for Swedish Nilsson 2005, 148; Kotsinas 1994, 93).

In addition to the turn-taking function, starting a new turn has a rhetorical function: The speaker has to position his or her contribution with respect to the thematic development of the conversation, i.e. he or she has to contextualize it (Lindström 2008, 209f.). When using *also* to start a turn, the speaker may signal up-take of the partner's utterance (Fischer 2000a): The turn-initial particle confirms that the speaker has heard and understood the partner's previous turn and is now about to say something that is related to the same topic.[11] Let us summarize this use of *also/alltså*:

---

11. Sometimes turn-initial *also* seems to refer to both the topic and the speech act of the previous turn, e.g. in protests, where both propositional information and the speech act asserting it can be refuted (Alm 2007: 97).

*Discourse particle with **up-take** function*

	Also	*Alltså*
Form	Position: turn-initial, host-unit initial (prefield w.r.t. the clause), syntactically nonintegrated Intonation: possibly unstressed and integrated into the following TCU Sentence types: all kinds of syntactic host units Before *also* another speaker is talking Used in interaction where the participants need to coordinate their speech	Position: turn-initial, host-unit initial (prefield w.r.t. the clause), syntactically nonintegrated Intonation: possibly unstressed, integrated into the following TCU Sentence types: all kinds of syntactic host units Before *alltså* another speaker is talking Used in interaction where the participants need to coordinate their speech
Meaning	Speaker has heard the partner's turn Speaker has understood the partner's turn signals that the speaker is about to say something that is relevant with respect to the topic of the previous turn (topic continuity) Provides an account for taking the turn (Fischer 2000b)	Speaker has heard the partner's turn Speaker has understood the partner's turn Signals that the speaker is about to say something that is relevant with respect to the topic of the previous turn (topic continuity) Provides an account for taking the turn (Fischer 2000b)

This function is very common for German *also*, but it is not as frequent for Swedish *alltså*.

The cross-linguistic difference between the Swedish and German uptaking constructions is thus a quantitative one.

4.2.2 *Turn-initial or turn-medial, prefield position*

Besides relating the current utterance to the partner's previous utterance as in the up-take function, prefield *also/alltså* may also introduce turn-constructional units that are situated either inside a turn, i.e. the prefield particle word will occur utterance-initially in a turn medial position, or turn-initially:

Table 4. Schematic representation of prefield *also/alltså*

same speaker/ new s peaker:	Prefield *also/alltså* unintegrated	Positions of the inner clause of a declarative clause				
		Front field	1st verbal position	Middle field	2nd verbal position	End field
		Any other host-unit type, including non-sentential units: single words, phrases, other main clauses or sub clauses				

Also/alltså introduce a new, yet previously ratified topic or return to an abandoned topic. In example (10) the instructor is using *also* in this framing function: Before this sequence, the instructor had to build the toy airplane herself. Now she is finished and turns to her partner, the constructor, to tell her how to build the airplane model. After making sure that she has her communication partner's attention (*Katja?*), the instructor turns to the real, previously ratified business of the conversation:

(10) Instr001 ((Lachen)) katja? ((Lachen)) **also** du musst jetzt aus diesen ((räus-pert sich)) wunderschönen bauteilen soll zum schluss erstmal (ei)n flugzeug dabei herauskommen (..) so 'n propellerflugzeug.

(Paar1)

Instr001 ((laughter)) Katja? ((laughter)) **PRT** now you'll have to out of these ((clears her throat)) wonderful building bricks in the end a there should be an air-plane (..) a kind of propeller-driven plane.

Prefield *also/alltså* can be used to introduce utterances that open up a new topic, or to return to a topic that is part of the communication partners' common ground (see also examples (3) and (6) above). These discourse-structuring and framing functions of *also/alltså* are found in both spoken and written language (cf. for German Alm 2007; Fernández-Villanueva 2007; Konerding 2004; Fischer 2000a; for Swedish Aijmer 2007; Lehti-Eklund 2003; Kotsinas 1994). For example, German *also* can be used to mark the beginning of a new discourse sequence. It then typically carries its own accent and is thus prosodically set apart from the following host unit (cf. Konerding 2004, 203, 214; Konerding 2002, 231). This can be done at the turn-beginning, in which case *also* is simultaneously turn-initial, or inside the turn after closing some other activity/topic (cf. example (10) above).

Unlike in German, in Swedish *alltså* has not been found to open up a new, though ratified topic, as has been seen in example (10), but both German and Swedish speakers use *also/alltså* to return to a previous topic of conversation, one that had been closed down or temporarily suspended. These uses fulfill structuring and framing functions. In example (11), the leader of a discussion group brings up a question, then interrupts his initiative to find the right page in the article, and with the *alltså*-prefaced utterance he returns to his question:

(11) J: ((...)) å sen hade ja faktiskt en annan- en egen fråga ((...)) nämligen / att man kunde neutralisera å förhöja semantiska / kontraster

[å] semantiska skillnader

X: [ha]

I: [ja] just de

E: m

J: var hade han den tanken nånstans (då)

((all participants turn over the leaves of their essays))

I: sidan tre- femhundratrettiofyra
J: just de{t} (..)
M: ((mumble))
J: äh (..) **asså** / fi / vilka mekanismer finns (..) i prat / för att (..) äh / >va
     ska man säja< (..) förhöja och äh / förminska meningsskilln- / ((...))
                                                                    (V4670011)
J: ((...)) and then I actually had a question of my own ((...)) namely / that
     you could neutralize and enhance semantic / contrasts
                                               [and] semantic differences
X: [yes]
I: [yes] that's right
E: m
J: where did he have that thought (then)
     ((all participants turn over the leaves of their essays))
I: page three- five hundred and thirty four
J: that's right (..)
M: ((mumble))
J: eh (..) **PRT** / is- / what mechanism are there (..) in talk / in order to (..)
     eh / >what do you say < (..) enhance and eh / diminish differences in
     meaning / ((...))

We can thus summarize the framing function of *also/alltså*:

*Discourse particle with **framing** function*

	Also	*Alltså*
Form	Position: host-unit initial, syntactically nonintegrated	Position: host-unit initial, syntactically nonintegrated
	Intonation: possibly carrying its own accent	Intonation: possibly carrying its own accent
	Sentence types: all kinds of syntactic host units	Sentence types: all kinds of syntactic host units
	Used in interaction where the participants need to coordinate their speech	Used in interaction where the participants need to coordinate their speech
	Before *also* there is a terminated turn-constructional unit from the same or another speaker	Before *alltså* there is a terminated turn-constructional unit from the same or another speaker
Meaning	Before *also* another activity is going on than after *also*	Before *alltså* another activity is going on than after *alltså*
	Signals either the beginning of a previously ratified topic/activity or the return to an old topic/activity	Signals the return to an old topic/activity

The difference between *also* and *alltså* thus concerns here the kinds of topics that can be (re-)opened by means of the framing particles.

Another use of turn-medial prefield *also/alltså* is that as a marker of a reformulative/explanatory comment (cf. for German Alm 2007; Fernández-Villanueva 2007; for Swedish Lindström 2008; Aijmer 2007; Lehti-Eklund 2003)[12]. This explanatory comment may constitute a deviation from the main activity/topic. Swedish *alltså* is used both initially and finally in this function and it is more often used with phrases than with whole sentences (Lehti-Eklund 2003, 140). German *also* is only used initially. In example (12), *also* introduces a metacomment:

(12)　Instr054　nee, ich hab auch n bisschen gefriemelt. bei mir ist es auch n
　　　　　　　　bisschen locker **also** ich glaub mein (.) ((lachend:)) flugzeug ist
　　　　　　　　nicht flugtauglich.　　　　　　　　　　　　　　　　　　(Paar5)
　　　　Instr054　no, I also tinkered a little. mine is also a little loose **PRT** I think
　　　　　　　　my (.) ((laughing:)) air plane is not capable of flying.

*Discourse particle with **reformulative** function*

	Also	*Alltså*
Form	Position: host-unit initial, syntactically nonintegrated Intonation: possibly unstressed and integrated into the following host-unit Sentence types: all kinds of syntactic host units	Position: host-unit initial or final, syntactically nonintegrated Intonation: possibly unstressed and integrated into the following or preceding host-unit Sentence types: all kinds of syntactic host units
Meaning	Before *also* there is a terminated or abandoned TCU The host-unit following *also* constitutes a reformulation, explanation or illustration of the previous utterance as a whole or of a part of it, or it is a metacomment on the previous utterance Signals an activity of local thematic concern; the host unit of *also* is not part of the superordinate ongoing topic/activity	Before *alltså* or its host unit there is a terminated or abandoned TCU The host-unit preceding or following *alltså* constitutes a reformulation, explanation or illustration of the previous utterance as a whole or of a part of it, or it is a metacomment on the previous utterance Signals an activity of local thematic concern; the host unit of *alltså* is not part of the superordinate ongoing topic/activity

---

12. Konerding (2004: 207f.) additionally identifies an apposition-marking function of German *also*, but we see no reason for singling out this function from the larger group of reformulations.

The two particles thus differ here with respect to the position of the particle concerning the reformulation, which can be both before and after the host unit in Swedish while being restricted to the host unit initial position in German.

> The cross-linguistic difference between the Swedish and German reformulative constructions consequently consists in a greater positional flexibility in Swedish.

For Swedish *alltså*, a *focusing* or *emphasizing* function is often discussed in the literature both for initial and final occurrences (Lindström 2008; Nilsson 2005, 146; Teleman 1999, 146; Kotsinas 1994, 90). The Swedish language has some discourse particles that can occur with great positional flexibility inside the sentence boundaries in order to emphasize an adjacent expression (Lindström 2008, 87ff.). They do not focus in the same way as focus particles (cf. König 1991), but they serve to highlight expressions that the speaker feels deserve extra attention from the listener. These "emphasizing" particles can be integrated prosodically into the surrounding speech and do not immediately stand out as syntactic parentheses, although it is clear that they are not used in any ordinary constituent function, as is apparent from the fact that they cannot occupy the front-field in German and Swedish on their own.[13] *Alltså* does not belong to the group of "emphasizing" particles in Lindström (2008), but Lindström discusses whether it may be fulfilling this function additionally to some of its other functions, for example as a hesitation or repair marker (see Section 4.2.6. below). According to Nilsson (2005), *alltså* in the following example has an "emphasizing" function since it serves to highlight a certain clause constituent:

(13)   S   här råder de lite delade åsikter (.) hälften av er tycker de ä (.)
              [okej]
       MK6   [a ja] tycker de e vidrit **asså** (.) huh   (Nilsson 2005, 146)
       S   here are some different opinions (.) half of you find it (.)
              [okay]
       MK6   [PRT I] find it gross **PRT** (.) PRT

For the same reasons, a "focusing" function has also been suggested for German *also* (Konerding 2004: 206). It is possible that *alltså* and *also* have an emphasizing function, but it is probably not a focus-particle function (cf. Alm 2006).

---

13.   An English example of a focusing particle like this is *like* (see Fox Tree 2006). It can be prosodically integrated.

Table 5. Schematic representation of sentence integrated, initial *also/alltså*

Positions of the inner clause of a declarative clause				
Front field	1st verbal position	Middle field	2nd verbal position	End field
alltså integrated				

4.2.3 *Sentence-integrated, initial position(s)*

Also and *alltså* also appear within the narrow bounds of the German and Swedish clause structure. When *also* and *alltså* are used in sentence-integrated positions, they will have scope over the whole sentence regardless of their exact position. They are then traditionally classified as conjunctional adverbs.

The so-called front field of a declarative clause is a sentence-integrated position. When occupying the front field, *also* and *alltså* will cause subject inversion, i.e. the subject will be placed in the middle field, after the finite verb, because the front field is already taken:

In written language, *also* and *alltså* are commonly used as the sole constituent in the front field. This is very rare both in spoken German and in spoken Swedish, but example (14) demonstrates it for German: The instructor explains to his conversation partner how to build a model air plane. *Also* directly precedes the finite verb *nimmst* "take", and the other clause elements then follow on the finite verb:[14]

(14) Instr61   =eins, (.) sechskant müssten das sein.
     Konstr55   ja.
     Instr62   ist egal.
     Konstr56   zwei, da habe ich zwei davon.
     Instr63   **also** nimmst du eine mit rille (..) und eine ohne rille.
     Konstr57   nee, die sind rund, die (.) mit rille.   (Paar12)
     Instr61   =a (.) that ought to be the kind with six sides.
     Konstr55   yes.
     Instr62   doesn't matter.
     Konstr56   two, I've got two of those.
     Instr63   PRT you take one with a groove (..) and one without a groove.
     Konstr57   no, they're round, those (.) with a groove.

---

14. For an illustration of the Swedish sentence structure with *alltså* in the front field, see example (7) above.

Conjunctional adverb signaling **conclusion**

	Also	*Alltså*
Form	Position: syntactically integrated, the only constituent in the front field of a declarative clause Intonation: integrated into the host unit sentence types: declarative clause	Position: syntactically integrated, the only constituent in the front field of a declarative clause Intonation: integrated into the host unit sentence types: declarative clause
Meaning	*Also* has sentence scope With the appearance of *also* in the front field, the host unit is signaled to be a conclusion based on information available from the previous conversation or the situational context Directs the attention of the listener backwards into the context	*Also* has sentence scope With the appearance of *alltså* in the front field, the host unit is signaled to be a conclusion based on information available from the previous conversation or the situational context Directs the attention of the listener backwards into the context

There is no cross-linguistic difference between German *also* and Swedish *alltså* used as conjunctional adverbs in the front field of a declarative sentence, and both uses are equally rare.

As mentioned earlier, sentence-integrated *also* and *alltså* in the front field are classified as conjunctional adverbs and their meaning and function is usually assumed to be fairly straight forward. However, Konerding (2002: 204) has shown that the function of conclusive conjunctional adverbs is often not as simple as connecting two propositions or even two adjacent sentences with each other. Often they connect their host utterance to a whole sequence of text, or to something even more abstract than that.

For Swedish front field *alltså*, Aijmer (2007)[15] makes a similar observation and distinguishes between the (conjunctional) adverb *alltså*, which signals that the host utterance is an inevitable conclusion of something already mentioned, and the inference particle *alltså*, which signals that the speaker bases his conclusion on background knowledge (Aijmer 2007, 40). The observation that the two particles under consideration may introduce a relationship between the host utterance and explicitly stated or implicitly inferred information or information from discourse memory, however, is true of connectives and conjunctions in general; many authors studying discourse connectives have noted similar indeterminacies (e.g. Roulet 2006; Pons Bordería 2006; Nemo 2006; cf. Fischer 2006a).

---

15.   Here Aijmer is following Vaskó/Fretheim (1997).

In German, there is a second position for *also* in the front field, namely as the second constituent of a doubly filled front field. This is a rare construction. The so-called post-initial position[16] of *also* in a doubly filled front field is demonstrated in example (15): In this example, both the adverbial prepositional phrase *ohne dieses Stichwort* "without this cue" and *also* "so" occupy the position preceding the finite verb *hätten* "would have", and both constituents are integrated into the sentence structure. When used in this construction, *also* helps to put emphasis (in the form of an accent) on the first constituent of the front field, namely the adverbial *without this CUE* (cf. Breindl 2008):

(15) Martin: [ohne dies-] ohne dies's STICHwort **allo** hätten wir das ALles
              jetzt nicht bekommen.   (BR001B)
      Martin: [without this] without this CUE **PRT** we would not have
              understood it all

The post initial position does exist for conjunctional adverbs in Swedish as well, but it is only used for certain adversative conjunctional adverbs (cf. Teleman 1999: 137). *Alltså* cannot be used in this position.

Since this use is rather rare in German and not applicable to *alltså* in Swedish, we just acknowledge its existence here and refrain from providing a constructional description of it at this point.

4.2.4 *Sentence-integrated, medial position*
Also the syntactically and prosodically integrated position of *also/alltså* in the middle field of a sentence belong to the sentence-integrated uses. This means that *also* and *alltså* have sentence scope and are traditionally classified as conjunctional adverbs or, in the German literature, as modal particles:

Table 6. Schematic representation of sentence integrated, medial *also/alltså*

Positions of the inner clause of a declarative clause				
Front field	1st verbal position	Middle field	2nd verbal position	End field
		also/alltså integrated		

---

16. This positional term is adapted from Breindl (2008). Breindl also presents several tests that show that the accent on the first constituent in the post-initial construction is *not* a focus accent.

In example (16) we can see that *also* is placed in the middle field since it appears after the finite verb *finde* "think/have the opinion" and in between the subject and the adjective phrase *vollkommen falsch* "completely wrong":

(16)   FF: (.) öh DAS finde ich **also** vollkomme:n öh falsch, im endeffekt wird
           DOCH gemacht was die:: erwachsenen wolln,   (NDR4)
      FF: (.) eh THAT I find **PRT** completely eh wrong, in the end it is done
           anyway what the grown-ups want,

The middle field in Swedish is much more restrictive than in German. Normally it only holds the subject (when the subject is not in the front field) and adverbials with sentence scope, such as sentence adverbials and conjunctional adverbials and – if you acknowledge their existence – modal particles. In example (17), *alltså* is situated in the middle field between the finite verb *va(r)* "was" and the subjective predicative *så ovanli(g)t* "so unusual," which is placed in the end field:

(17)   U: ((...)) de va **alltså** så ovanlit att se en färgad att / de: de va en sensation
                                                      (V0642011)
      U: ((...)) it was **PRT** so unusual to see a colored person that / it it was a
           sensation

Some German linguists divide the middle-field occurrences of *also* into two groups: the occurrences of the conjunctional adverb with an (allegedly) straight forward conclusive meaning and the occurrences of *also* that have to be something else because their meaning does not fit the linguists understanding of a conclusive meaning (e.g. Konerding 2004, 212; Kriwonossow 1977/[1963], 239). Sometimes the difficult middle-field occurrences are suggested to be modal particles. The middle field is the natural habitat of modal particles, and this category of words is famous for the elusive meanings of its members, thus an easy resort. Typically, this analysis is put forward when *also* is used in host utterances that syntactically consist of non-declarative sentences or of declarative sentences used in another function than making a statement. In example (18) *also* is used in a request with the finite verb in the imperative:

(18)   GEH **also** (endlich) nach Hause!
                                   (example noted by Konerding (2004, 212))
      GO **PRT** home (at last)!

Swedish grammarians rather assume some vagueness in the meanings of the conjunctional adverbs; e.g. Teleman (1999, 145) concludes that a conjunctional adverb can motivate the speech act as well as the propositional contents of the host-unit, but it is still a conjunctional adverb. Nonetheless, individual linguists do find a reason to differentiate between the middle-field occurrences. Lindström

(2008, 106) remarks that when *alltså* and other adverbs with sentence scope are used inside the sentence boundaries, it becomes difficult to distinguish between their use as adverbs and their use as "discourse markers". Examining the use of *alltså*, Lehti-Eklund concludes that "[i]n employing *alltså*, the writer no longer presents a conclusion, but merely makes a non-local connection in the text" (Lehti-Eklund 2003, 127), i.e. she describes middle-field *alltså* as a signal for returning to a previous topic.

In contrast to this view, Fischer (2007), following Diewald and Fischer (1998), holds all these functions to be instances of the same modal particle: *Also* – and it is likely that the same goes for Swedish *alltså* – used in the middle field connects its host utterance to a "proposition at hand", i.e. a proposition that is part of the argumentative common ground of the interlocutors. She defines this as the basic function that all modal particles have in common (cf. also Diewald & Fischer 1998; Diewald 2006). For instance, in example (16) above the speaker is signaling that it ought to be obvious for the listeners to understand his view on the matter considering what he has already told them about his observations on children and their parents, and in example (17), the speaker comment should be self-evident after telling how people reacted to seeing a colored person. In example (18), something in the common ground makes it obvious that the listener should be told to go home.

*Modal particle as a signal of **common ground***

	Also	*Alltså*
Form	Position: middle field, syntactically integrated Intonation: unstressed, integrated into the its host unit Sentence types: all kinds of sentence-formed host units Used in interaction where the participants jointly build up common ground	Position: middle field, syntactically integrated Intonation: unstressed, integrated into its host unit Sentence types: all kinds of all kinds of sentence-formed host units Used in interaction where the participants jointly build up common ground
Meaning	*Also* has sentence scope Signals that the information conveyed by the host unit belongs to the common ground of the speaker/writer and the listener/reader and that it is therefore in some way 'at hand' (cf. Diewald 2006; this volume) Signals that the host unit is non-initial	*Alltså* has sentence scope Signals that the information conveyed by the host unit belongs to the common ground of the speaker/writer and the listener/reader and that it is therefore in some way 'at hand' (cf. Diewald 2006; this volume) Signals that the host unit is non-initial

Both in German and Swedish, *also* and *alltså* are used syntactically integrated in a sentence-medial position as signals of common ground. We define this as a **modal particle** function.

4.2.5   *Final positions: post-field and turn-final position*

As we have seen already, *also* and *alltså* can also appear at the end of their host units. For Swedish, a final position of *alltså* at the end of a sentence-formed host unit is already non-integrated, i.e. it is in the post field. This is shown in Table 7.

For German, the position at the end of a sentence-formed host unit could still be a sentence-integrated position since the German end field is open to sentence constituents normally placed in the middle field. On the other hand, *also* could also be positioned in the post field, which is a sentence-peripheral position just as in Swedish. There is no way to tell from a simply linear perspective. This is illustrated in Table 8.

In spoken German, the final position of *also* is rare. Fernández-Villanueva (2007, 105), who examines the use of *also* in spoken German, does not report a single occurrence of post-field *also* out of a total of 539 occurrences, and in the preparatory work for Alm (2007), only 14 out of 499 occurrences of *also* were considered to be final, and some of these were tentative. In spite of the overwhelming preference in German for *also* to be initial, *also* can be found in final position as in example (19):

Table 7.   Schematic representation of final *alltså* in Swedish

Positions of the inner clause of the Swedish declarative clause					Post field
Front field	1st verbal position	Middle field	2nd verbal position	End field	
Any other syntactic host-unit type, including non-sentential units: single words, phrases, other main clauses or sub clauses					*alltså* unintegrated

Table 8.   Schematic representation of final *also* in German

Positions of the inner clause of the German declarative clause					Post field
Front field	1st verbal position	Middle field	2nd verbal position	End field	
				also? integrated	*also?* unintegrated
Any other syntactic host-unit type, including non-sentential units: single words, phrases, other main clauses or sub clauses					

(19) Dirk: das BURG ist eine seh:r (.) roMANtische, ((dramatisch)) .hh
WILde FEStung noch, (.) ich hab NICH rauskriegen können, .hh
also aus welchem jahrHUNdert die (äh) STAMMt da **also:**
(BR001B)
Dirk: the castle is a very (.) romantic, ((dramatic)) .hh wild fortress still,
(.) I have not been able to find out, .hh PRT from what century it
(eh) originates there **PRT**

In contrast to German *also*, Swedish *alltså* occurs very frequently in the post field.
It is used in the post field in the corrective/reformulative function (Lindström
2008; Nilsson 2005; Kotsinas 1994) and as an emphasis marker (Nilsson 2005;
Kotsinas 1994). It also signals the end of units, especially in Swedish reformulations (Kotsinas 1994). The examples of *alltså* as a discourse particle in the literature often presents final occurrences, and in Nilsson's data (2005, 146), more than
half of the 116 occurrences analyzed are final. Analyzing the same corpus that
Nilsson uses (GSM), we have found that 40 out of 129 occurrences are definitely
turn final.

Example (20) shows a post-field occurrence of Swedish *alltså*. It occurs after
the non-finite verb *va(ra)* "be" of the preceding sentence and is thus located after
the middle field of that sentence, and as it cannot occupy the end field in Swedish,
it has to be outside the inner clause. It is followed by the coordinating conjunction
å "and," which means that it cannot belong to the following sentence, since
coordinating conjunctions precede *alltså* in turn-constructional initial position
(Lindström 2008, 227). It is thus clearly in the post field:

(20) C: ((...)) så säger man alltså så mycke från medelvärdet / på den ena sidan
får det va så mycket från den andra sidan får de va **alltså** å sedan de
som ligger där ut- de som ligger där utöver alltså de e avvikande
(V0642011)
C: ((...)) then you say PRT so much it is allowed to be from the mean
value on the one side so much it is allowed to be from on the other side
PRT and then what exceeds that what exceeds that PRT that is
deviant

As we saw in the discussion of host-unit initial occurrences, *also/alltså* seem to
fulfill an array of different functions regarding discourse structuring and discourse
management when used in the prefield or the post field. Prefield and post field
also/alltså may even co-occur with the same host unit as in example (19) above.
Although the final position thus clearly exists, it is the position about which we
still know the least (cf. Traugott 2010). However, if the post-field occurrences of
also/alltså are also turn-final, they fulfill a clear turn-yielding function. This

function typically involves projective expressions like conjunctions, and per definition, conjunctions relate two units to each other, and thus they cannot be used
alone, nor can they be added in a host-unit final position in German and Swedish.
Still, a speaker can use them to yield the turn if the contents of the projected clause
can be predicted by the communication partner. In this way, the speaker can be
understood to mark the turn as *conditionally* terminated; he or she is prepared to
yield the turn if one of the interlocutors would like to take over. Yet, if they do not,
the speaker may continue him- or herself (Lindström 2008, 252). Lindström demonstrates this for Swedish with the subordinating conjunction *så att* "so that," and
Fischer (2001) has made the same point for German concerning the coordinating
conjunction *aber* "but."

Both *also* and *alltså* can be found in this turn-yielding function. Example (21)
is a typical turn-final *alltså* in Swedish:

(21) EK2   de e ju inget man lyss- man kan lyssna på så. tycker jag. i en hel
              skiva igenom.
      EK3   man sätter sej liksom   [inte-]
      EK2   [för att] de e: (.) de e ju bara=
            =[för jobbigt för hjärnan **alltså.**]
      EK1   [nää jag lyssnar inte nån[ting].   ]   (GSM10)
      EK2   that is nothing you can list- you can listen to like that. I think. right
              through a whole album.
      EK3   you like do [not] sit down-
      EK2   [because] it is (.) it is just too hard=
            [for the brain **PRT**.   ]
      EK1   [no I do not listen to any[thing].]

The syntactic status *also/alltså* when used in this turn-yielding function is still
unclear. When conjunctions like *but* or *so that* are used in a turn-yielding function, their semantic meaning is still projective, even if the speaker does not intend
to produce the projected host unit. Turn-final *alltså* and *also* could be used like
that. However, they could also be used in the post-field position of their host unit.
Then their projective meaning would be directed backwards into the conversation,
not forwards like the conjunctions. To conclude, the turn-yielding function of *also*
and *alltså* needs to be investigated further, and for this reason we are not presenting a turn-yielding construction here.

4.2.6 *Positionally unbound, non-integrated particles*
In spoken interaction, *also* and *alltså* can furthermore be used as repair markers
and as hesitation markers (e.g. for German Alm 2007, 65ff.; Konerding 2004, 209f.;

Table 9. Positioning of the hesitation marker with respect to the German and Swedish sentence structure

Prefield	Positions of the inner clause of a declarative clause					Post field
	Front field	1st verbal position	Middle field	2nd verbal position	End field	
	Any other syntactic host-unit type, including non-sentential units: single words, phrases, other main clauses or sub clauses					
↑	↑	↑	↑	↑	↑	↑

In the function as hesitation or repair marker, *also* and *alltså* can occur anywhere in a syntactic structure without being syntactically integrated.

for Swedish Lehti-Eklund 2003, 152f.).[17] Used in this function, *also/alltså* are syntactically unintegrated as well as positionally unbound:

Hesitation and repair markers are thus syntactically unrestricted with respect to the sentence positions demonstrated in Table 9 above. For instance, they can appear in the middle of a PP, between a preposition and its noun phrase, or inside any other kind of constituents.

With a repair, in the strict sense, the speaker wants to cancel a previous expression and to replace it with another. Alm (2007, 68ff.) reports some examples of repairs involving German *also*, yet the strict repairs are unusual with *also/alltså*. Instead, repairs often concern a belated specification of a previous expression. In this case, it does not seem necessary to cancel the reparandum completely, but the speaker seems to decide, possibly based on the communication partner's contingent, non-verbal feedback, that his or her utterance might be difficult to understand or misleading if the previous formulation is not put more precisely; that is, the two particles introduce some kind of preventive self-initiated self-repair. *Also* and *alltså* are both frequently involved in this kind of repair; they thus cover a functional spectrum from strict repairs to the reformulation function demonstrated above (cf. for German Alm 2007, 74ff.; for Swedish Lindström 2008, 108; Nilsson 2005, 146; Kotsinas 1994, 87). In German, the repair marker is initial but in Swedish it can be either initial or final:

(22)   det e jättefint där / i Småland **asså**   (Kotsinas 1994, 87)
       it is really beautiful there / in Småland **PRT**

---

17.   It is surprising that Fernández-Villanueava (2007) does not mention these functions although she explicitly states that she is analyzing spoken German looking for differences in the use of *also* in comparison to written German.

*Discourse particle with **repair** function*

	Also	*Alltså*
Form	Position: usually initial, but final position not ruled out, syntactically nonintegrated Intonation: possibly unstressed and integrated into its host-unit Sentence types: all kinds of syntactic host units Used in interaction where the participants need to formulate their speech online Before *also* there is a terminated or abandoned TCU	Position: host-unit initial or final, syntactically nonintegrated Intonation: possibly unstressed and integrated into its host-unit Sentence types: all kinds of syntactic host units Used in interaction where the participants need to formulate their speech online Before *alltså* there is a terminated or abandoned TCU
Meaning	The host-unit of *also* replaces or specifies a previous expression Signals an activity of local communication management: The speaker wants to cancel a previous expression and to replace it	The host-unit of *alltså* replaces or specifies a previous expression Signals an activity of local communication management: The speaker wants to cancel a previous expression and to replace it

Just like the reformulation markers, *also* and *alltså* with a repair function differ regarding the more flexible position of the Swedish particle.

   (23)   Dirk: =ottilie bereits vorhin erZÄHLt, dass ich: glau:bte irgendwo (1 Sek) .h (.) **also** den (.) den GRABstein NIEtzsches völlig (.) ver- (.) verMOdert zu finden,   (BR001B)

             Dirk: =told Ottilie already a moment ago, that I: thought that I would find (1 sec) .h (.) **PRT** the (.) Nietzsche's gravestone completely (.) de- (.) decayed,

Some linguists may not characterize *also/alltså* used inside the inner sentence boundaries as syntactically peripheral but as sentence-medial, but we define sentence-medial occurrences as having sentence scope (see the discussion in 4.2.4).

*Discourse particle with **hesitation marking** function*

	Also	*Alltså*
Form	Position: syntactically nonintegrated Intonation: typically produced in a low pitch and slower than the surrounding speech Sentence types: all kinds of syntactic host units Used in interaction where the participants need to formulate their speech online The speech surrounding *also* contains prosodic breaks and pauses and restarts	Position: syntactically nonintegrated Intonation: typically produced in a low pitch and slower than the surrounding speech Sentence types: all kinds of syntactic host units Used in interaction where the participants need to formulate their speech online The speech surrounding *alltså* contains prosodic breaks and pauses and restarts
Meaning	Signals delay coming up (Clark and Fox Tree 2002) Signals an activity of local communication management: The speaker is busy with the formulation process itself	Signals delay coming up (Clark and Fox Tree 2002) Signals an activity of local communication management: The speaker is busy with the formulation process itself

Also and *alltså* are both used as hesitation markers alike.

4.2.7 Stable collocations

As an example of how construction grammar deals with stable collocations, we briefly discuss the fixed expression *na also* "just as I thought!" here. Construction grammar postulates a continuum between general and specific, schematic and idiosyncratic information. While the constructions identified so far are all schematic such that they can be filled with other particles as well (see Section 5 below), *na also* is entrenched as an idiomatic unit with non-compositional meaning.

(24)   12:1 Höhe des gestrigen Testspielsieges der deutschen Fußball-National-
        mannschaft über die Türkei. **Na also**, es geht doch – zumindest bei
        den Frauen.
        (L99/FEB.04974 Berliner Morgenpost, 15.02.1999, S. 24, Ressort:
        SPORT; 12:1)
        12:1 is the victory of the German national soccer team over Turkey in
        yesterday's test game. **PRT**, it does work after all – at least among the
        women.

In this example, *na also* suggests that the German soccer teams' quality had been in doubt, yet that their success could nevertheless be expected, which is now supported by the women's team's victory over the Turkish team. Thus, the idiomatic expression indicates a pragmatic meaning confirming a hypothesis that is suggested to have been problematic.

Entrenched stable collocation **na also**

	Na also
form	usually turn-initial, independent utterance, prosodically unintegrated
meaning	confirms a hypothesis that had been in doubt

The idiomatic expression *na also* is restricted to German and is represented as a construction of its own in construction grammar.

4.2.8 *Functions yet to be described*

The descriptions of *also* and *alltså* provided here can self-evidently not be complete, yet we have presented some of the most frequent constructions that are easy to find in spoken language. There are some other possible functions to be described: The focusing function of *also/alltså* is one of them (see example (22) above), and so are some other suggested segmenting functions of *also* and *alltså*. The post-initial position for *also* (see example (15) above) remains to be examined. The turn-yielding function (see example (21) above) probably exists for *also* and *alltså* alike, but the exact characteristics for the particle words used in this construction still need to be examined before the construction can be defined.

To sum up, the analysis of the uses of German *also* and Swedish *alltså* in their different contexts has shown a) that certain functions can be associated with the constructions in which the respective items occur, and b) that even two as closely related language as German and Swedish differ with respect to the functions discourse particles and modal particles fulfill.

5.   Constructions as general form-meaning pairs

In this section, we briefly illustrate the point made in Section 3 above, that the constructions accounting for the different uses of *also* and *alltså* identified in Section 4 are in fact general constructions and account for the interpretations of several different discourse and modal particles.

In example (25), we find several particles functioning in the uptaking construction we saw in example (8) and (9) above. The interlocutors are discussing the fact that they lived in Eastern Germany and still noticed so little of the doings of the regime:

(25) Gisela: ((...)) da denk ich na mensch war ich WIRklich so verBIEStert in meine bücher und so dass ich=

Thomas: **ja₁**, ich hab das OOCH gewusst, dass die überall sind, und dass man äh bei MANchen leuten vielleicht VORsichtig sein sollte, aber / ich hab also- mich NIE hingesetzt und hab das DURCHgerechnet und überLEGT äh ((Schnauben)) wie viel hunderttausende das SEIN könnten.

Gisela: ja.
(.)

Barbara: **und₁** ICH war total schockiert, als sie bei uns bei rostock in kabelsdorf / einen RIEsen munitions
[depot] auf [machten   ]=

Thomas: [ja   ]   [**ja₂**, davon hab ich äh in der zeitung gelesen]

Barbara: =**und₂**,
(..)

Barbara: **und₃** es stand **ja₃** im selben text dass wir damit (.) na (..)

Gisela: handel   [ten.]

Barbara: [kon]flikt-

Thomas: ja.

Barbara: -gebiete be[liefert] haben.   (BR006B)

Gisela: ((...)) then I think well man was I REALly so badly cought UP in my books and all such that I =

Thomas: **ja₁**, I ALSO knew that, that they are everywhere, and that you eh perhaps should be CAREful with SOME people, but / I never PRT- Never sat down and CALculated and conSIDered eh ((snort)) how many hundreds of thousands that could BE.

Gisela: yes.
(.)

Barbara: **und₁** I was totally shocked, when they here with us in Rostock in Kabelsdorf / a GIANT ammunition
[depot]   [opened   ]=

Thomas: [ja   ]   [**ja₂**, I read in the news paper about that]

Barbara: =**und₂**,
(..)

Barbara: **und₃** it said **ja₃** in the same text that we with that had (.) na (..)

Gisela: trad [ed.]
Barbara: [con]flict-
Thomas: yes.
Barbara: -areas sup[plied].

With ja_1 "yes", which is used in the prefield position, the conversation partner Thomas signals that he has heard and understood the partner's utterance, that he wants to speak and that he has something to say that is thematically relevant with respect to the previous speaker's turn, i.e. ja_1 is an up-take. With und_1 "and," which is also used in the prefield, Barbara signals that she has heard and understood the previous speaker's utterance and that she has something to say that is thematically relevant with respect to the topic of the previous turns, i.e. und_1 is also an up-take. Ja_2 "yes" is another up-take. Und_3 "and" is probably also an up-take after a long pause during which none of the conversation partners wants to take the floor.

Und_2 "and" opens up for different interpretations. It could be analyzed as an ordinary host-unit initial but turn-medial marker and would in this case mark that the speaker is continuing her story. Still, since it is followed by a long pause, it could also be interpreted as a hesitation marker signaling that the speaker is working on finding the right words. The long pause during which none of the conversation partners wants to take the floor could then be an indication of them understanding the hesitation marker as a turn-holding signal and giving the speaker time to formulate her message. However, since we know that the adversative conjunction *aber* "but" is often used turn-finally in the turn-yielding function discussed in the section above (Fischer 2001), the long pause after und_2 during which none of the conversation partners wants to take the floor could also indicate that Barbara is offering to yield the floor, but when nobody seems interested, she produces the additional turn-constructional unit that she projected with und_2. The repeated und_3 could then be understood as a confirmation of the kind of additional turn-constructional unit that she has been intending to make, namely an addition to her previous story.

Ja_3 "yes" is prosodically and syntactically integrated into the middle field of a sentence-formed host-unit. This is one of the traditionally accepted modal particles and its meaning is often described as "as you know". This fits an interpretation of ja_3 signaling that the information conveyed by the host utterance belongs to the conversation partners' common ground. In this case it probably has not really been part of shared knowledge – even though Barbara may suspect that her conversation partners have read about the story she is referring to, she cannot be sure – but this is in fact irrelevant; modal particles serve to construe common ground as much as they refer to it (Fischer 2007).

Finally, *na* "well", an interjection which can only be used in the prefield, is surrounded by pauses, which could indicate that *na* in this case has a hesitation function. Actually, this seems to be the way the conversation partners interpret it since Gisela supplies a suggestion that would fit the context: *handelten* "traded."

In example (26) we have a situation from a Swedish dialogue corresponding to example (10) above: The participants in an air-plane construction dialogue have been waiting for the set-up, and the excerpt starts with the very first "real business"-contribution of the dialogue. As a framer marking the transition from small talk to real work we find *okej* "okay":

(26) instr: får vi (..) börja
        techn: ja
        instr: leka nu / **okej** ja har alltså ett plan framfö mej som / har äh / två hjul / å så e de liksom ett hjulchassi / å / en lång kropp å så e de TVÅ vingar ((...))   (V3001011)
        instr: can we (..) start
        techn: yes
        instr: playing now / **okej** I have PRT a plane in front of me that / has eh / two wheels / and then there are like wheel chassis / and / a long body and then there are TWO wings ((...))

In example (27) we have another excerpt from the same dialogue: In example (26) above, the instructor starts out the "real business" of the dialogue with a detailed description of the end product, i.e. what the model air plane looks like when it is ready. After that the conversation partners have to turn to the construction phase itself. The very first proper instruction to the constructor in example (27) below is prefaced by the initial particle *så* "so":

(27) instr: va .h då började jag enlit instrtionena me å ta en sån där (...) me att göra stjärten och kroppen så att säja
        constr: okej
        instr: **så** du tar en sån här me fem hål i,
        constr: (j)a / klart   (V3001011)
        instr: be .h then I started according to the instructions with taking one of those (...) with making the tail and the body so to say
        constr: okay
        instr: **så** you take one of these with five holes in it,
        constr: yes / done

Thus, all discourse particles in the uptaking construction share common functional characteristics, which are therefore not due to the respective discourse particles, but rather meaning components directly connected to the respective

construction. In this case, all examples share the functions of signaling success-
ful perception and understanding to the communication partner and to indicate that the current host utterance relates relevantly to the partner's previous
turn, which are thus part of the constructional meaning of the uptake--
construction. Similarly, concerning turn-medial occurrences of particles,
i.e. occurrences of modal particles, Diewald (2006) has argued for a particular
grammatical function of modal particles, namely to mark the current utterance
as non-initial (evoking common ground); this function can be understood as
the constructional meaning of the modal particle construction in German,
which is shared by all modal particles in the sentence-integrated, turn-medial
middle-field position. The same holds for items used as framing signals or as
hesitation markers: the constructions in which they occur carry meaning components that are not part of the meaning of individual particles but rather constructional meanings.

However, if a particle is used in a given construction, it brings its own meaning components with it, which may interact with the functions connected to the
construction; in the examples above, in addition to the constructional meaning
that all examples in a given construction share, the different lexemes play different roles within the construction. For instance, while *also* "so" provides an account for taking the turn by signaling that the new turn is a direct consequence
of the partner's previous turn (see Section 4.2.1. above), *ja* "yes" suggests that the
current speaker's utterance is in accordance with the partner's statement and
und "and" suggests that the speaker is making an addition to what has previously been said (see example (25) above), whereas *oh* serves a turn-taking
function by indicating a spontaneous reaction to the partner's turn (Fischer
2000b; 2010).

Consequently, while all these particles serve to provide accounts (cf. Heritage
1988) of the fact that the speaker is taking the turn, they do so in different ways
(Fischer 2000b). Thus, both the particle lexeme and the construction contribute to
the interpretation in ways predictable from the meanings of the respective parts.

6. Cross-linguistic differences

We have observed that even though German and Swedish are so closely related
that they use similar sentence structures (see Section 4.1. above) and phonetically
similar items for very similar purposes (i.e. *also* and *alltså*), there are also some
important differences with respect to their inventory of constructions and the
relationships between constructions and lexical items. For example, we have seen

that while both German and Swedish use turn- and utterance-initial discourse particles for similar purposes, they show differences in the frequency of these constructions.

Alltså as a framer in Swedish differs from *also* in German since in Swedish since has not been found to be used to open up previously ratified, yet as yet undiscussed topics. Reformulation markers furthermore have been found to be always initial in German, yet predominantly final in Swedish. And finally, while utterance-final discourse particles in the post field are rather rare in German, they are extremely frequent in Swedish. This means that certain functions are fulfilled by particles in German that are not fulfilled to the same extent by the cognate particles in Swedish and vice versa, and that the formal features by means of which particles fulfill their tasks in the two different languages may differ. Such findings make the definition of linguistic categories such as discourse particles and modal particles across languages highly problematic.

However acute for the definition of discourse particles and modal particles, the problems we are facing here are by no means peculiar to the current domain; as Croft (2001, 29) points out: "languages differ in the constructions that they possess". Similarly, the fact that the categories of discourse particles and modal particles may fulfill different functions in different languages is a common typological finding: "like the problem of missing constructions, the problem of widely different distribution is a cross-linguistic common one" (Croft 2001, 30).

6.1   Radical construction grammar

Croft is the main representative of construction grammar approaches to linguistic typology. His considerations have led him to the development of Radical Construction Grammar (Croft 2001). In this approach, constructions "are language-specific in their morphosyntactic properties, but their function in structuring and communicating information is not" (Croft 2001, 60). These "functional properties define a conceptual space, also known as a mental map, cognitive map, semantic map, or semantic space" (Croft 2001, 92). Even though according to cognitive linguists there is no universal inventory of atomic syntactic primitives, Croft suggests that languages can be related to each other on the basis of the conceptual space (Croft 2001, 32); thus, typological comparison has to rely on comparisons of functions only.

The approach taken in radical construction grammar seems highly useful to address the issues observed in the current study. In particular, we would like to argue that while we have identified certain formal criteria which are reliably associated with particular meanings in a given language, the form-function correlations cannot be assumed to hold across languages. Furthermore, even though many of the functions observed are similar across the two languages studied, and even though some functions are most likely directly associated with a certain formal property, like, for instance, a turn-yielding function with a turn-final position, we still have no basis to claim that the constructional features identified are cross-linguistically valid or even universal.

For instance, the function worked out here for modal particles in German and Swedish is similar to what Ler (2006) suggests to be the function of utterance-final particles in Singlish, colloquial English spoken in Singapore. Thus, the functions expressed by utterance-medial, integrated modal particles in German and Swedish are expressed by utterance-final particles in Singlish. Likewise, it has been suggested that French "mots de discours," which may include relatively long fixed expressions, fulfill argumentative functions like those suggested here for German and Swedish modal particles (Nemo 2006; Nyan 2006; cf. also Waltereit 2001). Taking a radical construction grammar approach thus means that we can relate the different constructions in the different languages, i.e. turn-medial German and Swedish modal particles, utterance-final particles in Singapore Colloquial English and French fixed expressions, by means of their common functions; on the basis of this common function, we can compare the contributions of the different formal features across languages.

Following Croft (2001), we therefore take constructions to be language-specific. There is consequently no cross-linguistic category discourse particle or modal particle; instead, a methodologically sound starting point for cross-linguistic comparison is the conceptual space the items under consideration evoke in a particular language. Such an approach allows us to see how these functions are realized differently in the different languages and only in a next step to identify universal relationships between certain functions and their grammatical, i.e. constructional, realizations in the languages of the world. However, such a comparison presupposes a systematic description of the conceptual space.

6.2   The conceptual space

The conceptual space to be assumed is not an objectively given entity in the world; instead, numerous studies of discourse particles and modal particles have attempted to define the functional spectrum covered by these items. Most interesting for our purpose are those approaches that postulate different functional domains to which discourse particles and modal particles may contribute (see Fischer 2006a); the first such model for discourse particles is certainly Schiffrin (1987), who suggests that discourse particles (which she calls discourse markers) contribute to three different discourse planes: the ideational, the exchange and the action plane, which are connected to information and participation structure respectively. In

Schiffrin's model, discourse markers index different planes (possibly simultaneously) and are thus multifunctional.

Fischer (2006, ed.) provides an overview of the most important approaches to
discourse particles; for instance, besides the three domains identified by Schiffrin
(1987, 2006), also rhetorical, information structuring, thematic, epistemic, affective, among other functional domains have been proposed (e.g. Redeker 1990;
Frank-Job 2006; Lewis 2006; Aijmer et al. 2006). In addition, it has been suggested
that discourse particles fulfill connecting functions, marking, for instance, connections between events in the world (Fraser 1999; 2006) or between textual elements
and events in discourse memory (Roulet 2006). Thus, the list of possible functions
discourse particles may fulfill is considered to be generally rather broad.

Diewald and Fischer (1998), Diewald (2006; this volume) and Fischer (2007)
have suggested to divide the conceptual space in three broad areas; in this model,
the communicative tasks speakers have to fulfill in interaction concern a) the
reporting of events, i.e. what is talked about, b) the anchoring of the current
utterance in the argumentative structure of the discourse, i.e. it concerns why
something is said and participants' attitude towards it, and c) responding to the
contingencies of the current interaction, including the management of the communicative event itself. Diewald and Fischer (1998), Diewald (2006), and Fischer
(2007) suggest that in German, very generally, adverbs and conjunctions refer to
aspects of the events presented, i.e. to the ideational domain, modal particles refer
to the rhetorical or argumentative domain while discourse particles refer to aspect of the communicative situation, i.e. to a communicative background frame
(Fischer 2000a, 2006b).

We suggest here that these three broad areas constitute the conceptual space
against which the constructions identified for *also* and *alltså* above can be compared. However, our model does not lose anything by allowing epistemic, attitudinal, participation structuring or other tasks to be added; the more elaborate the
conceptual space, the more fine-grained the cross-linguistic description; for instance, Diewald and Kresic (2010) provide a detailed model for the cross-linguistic
comparison of modal particles. They introduce a procedure in three steps which
associates (a) a particular modal particle lexeme with (b) a particular rhetorical
context and (c) a particular surface realization of the utterance containing the
modal particle.

Similarly, the detailed domain model presented in Fischer (2000a; 2006b) allows the definition of particular tasks speakers attend to in discourse with respect
to which particles in different languages can be compared. Thus, no claims are
made regarding the completeness of the conceptual space – on the contrary: We
regard the definition of the conceptual space to be an important empirical task for
future work. For the functions of the two particles analyzed above, however, the

broad division into ideational, argumentational and communicational is sufficient. We thus suggest that the constructions that define the classes of particles within a given language can be compared with each other across languages on the background of the conceptual space. This enables us to relate the language-specific realizations of pragmatic functions in languages as close as German and Swedish, but also very different constructions, such as the utterance-final particles in Singlish (see Ler 2006), to each other.

7.   Conclusion

The construction grammar approach taken in this study turned out to be useful for putting the search for the definition of discourse and modal particles on a solid methodological basis. First, we have shown that construction grammar allows us to distinguish between the contributions of lexical items and constructions. While the particles themselves are not specified for word class, it is the constructions that make a particle a discourse or a modal particle. Consequently, within a language the definition of the two classes of discourse particles and modal particles has to be construction-based and thus language-specific.

Second, we have argued that a construction-based account allows us to define a set of form-meaning pairings that contribute to the interpretation of each particle occurrence. Thus, a construction grammar framework allows the language-specific definition of the exact conditions under which discourse and modal particles fulfill their functions.

Third, the construction grammar account, especially the radical construction grammar model presented by Croft (2001), has been shown to be highly suited for the cross-linguistic comparison of particles and their uses on the basis of a common conceptual space. While we have illustrated how German *also* and Swedish *alltså* are associated with particular language specific constructions, corresponding to specific functions with respect to a particular conceptual space, how other languages carve up the functional spectrum is an empirical question. The word classes can be defined cross-linguistically only on the basis of the particular slice of the conceptual map that they refer to.

Transcription conventions

The transcriptions for the examples of spoken language originate from different corpora where transcription conventions are used. We have aimed to standardize them using the following conventions:

((...))	parts of a speaker's turn are left out
((laughing))	metacomments
.h .hh	short or long inbreath, respectively
=	turn transition without any gap
[overlap]	overlapping parts of speech are marked in square brackets
STICHwort	stressed syllables are marked with capital letters
. , ?	terminal intonation is marked with a full stop, progressive intonation with a comma, interrogative intonation with a question mark
also:	colon marks the prolongation of a sound
/	slash marks a prosodic break
(.) (..) (1 sec)	short pause, longer pause, measured pause
(al)so	word parts in brackets are difficult to hear
>faster<	pointed brackets mark a stretch of speech that is produced fastert than surrounding speech

Material

BR001B + BR006A originate from the corpus Biographic- and Travel Stories from the German Language Archives in Mannheim, Germany. These conversations were recorded in 1985 and 1990, respectively. They consist of rather free discussions on a broad main topic.

Paar1 + Paar12 originate from the corpus of the Special Research Project (SFB) 360 at the Bielefeld University, Germany, in 1993. An instructor is explaining to a constructor how to build a model air plane.

NDR4 is a discussion program of the regional German radio channel NDR. The speakers are a presenter and some invited guests, and additionally listeners can call in. The topic of this show is "Do children need limits?" and it was recorded and transcribed by Maria Alm in 2001.

The transcriptions beginning with "V" belong to the Gothenburg Corpus of spoken language at the Department of Philosophy, Linguistics and Theory of Science, Gothenburg, Sweden. V4670011, V0642011 + V0236011 are probably seminar discussions. V3001011 is an "air plane experiment dialogue" analogous to the corpus SFB 360 above.

GSM is a corpus of Swedish teenagers discussing music. For details: Wirdenäs, Karolina. 2002. *Ungdomars argumentation: Om argumentationstekniker i gruppsamtal.* Göteborg.

References

Aijmer, Karin, Ad Foolen, and Anne-Marie Simon-Vandenbergen. 2006. "Pragmatic markers in translation: A methodological proposal." In *Approaches to Discourse Particles*, ed. by Kerstin Fischer, 101–114. Amsterdam: Elsevier.

Aijmer, Karin. 2007. "The meaning and functions of the Swedish discourse marker *alltså*: Evidence from translation corpora." *Catalan Journal of Linguistics* 6: 31–59.

Alm, Maria. 2006. "German *also*: A focus particle or a discourse-pragmatic focus marking device?" *The Department of English in Lund: Working Papers in Linguistics* 6: 1–17.

Alm, Maria. 2007. *Also darüber lässt sich ja streiten! Die Analyse von also in der Diskussion zu Diskurs- und Modalpartikeln*. Stockholm: Almqvist & Wiksell International.

Antonopoulou, Eleni and Kiki Nikiforidou. 2011. "Construction grammar and conventional discourse: A construction-based approach to discoursal incongruity." *Journal of Pragmatics* 43, 10: 2594–2609.

Auer, Peter. 1996. "The pre-front field in spoken German and its relevance as a grammaticalization position." *Pragmatics* 6: 295–322.

Breindl, Eva. 2008. "*Die Brigitte nun kann der Hans nicht austehen*: Gebundene Topiks im Deutschen." *Deutsche Sprache* 36: 27–40.

Clark, Herbert H. and, Jean E. Fox Tree. 2002. "Using *uh* and *um* in spontaneous speaking." *Cognition* 84: 73–111.

Couper-Kuhlen, Elizabeth and, Sandra A. Thompson. 2008. "On assessing situations and events in conversation: *Extraposition* and its relatives." *Discourse Studies* 10: 443.

Couper-Kuhlen, Elizabeth and, Margret Selting. 2001. "Introducing interactional linguistics." *Studies in interactional linguistics,* ed. by Margret Selting and Elisabeth Couper-Kuhlen, pp. 1–21. Amsterdam/Philadelphia: John Benjamins.

Croft, William. 2001. *Radical Construction Grammar*. New York: Oxford University Press.

Deppermann, Arnulf. 2007. *Grammatik und Semantik aus gesprächsanalytischer Sicht*. Berlin/New York: de Gruyter.

Diewald, Gabriele and, Kerstin Fischer. 1998. "Zur diskursiven und modalen Funktion der Partikeln *aber, auch, doch* und *ja* in Instruktionsdialogen." *Linguistica* 38: 75–99.

Diewald, Gabriele. 2006. "Discourse particles and modal particles as grammatical elements." In *Approaches to Discourse Particles,* ed. by Kerstin Fischer, 403–425. Amsterdam: Elsevier.

Diewald, Gabriele. 2008. "The catalytic function of constructional restrictions in grammaticalization." In *Studies on grammaticalization,* ed. by Elisabeth Verhoeven, Stavros Skopeteas, Yong-Min Shin, Yoko Nishina, and Johannes Helmbrecht, 219–240. Berlin: de Gruyter.

Diewald, Gabriele. 2011. "Pragmaticalization (defined) as grammaticalization of discourse functions." *Linguistics* 49: 365–390.

Diewald, Gabriele and, Marijana Kresic. 2010. "Ein übereinzelsprachliches kontrastives Beschreibungsmodell für Partikelbedeutungen." *Linguistik Online* 44.

Duden Vol. 4 *Die Grammatik*. 2006. Mannheim: Dudenverlag.

Fernández-Villanueva, Marta. 2007. "Uses of *also* in oral semi-informal German." *Catalan Journal of Linguistics* 6: 95–115.

Fillmore, Charles J., Paul Kay, and Mary O'Connor. 1988. "Regularity and idiomaticity in grammatical constructions: The case of *let alone*." *Language* 64: 501–538.

Fischer, Kerstin (ed.). 2000a. *From Cognitive Semantics to Lexical Pragmatics: The Functional Polysemy of Discourse Particles*. Berlin/New York: de Gruyter.

Fischer, Kerstin. 2000b. "Discourse particles, turn-taking, and the semantics-pragmatics interface." *Revue de Sémantique et Pragmatique,* 8: 111–137.

Fischer, Kerstin. 2001. "Pragmatic methods for construction grammar." In *Proceedings of the 18th Scandinavian Conference of Linguistics,* ed. by Arthur J. Holmér, Jan-Olof Svantesson and Åke Viberg, 153–162. Lund: Univ. Dept. of Linguistics and Phonetics.

Fischer, Kerstin. 2006a. "Towards an understanding of the spectrum of approaches to discourse particles: Introduction to the volume." In *Approaches to Discourse Particles*, ed. by Kerstin Fischer, 1–20. Amsterdam: Elsevier.

Fischer, Kerstin. 2006b. "Frames, Constructions and Invariant Meanings: The Functional Polysemy of Discourse Particles." In *Approaches to Discourse Particles*, ed. by Kerstin Fischer, 427–447. Amsterdam: Elsevier.

Fischer, Kerstin. 2006 (ed.). *Approaches to Discourse Particles*. Amsterdam: Elsevier.

Fischer, Kerstin. 2007. "Grounding and common ground: Modal particles and their translation equivalents." In *Lexical Markers of Common Grounds*, ed. by Anita Fetzer and Kerstin Fischer, 47–66. Amsterdam et al.: Elservier.

Fischer, Kerstin. 2010. "Beyond the sentence: Constructions, frames and spoken interaction." *Constructions and Frames* 2: 1–28.

Fischer, Kerstin. Forthcoming. "Conversation, Construction Grammar, and Cognition." *Language and Cognition.*

Fox Tree, Jean E. 2006. "Placing *like* in telling stories." *Discourse Studies* 8: 749–770.

Frank Job, Barbara. 2006. "Discourse marker research and theory: Revisiting *and*." In *Approaches to Discourse Particles*, ed. by Kerstin Fischer, 167–190. Amsterdam: Elsevier.

Fraser, Bruce. 1999. "Pragmatic markers." *Pragmatics* 6: 167–190.

Fraser, Bruce. 2006. "Towards a theory of discourse markers." In *Approaches to Discourse Particles*, ed. by Kerstin Fischer, 189–204. Amsterdam: Elsevier.

Fried, Miriam and, Jan-Ola Östman. 2005. "Construction grammar and spoken interaction: The case of pragmatic particles." *Journal of pragmatics* 37: 1752–1778.

Goldberg, Adele E. 1995. *Constructions: A Construction Grammar Approach to Argument Structure.* Chicago: University of Chicago Press.

Helbig, Gerhard and, Agnes Helbig. 1995. *Deutsche Partikeln – richtig gebraucht?* Leipzig et al.: Langenscheidt.

Heritage, John. 1984. "A change-of-state token and aspects of its sequential placement." In *Structures of Social Action: Studies in Conversation Analysis*, ed. by Jean Atkinson and John Heritage, 299–345. Cambridge: Cambridge University Press.

Hultman, Tor G. 2003. *Svenska Akademiens språklära.* Stockholm: Svenska Akademien.

Imo, Wolfgang and, Susanne Günthner (eds.). 2007. *Konstruktionen in der Interaktion.* Berlin/New York: de Gruyter.

Jörgensen, Nils and, Jan Svensson. 1986. *Nusvensk grammatik.* Stockholm: Liber.

Kay, Paul. 1995. "Construction grammar." In *Handbook of Pragmatics*, ed. by Jef Verschueren, Jan-Ola Östman, Jan Blommaert and Chris Bulcaen, 171–177. Amsterdam/Philadelphia: John Benjamins.

Kay, Paul. 2003. "Pragmatic aspects of grammatical constructions." In *Handbook of pragmatics*, ed. by Laurie Horn and Gregory Ward, 675–700. Oxford: Blackwell.

Kay, Paul and, Laura Michaelis. 2012. "Constructional meaning and compositionality." In *Semantics: An International Handbook of Natural Language Meaning*, ed. by Claudia Maienborn, Klaus von Heusinger and Paul Portner, 2271–2296. Berlin: de Gruyter.

Konerding, Klaus-Peter. 2002. *Konsekutivität als grammatisches und diskurspragmatisches Phänomen.* Tübingen: Stauffenburg.

Konerding, Klaus-Peter. 2004. "Semantische Variation, Diskurspragmatik, historische Entwicklung und Grammatikalisierung: Das Phänomenspektrum der Partikel *also*." In *Stabilität und Flexibilität in der Semantik: Strukturelle, kognitive, pragmatische und historische Perspektiven*, ed. by Inge Pohl and Klaus-Peter Konerding, 199–237. Frankfurt a/M et al.: Peter Lang.

König, Ekkehard. 1991. *The Meaning of Focus Particles: A Comparative Perspective*. London/New York: Routledge.

Kotsinas, Ulla-Britt. 1994. *Ungdomsspråk: Ord och stil* [Språkvårdssamfundets skrifter 25]. Hallgren & Fallgren: Uppsala.

Kriwonossow, Alexej. 1977/[1963]. *Die Modalpartikeln in der deutschen Gegenwartssprache*. Göppingen: Kümmerle.

Langacker, Ronald W. 2008. *Cognitive grammar: A basic introduction*. New York: Oxford University Press.

Lehti-Eklund, Hanna. 2003. "The grammaticalization of *alltså* and *således*: Two Swedish conjuncts revisited." In *Cognitive Approaches to Lexical Semantics*, ed. by Hubert Cuyckens, Rene Dirven and John R. Taylor, 123–162. Berlin: de Gruyter.

Ler, Vivien. 2006. "A relevance-theoretic approach to discourse particles in Singapore English." In *Approaches to Discourse Particles*, ed. by Kerstin Fischer (ed.), 149–166. Amsterdam: Elsevier.

Lewis, Diane. 2006. "Discourse markers in English: A discourse-pragmatic view." In *Approaches to Discourse Particles*, ed. by Kerstin Fischer, 43–59. Amsterdam: Elsevier.

Lindström, Jan. 2008. *Tur och ordning: Introduktion till svensk samtalsgrammatik*. Stockholm: Norstedts akademiska förlag.

Meibauer, Jörg. 1994. *Modaler Kontrast und konzeptuelle Verschiebung. Studien zur Syntax und Semantik deutscher Modalpartikeln*. Tübingen: Niemeyer.

Nemo, Francois. 2006. "Discourse particles as morphemes and as constructions." In *Approaches to Discourse Particles*, ed. by Kerstin Fischer, 375–402. Amsterdam: Elsevier.

Nilsson, Jenny. 2005. *Adverb i interaktion*. Göteborg: Institutionen för svenska språket, Göteborgs universitet.

Nyan, Than. 2006. "From procedural meaning to processing requirement." In *Approaches to Discourse Particles*, ed. by Kerstin Fischer, 167–188. Amsterdam: Elsevier.

Pasch, Renate, Ursula Brauße and, Eva Breindl. 2003. *Handbuch der deutschen Konnektoren*. Berlin/New York: de Gruyter.

Pons Bordería, Salvador. 2006. "A functional approach to the study of discourse markers." In *Approaches to Discourse Particles*, ed. by Kerstin Fischer, 77–100. Amsterdam: Elsevier.

Redeker, Gisela. 1990. "Ideational and pragmatic markers of discourse structure." *Journal of pragmatics*14: 367–381.

Roulet, Eddy. 2006. "The description of text relation markers in the Geneva model of discourse organization." In *Approaches to Discourse Particles*, ed. by Kerstin Fischer, 115–132. Amsterdam: Elsevier.

Schiffrin, Deborah. 1987. *Discourse Markers*. Cambridge: Cambridge University Press.

Schiffrin, Deborah. 2006. "Discourse marker research and theory: Revisiting *and*." In *Approaches to Discourse Particles*, ed. by Kerstin Fischer, 315–338. Amsterdam: Elsevier.

Schourup, Lawrence. 1999. "Discourse markers." *Lingua* 107: 227–265.

Thurmair, Maria. 1989. *Modalpartikeln und ihre Kombinationen*. Tübingen: Niemeyer.

Teleman, Ulf (ed.). 1999. *Svenska Akademiens grammatik. Vol. 4 Satser och meningar*. Stockholm: Svenska Akademien.

Tomasello, Michael. 2003. *Constructing a language*. Cambridge, Mass.: Harvard University Press.

Traugott, Elizabeth. 2008. "Grammaticalization, constructions and the incremental development of language: Suggestions from the development of degree modifiers in English". In *Variation, Selection, Development--Probing the Evolutionary Model of Language Change*, ed.

by Regine Eckardt, Gerhard Jäger, and Tonjes Veenstra, 219–250. Berlin/New York: Mouton de Gruyter.

Traugott, Elizabeth. 2010. "Revisiting Subjectification and Intersubjectification". In *Subjectification, Intersubjectification and Grammaticalization,* ed. by Kristin Davidse, Lieven Vandelanotte, and Hubert Cuyckens, 29–70. Berlin: De Gruyter Mouton.

Vaskó, Ildikó and Fretheim, Thorstein. 1997. "Some central pragmatic functions of the Norwegian particles *altså* and *nemlig*." In *Modality in Germanic languages,* ed. by Toril Swan and Olaf Jansen Westwik, 233–292. Berlin: Gruyter.

Waltereit, Richard. 2001. "Modal particles and their functional equivalents: A speech-act theoretic approach". *Journal of Pragmatics* 2001, 33(9), 1391–1417.

Zifonun et al. 1997. *Grammatik der deutschen Sprache.* Berlin/New York: de Gruyter.

Analyzing modal adverbs as modal particles and discourse markers

Karin Aijmer
University of Gothenburg

Modal particles have been discussed primarily in languages such as German or the Scandinavian languages. English is not usually said to have modal particles. In this chapter it is argued on the basis of the translations of *of course* into Swedish that it has uses as a modal adverb, discourse marker and modal particle although the distinction between the categories is fuzzy. *Of course* as a discourse marker is adversative or concessive. *Of course* as a modal particle has striking similarities with the modal particle *ju* in Swedish. It is used to signal consensus, for argumentative functions and to introduce background information.

1. Introduction

In a discussion article Traugott (2007) raised the question about the affinities between modal expressions and discourse markers and that question has been very much on the agenda since then. In her article she pointed to three different approaches. One approach is to distinguish between discourse markers and modal particles on formal and functional grounds. Another is "to make no difference between the terms, apparently on discourse pragmatic grounds, while recognizing that 'formally' clause-internal position is the modal particle position" (p. 141). A third approach 'is to show that certain discourse marker uses have epistemic inferential modal values' (Traugott 2007, 142). In this article it will be argued that we need to distinguish between modal particles and discourse markers primarily on functional grounds.

Modal particles have been discussed mainly in languages such as German or the Scandinavian languages. English, on the other hand, has been said to lack words which can be regarded as modal particles. However it is interesting to ask the question whether English has modal particles in the light of the recent discussion about the classification of pragmatic markers into sub-categories. Functional criteria which have been mentioned for modal particles are for instance 'that they express the speaker's attitude to the proposition, the relationship between the proposition and the real world, and the speaker's relationship with the hearer' (Hasselgård 2006, 95). The aim of this study is to show on the basis of a case study of *of course* that we need to make a functional split between uses which can be regarded as adverbs, discourse markers and modal particles.

The paper has the following structure. I will first discuss previous work on *of course* as a modal adverb within the framework of Quirk et al's (1985) classification of modal adverbs as conjuncts, disjuncts and subjuncts (Section 2). Section 3 will discuss discourse markers and modal particles in a grammaticalization perspective. Section 4 deals with translations as a methodology providing 'paradigms' which can be the basis for categorizing the different functions of *of course*. Section 5 is concerned with *of course* as a discourse marker and Section 6 gives examples where it is a modal particle. Section 7 is a discussion of the issues raised and the conclusion.

2. Modal adverbs

Of course, certainly, actually, etc. have mainly been discussed as modal adverbs.[1] However it can be argued that modal adverbs also have functions which can be associated with their status as discourse markers or modal particles.

Of course is an adverbial disjunct in:

(1)   of "course he'll be working with overseas students
(2)   of course, when the subject matter concerns very recent events it may not be easy to convey new techniques   (Hoye 1997, 190)

Disjuncts "have a superior role as compared with the sentence elements; they are syntactically more detached and in some respects 'superordinate', in that they seem to have a scope that extends over the sentence as a whole" (Quirk et al 1985, 613).

In addition, *of course* can be a conjunct encouraging 'a particular attitude in the addressee as well as expressing the nature of the connection between the units they conjoin' (Hoye 1997, 154). In (3), *of course* expresses the nature of the connection between the utterances it conjoins:

(3)   A: She could be waiting at the hairdresser's, I suppose ...
       B: Of course she could but all the same I don't think it likely.

Of course signals concession and implies that 'one unit is seen as unexpected in the light of the other' (Quirk et al. 1985, 639). Conjuncts can be regarded as discourse markers. Fraser (1996, 188), for example, regards *of course* as belonging to a class

---

1.   Compare the discussion in Aijmer (2009).

of inferential markers, 'expressions which signal that the force of the utterance is a conclusion which follows from the preceding discourse.'

Of course as a subjunct is illustrated in (4). It functions as an emphasizer with 'a reinforcing effect on the truth value of the clause or part of the clause' to which it applies (Quirk et al. 1985, 583):

(4)   Many young people may of course prefer hip hop to rock music.

Modal adverbs have sometimes been regarded as discourse markers (discourse particles, pragmatic markers). According to Holmes (1988, 49), it is 'abundantly clear' that *of course* is 'a discourse particle or verbal filler like *you know* or *I think*'. This is the position taken by Simon-Vandenbergen and Aijmer (2002/2003, 19): Our own position is 'to treat *of course* as a pragmatic marker in all its occurrences, regardless of its position, syntactic integration, prosody and realization as full or reduced form'.

It has also been suggested that modal adverbs in English should be considered modal particles in some of their senses, 'primarily those adverbs with only faint shades of meaning' (Hoye 1997, 209). According to Hoye (1997, 212), "it would not be implausible to redefine subjuncts expressing modality as 'modal particles', subdivided into the following categories: evidential particles (*clearly, obviously*); hearsay particles (*apparently*); reinforcement or emphasizing particles (*certainly, surely, well*); and focus particles (*only, simply*)". *Of course* (not mentioned by Hoye) could presumably be regarded as a modal particle with evidential meaning. This idea fits in well with the hypothesis proposed by several linguists (Diewald 2006, Waltereit and Detges 2007) that modal particles are derived by grammaticalization from adverbs.

3.   *Of course* and grammaticalization

It is characteristic of *of course* that it has a large number of functions some of which are more closely related to each other. The explanation for the multifunctionality of *of course* is diachronic and involves grammaticalization. According to Lewis (2002), *of course* comes originally from a French/Middle English noun *cours* which combines with the preposition *of* into a VP adverbial which is further reanalyzed as a sentence adverb. As a sentence adverb it splits into two typical meanings: a) normally/as a rule and b) naturally, in the order of things. *Of course* ('naturally') first acquires causal meanings ('consequently') and later epistemic meaning ('obviously') by means of inference. "The reasonable inference is that if something happens as a consequence of the natural order, it can be assumed definitely to happen." (Lewis 2002, 84). *Of course* also starts occurring in rhetorical patterns favoring a concessive interpretation. In present-day English additional patterns of use are found such as a) the introduction of background material, b) topic shift (*of course* is replaceable by *but, however*), c) introducing a new, final idea on a particular topic. However Lewis does not discuss the multifunctionality of *of course* in terms of whether we can distinguish between a discourse marker and a modal particle use. The relationship between discourse marker and modal particle will be explored here on the basis of translations.

4.   Translations as a model to study multifunctionality

Of course has several functions which are not always easy to distinguish from each other. Paraphrasing goes some way towards describing what *of course* means in different contexts. However translations are particularly interesting when lexical elements are multifunctional since the translator has to interpret the meaning of the lexical item in its context (cf. Dyvik 1998, 1999, Aijmer and Simon-Vandenbergen 2003, Aijmer et al. 2006). The translations can thus be seen as a complement to the linguist's analysis of the meanings of lexical items based on features such as position, collocation and the linguistic and non-linguistic context.

The translations serve as a clue to the 'functional potential' of *of course*. Depending on the formal properties and contextual features of *of course* a particular function is selected in the communication situation. However the functions revealed by the translations have to be further analyzed as sub-senses, implicatures and connotations associated with the uses of *of course* as a discourse marker or a modal particle. The translations may also reflect the literal meaning of *of course* 'something is taken for granted' (something is definitely or obviously the case).

The examples of *of course* and their translations are taken from the English-Swedish Parallel Corpus (Altenberg and Aijmer 2000), a corpus of almost three million words of fiction and non-fiction. Table 1 shows the translations of *of course* into Swedish (English originals -> Swedish translations) and in Swedish sources of English *of course* (English translation ->Swedish originals). Only the most frequent correspondences (occurring four times or more) have been shown. In all 32 different patterns were represented. The zero-expressions are also important. When *of course* has not been translated this can be taken as proof that it has a weakened literal meaning and mainly pragmatic function as a modal particle or a discourse marker. [2]

---

2.   For more detailed analysis of the translations of *of course* into Swedish including less frequent examples, see Aijmer (2009). Simon-Vandenbergen and Aijmer (2002/2003) has translations of *of course* both into Swedish and into Dutch.

Table 1. Swedish correspondences of *of course* in the English-Swedish Parallel Corpus (SO->ET, EO->ST)

naturligtvis	165
förstås(s) ('of course')	141
ju ('as you know')	70
givetvis ('of course')	53
visst ('certainly', 'by all means')	25
det är klart (att), så klart ('it is clear that')	25
visserligen ('admittedly')	10
javisst (ja), jovisst ('certainly')	10
självfallet, självklart ('of course')	10
nog ('probably')	7
väl ('surely')	4
zero	20

Of course can be translated literally in its meaning of something being taken for granted, definitely, obviously (reflected by translations such as 'naturligtvis', 'givetvis', 'förstås', 'självfallet', 'självklart'). Other meanings have to do with certainty (such as *nog* 'probably').

The translator also used the modal particle *ju* when that was appropriate instead of a more literal translation. The Swedish *ju* can be described as a versatile marker conveying that the speaker believes that the hearer believes or knows something (paraphrased as 'as you know'). It is also an important tool to show what is foregrounded and backgrounded information. If something is known, it constitutes the background to what is new information. It will be argued that when *of course* is translated as *ju* it has certain properties which distinguish it from the discourse marker (or the adverb). This is not a new idea. According to Fischer (2007, 57), 'in particular the function of modal particles to relate the current utterance to the common ground can usually be found in the translation'.

5. *Of course* as a discourse marker

Of course can be used in two different ways depending on the speaker's motives in the discourse. We can distinguish between *of course* as a discourse marker and as a modal particle. In the well-known definition of discourse markers by Schiffrin (1987, 31) they are 'sequentially dependent elements which bracket units of talk'. 'That is, they do not add so much to the propositional content of utterances as flag the sequential structure of discourse by indicating how discourse *relates* to other discourse' (Rühlemann 2007, 116).

When *of course* is a conjunct with concessive meaning it is a discourse marker expressing the connection between two utterances. The translators' *visserligen* (cf. *visst* with the same meaning) signals that *of course* introduces an argument which is later dismissed in a *but*-clause which contains the 'favoured' interpretation (Lewis 1998).

(5)   Of course you haven't been here long, but you 'll have heard of Davina Flory?"   (RR1)
      Visserligen har ni inte varit här så länge, men nog måste ni ha hört talas om Davina Flory?"

Of course as a conjunct can also can also convey that one event follows logically from another event (resultative meaning; cf. Quirk et al. 1985, 635 'resultive' role).

(6)   He was impressed; it was from the General Secretary of the CPSU personally, handwritten in the Soviet leader's neat, clerkish script and, of course, in Russian.   (FF1)

      Han blev imponerad; det var från kommunistpartiets generalsekreterare personligen, handskrivet med den sovjetiske ledarens prydliga, bokhållaraktiga stil, och givetvis på ryska.

The letter was from the secretary of the Communist party personally which explains that it was written in Russian.

Disjuncts, on the other hand, express the speaker's attitudes or comments on the message and are less clearly discourse markers. In (7) *of course* is an emphatic adverb:

(7)   "You are a fool!" Hilary had banged on a kitchen cupboard as she spoke and the cups and plates inside trembled.
      "Of course he's not coming back.
      The petty cash is empty.   (FW1)
      "Ni är en idiot!"
      Hilary hade slagit näven i köksskåpen när hon talade, så att kopparna och tallrikarna därinne skakade.
      "Det är klart att han inte kommer tillbaka.
      Handkassan är borta, och jag ringde banken.

Of course is thematic and stressed. However, as Thompson and Zhou (2000) have shown, disjuncts can also be weakly connective although it may be difficult to label or explicate the relation to the preceding utterance in many cases (Thompson and Zhou 2000, 137). As a discourse marker *of course* guides the hearer through the discourse (what's happening next?). When *of course* combines with *but* or can be replaced by *but* it can be regarded as a discourse marker with adversative function.

In (8) *but of course* strengthens the contrast with the preceding utterance:

(8) Then there might possibly be an interaction, <u>but</u> all the time, <u>of course</u>, he'd dominate it with his grasp of the thing and if we were able to come up with anything, if he took hold of it, then he 'd elaborate it in his own par-ticular way.   (CE1T)
   Då kunde det möjligtvis ske en växelverkan, <u>men det är ju klart att</u> det var hela tiden han som dominerade med sitt grepp på det och om vi då kunde komma med bidrag, om han högg tag i dem, så vidareutvecklade han ju dem på sitt speciella sätt.

But of course is more emphatic than the simple *but* (and potentially contentious). In the following example the translator has added *men* 'but' in the Swedish translation thus making explicit the adversative or 'oppositional' meaning of *of course*.

(9) That left him and Blake, the old man thought.
   In a way he envied Blake, completely assimilated, utterly content, who had invited him and Erita round for New Year's Eve.
   <u>Of course</u>, Blake had had a cosmopolitan background, Dutch father, Jewish mother.   (FF1)
   Nu var det han och Blake kvar, tänkte den gamle mannen.
   På ett sätt avundades han Blake, som var helt assimilerad och fullständigt belåten och hade bjudit hem honom och Erita på nyårsafton.
   <u>Men</u> Blake hade <u>förstås</u> också en kosmopolitisk bakgrund –holländsk mor och judisk far.

The old man envied Blake who had been completely assimilated (both had been spies during the war). However (but) Blake had had a cosmopolitan background with a Dutch mother and a Jewish father.

   In (10), *of course* is shown to be a discourse marker by its translation as *fast det är klart* ('however it is clear that'). Harry Harris has run off with a young blonde (it was not a joke). But you can't blame HH for this.

(10) ...and he thought perhaps she wasn't joking.
   A little later she said:
   "<u>Of course,</u> you can't blame Harry Harris too much, considering what his wife's like."   (FW1)
   Kanske ligger det i alla fall något bakom det hon säger, tänkte han.
   Lite senare sa hon:
   "<u>Fast det är klart</u>, man kan inte bara skylla på Harry Harris, eftersom man vet hurdan hans hustru är."
   Lit. 'though it is clear that one cannot only blame HH since one knows what his wife is like'.

As shown by the translations, *of course* not only expresses certainty or emphasis but it has developed discourse-marking functions e.g. to express contrast or concession. Because of its close relationship with adversative markers like *but* and with additive markers (*and*) it should be regarded as a discourse marker with the function of achieving interpersonal and textual coherence. The close association with adversativity and concession suggests that it is basically argumentative. *Of course* as a discourse marker is placed initially (followed by a comma) as in example (10) or after a conjunction ('and, of course, (it is) in Russian' as in example 6). [3]

6.   *Of course* – a modal particle?

The meaning of both the discourse marker and the modal particle can be understood from the presuppositional properties of the adverb. Because of its evidential or modal meaning (something is self-evident, certain or uncontroversial) *of course* presupposes that something is given or known information. *John is of course a factory worker* presupposes for example that it is true that John is a factory worker. The notion of (pragmatic) presupposition means that circumstances, events, beliefs are part of a shared pool of beliefs or common ground. Lambrecht (1994) defines pragmatic presupposition as follows:

> The set of of propositions lexicogrammatically evoked in a sentence which the speaker assumes the hearer already knows or is ready to take for granted at the time the sentence is uttered (1994, 52).

The examples I will discuss as modal particles are those where *of course* has been translated as *ju*, i.e. the translator has interpreted *of course* as having the meaning 'as you know', 'as you and I know', 'as everyone knows'.

There may be additional linguistic cues indicating that something is given information or shared knowledge. In example (11) *of course* co-occurs with 'as mentioned earlier'. *Of course* contributes to the speaker's argument by referring to the store of shared knowledge which has been established in the preceding discourse:

(11)   And not only America.Trading vessels from most of the European countries were to be seen in the ports of Cádiz.
But the great tradition in Cádiz is, <u>of course, as mentioned earlier</u>, dance and song. There was a *barrio gitano* (gypsy quarter) in the city from which

---

3.   *Of course* is also a discourse marker when it is used as a 'response marker':
"Can you see all right?" Sarah asked."<u>Of course</u>," Macon said.(AT1)
Ser du ordentligt?" frågade Sarah. <u>Javisst</u>.

many well-known flamenco singers and dancers came as well as from the surrounding ports. (BTC1T)

Men det var inte bara med Amerika man hade handelsutbyte – fartyg från de flesta europeiska länderna sågs i Cádiz' hamnar.
Från Sverige fraktades bl a trävaror och tjära i utbyte mot salt, olja och vin.
Men den stora traditionen i Cádiz är ju, som tidigare nämnts, dansen och sången.
I staden fanns en *barrio gitano* och därifrån, och från hamnarna runt omkring, kom många kända flamencosångare och dansare.

An important function of the modal particle is to refer to shared knowledge in order to establish or maintain rapport (Holmes 1988):

(12) But sometimes I ca n't get my breath, I have difficulty in breathing. I'm not as young as I was, of course, and you 've got to have some ailment. (SC1T)

Men ibland har jag svårt för att få luft, svårt att andas.Jag är ju inte så ung längre och nån krämpa ska man ju ha.

And of course can introduce a 'new, final idea on a particular topic' (Lewis 2002, 87):

(13) "We became friends because we shared some artistic enthusiasms – music, and manuscripts, and calligraphy, and that sort of thing – and of course he made me one of his executors. (RDA1)

"Vi blev vänner för att vi hade en del konstnärliga intressen gemensamt – musik och manuskript och kalligrafi och sådana saker, och han gjorde ju mig till en av sina testamentsexekutorer.

In (14) the reference to shared information has the function of making the following question less abrupt. (I wonder if you know anything about what they call jazz. I'm asking you since jazz comes from America and as we both know your wife comes from America).

(14) And now the Boss stands there, several years closer to Modern Times, and wants to placate, shouts down the stairs."There was one thing, Aron. I've purchased a gramophone and wonder if you know... your wife was from America, of course. Do you know anything about what they call *jazz*? (GT1T)

Och nu står Patron där, några år närmare det Moderna och vill blidka; ropar neråt trappan.
– Det var en sak till, Aron.

Jag har inköpt en grammofon och undrar, känner du till... din hustru hon
var ju från Amerika. Kan du något om den där *jazzen*?

Of course also contributes to the structuring of the information into what is foregrounding and what is backgrounding. Consider example (15). The three Spanish
cities Sevilla, Cádiz and Jerez all claim to be the cradle of flamenco. *Of course* introduces the background information which is needed in order to understand this
claim (the sweet grape is grown, several famous wine cellars are located there).
Lewis refers to this use as a metatextual backgrounding function: 'the thread of the
narrative is broken... to inform the hearer of a circumstance that will make the
narrative more coherent' (Lewis 2002, 87).

(15)   Sevilla, Cádiz and Jerez all claim to be the cradle of flamenco, and all three
       cities are, in fact, important names in the history of flamenco. Jerez, of
       course, is best known as the city of wine. Between the mouths of the Gua-
       dalquivir and Guadalete rivers the sweet grape is grown from which the
       sherry wine with all its variants comes.The great *Bodegas* (wine-cellars)
       with famous names like Domecq, González Byass, Sandeman and several
       others are located there. In the world of flamenco two types of flamenco
       song can be identified: *cante flamenco andaluz* and *cante flamenco gitano*,
       Andalusian flamenco song which is sung by a *payo* (non-gypsy) and gyp-
       sy-flamenco song which is sung by a *calé* (gypsy).   (BTC1T)
       Sevilla såväl som Cádiz och Jerez gör anspråk på att vara den ort där fla-
       mencons vagga stod. Säkert är dock att alla de tre städerna är viktiga namn
       i flamencons historia. Jerez är ju framförallt känd som vinets stad. Mellan
       Guadalquivirs och Guadaletes mynningar odlas den ljuva druvan som ger
       sherryvinet i alla dess varianter. Där finns de stora bodegorna med sina
       kända namn som Domecq, González Byass, Sandeman och flera till.I fla-
       mencovärlden skiljer man på två typer av flamencosång: *cante flamenco
       andaluz* och *cante flamenco gitano*. Andalusisk flamencosång som sjungs
       av en *payo* – icke-zigenare – och zigenarflamencosång som sjungs av en
       calé – zigenare.   (BTC1)

Similarly in (16), *of course* refers to what is backgrounded as is also suggested by
the translation with *ju* and the switch from past tense to the past perfect:

(16)   Pasqual Pinon's two heads are shown on a series of photographs from the
       1920s and 1930s; the last was taken only a few days before his death.He
       had of course acquired a certain international fame by then, and had been
       the subject of a biography, which was published after his death: this was

written by the impresario John Shideler, and called A Monster's Life. There
are pictures enough.

They all express sadness and dignity; as if the two heads always looked
into the camera conscious that they would never be understood, that those
seeing the pictures would never understand.   (PE1T)

Pasqual Pinons två huvuden finns återgivna på en rad fotografier från
20- och 30-talen; det sista är taget bara några dagar före hans död.Han
hade <u>ju</u> då uppnått en viss internationell ryktbarhet, och blev föremål för
en biografi publicerad efter hans död: det var impressarion John Shideler
som skrivit denna biografi, "A Monster's Life". Bilder finns det gott om.

De ger alla uttryck för sorg och värdighet; som om de två huvudena alltid
såg in i kameran medvetna om att de som såg bilderna aldrig skulle
förstå.

The function of *of course* is to show that the information is backgrounded in relation to the main topic. The topic (Pinon's two heads are shown in a series of photographs) is resumed after the addition of the information that Pinon had achieved
international fame by then.

A closer analysis of the contexts where *of course* means 'ju' shows that that it
typically introduces a topic which is subordinate to another topic (e.g. the explanation for a claim, background information needed to facilitate the progression of a
narrative).

(17) "Yes," said Asplund, "that 's the whole idea."

I had a few meetings with Lewerentz when we were drawing the Breden-
berg department store.

Lewerentz <u>of course</u> took over his father's factory in Eskilstuna and used a
metal window that was n't so common in those days, with interlinked
arches and double It was absolutely new, because we had invited tenders
from German companies for that sort of design. Then Lewerentz came
along and said that he could do it cheaper, but he could n't meet the deliv-
ery deadlines.   (CE1T)

"Jo," sa Asplund, "det är ju det som är meningen."

Jag hade en del sammanträffanden med Lewerentz när vi ritade Breden-
bergs varuhus.

Lewerentz övertog <u>ju</u> sin fars fabrik i Eskilstuna och körde med ett metall-
fönster som inte var så vanligt på den tiden med kopplade bågar och dub-
bla glas. Det var alldeles nytt, för vi hade tagit in anbud från tyska firmor
på en sån konstruktion. Då kom Lewerentz och menade att han kunde
göra det där billigare, men han kunde inte klara leveranstiderna.

Of course relates a proposition to the preceding utterance which contains the new information (I had a few meetings with Lewerenz). By introducing a reference to shared evidence for the information in the first utterance the speaker makes sure that misunderstandings are avoided and that the progression of the narrative is facilitatated.

In (18) the new information is that the shipping company was obliged to lay the vessels up. *Of course* signals that the sentence to which it is attached fits into the context as backgrounded information. The backgrounded utterance marked by *of course* is followed by a resumption of the topic (in 1901 renegotiations took place).

(18)   Export volumes to Belgium and France were small and the Gällivare com-
        pany was periodically compelled to lay the vessels up.Narvik did not come
        into use before the beginning of 1903, <u>of course.</u> In October 1901, both
        time charters were renegotiated so that they applied only to the season
        when Luleå was open.   (TR1T)
        Exportkvantiteterna till Belgien och Frankrike var små och Gällivarebo-
        laget fick periodvis lägga upp fartygen.Narvik kom <u>ju</u> ej i bruk förrän
        1903. I oktober 1901 omförhandlades dessa bägge timecharterkontrakt så
        att de kom att gälla enbart under Luleå-säsongen.

When *of course* is found in a non-restrictive relative clause as in (19), the information is already backgrounded or 'parenthetical'. By sneaking in *of course* the speaker
makes it even more difficult for the hearer to avoid the implication that there is
consensus about the facts. *Of course* has the function of upgrading backgrounded
information:

(19)   But one must not forget the long winters <u>which, of course,</u> for seventy to
        eighty percent consist of *complete* darkness."   (GT1T)
        Men man får då inte glömma de långa vintrarna <u>som ju</u> till sjutti, åttio
        procent består av *rent* mörker.

Of course in an explanatory *because*-clause as in (20) signals that the information
is backgrounded:

(20)   How do you do, Franklin,' said Auntie, shaking the boy's hand (she found
        herself wondering just whom it had originally belonged to, because <u>of</u>
        <u>course</u> it was, as you might say, second-hand).   (ARP1T)
        – Goddag Franklin, sa fastern och tog gossens hand (och hon kom på sig
        med att undra vem den hade tillhört i original, den var <u>ju</u> numera så att
        säga second hand).

Of course as a modal particle is both consensus-seeking and rhetorical. If the
speaker knows that the hearer (or 'everyone') does not agree *of course* is subtly

argumentative. The following example is taken from the debates in the European Parliament.

(21)   Of 47 states invited from all corners of the world, not one of them, however, is an Arab state included in the EU's Barcelona process. This has been interpreted as indicating that the Arab attitude towards Israel should be regarded by Europeans as being similar to the Nazis' anti-Semitism, <u>which of course</u> is completely incorrect.   (EGAH1T)
Bland fyrtiosju inbjudna stater från samtliga världsdelar finns emellertid inte en enda av de arabstater som ingår i EU:s Barcelonaprocess. Detta har tolkats som att den arabiska hållningen gentemot Israel av européer skulle betraktas på samma sätt som nazismens antisemitism, vilket <u>ju</u> är fullständigt felaktigt.

Instead of arguing explicitly that excluding the Arab states from the EU's Barcelona process could be interpreted as similar to anti-Semitism the speaker adopts the stance that this is a fact and not controversial. The use of *of course* enables the speaker to make a controversial statement in the guise of what is shared knowledge or self-evident.

Of course is also used if the argument is less controversial and consensus may be expected (must of course).

(22)   If global decisions are to have legitimacy, then <u>of course</u> they <u>must</u> be representative.   (EISC1T)
För att globala beslut skall ha någon legitimitet, <u>måste</u> de <u>ju</u> vara representativa.   (EISC1)

The speaker takes for granted that no one in the audience will dispute that global decisions must be representative.

The syntactic distribution is another indication of how *of course* should be interpreted. The left-detached position (marked by commas) is reserved for the discourse marker. On the other hand, the modal particle is integrated in the syntactic structure and is non-initial. The modal particle *of course* can also have end position (at the end of a clause).

7. Conclusion

Cross-linguistically a distinction can be made between discourse markers and modal particles. However in spite of intensive research there is still little agreement on basic issues such as terminology and how these categories should be distinguished. In particular the problems of categorizing discourse markers and modal particles have attracted considerable attention recently. The discussion of this issue is not restricted to typical particle languages such as German but has been fuelled by the question of whether all languages can be said to have modal particles.

It can be argued that the distinction between discourse markers and modal particles need to be made also in languages where the criteria for particlehood are less strict. The importance of this distinction has been illustrated by a study of the different uses of English *of course*. Its multifunctionality can be explained diachronically in a grammaticalization framework. Grammaticalization can explain the emergence of new meanings and functions but only provides the raw material for further sub-classification. The method used in this chapter has been to look at the translations of *of course* into Swedish. When *of course* is potentially a modal particle, *ju* appears in the translation. The discourse marker, on the other hand, has translations such as *men* ('but') and it appears in collocations with *but*. Table 2 summarizes the meanings of the modal particle and the discourse marker.

Of course as a discourse marker is used at boundaries of the discourse (signaled by utterance-initial position) and signals connection between utterance units (adversative, concessive or resultative function). The modal particle *of course*, on the other hand, is used to metapragmatically comment on the proposition in the context of the language users' common ground. It can be described as 'context-adjusting', a notion I have borrowed from Vaskó and Fretheim (1997). Vaskó and Fretheim (1997, 253) refer to the context-adjusting function as follows:

> With the context-adjusting particle the speaker gives the hearer information which it seems reasonable to think that the hearer has failed to access, or else accessible information which the speaker feels that the hearer has ignored.

Table 2. The discourse marking and modal particle functions of *of course*

Discourse marker	
	Adversative (contrast) (but of course)
	Concessive (of course... but)
	Resultative
Modal particle	
Consensus	Solidarity (positive politeness) (as we both know)
Argumentative	Persuasion (as everyone knows, as you should know, must of course)
	Making a final point (and of course)
Backgrounding	Explaining, elaborating, correcting, remedying a break in the narrative thread
	Emphasising the backgrounding of information (which of course)

The speaker can say either *John of course took over his father's factory* or *John took over his father's factory*. In the first example *of course* draws attention to the fact that the speaker and hearer do not have the same access to knowledge and that the information may be more or less accessible (to the hearer). Both the speaker and the hearer can have access to the same information (this is related to given information); only the speaker knows something but the hearer does not know (this is related to new information). However there are degrees of accessibility to knowledge. The hearer may have momentarily forgotten something or intentionally ignored the information. The function of *of course* is to check that the speaker's and hearer's contextual assumptions (beliefs, expectations) converge (as we both know) or to remind the hearer of information which has been given.

Of course is potentially argumentative. The speaker can smuggle new information or ideas into the discourse pretending that it is shared knowledge. *Of course* can also be used for marking consensus and consolidating a harmonious relationship with the hearer. Both functions are dependent on the shared context. According to Simon-Vandenbergen et al. (2007, 61):

> [s]uch expressions [e.g. *of course*] are indeed manipulable because speakers use them for presenting non-shared and even highly contested propositions as if they were shared knowledge. The effect is on one hand that solidarity is confirmed with those who share the speaker's viewpoint and on the other hand that those who hold alternative opinions are put in a position where more interactive work needs to be done if they want to challenge the speaker's view.

Of course as a modal particle can introduce background material into the discourse. It is used with 'remedial effects' for example to introduce an explanation or to interrupt a narrative by some additional information.

The existence of a category of modal particles in one language does not automatically mean that there must be a corresponding category in another language. English is for instance not usually thought to have modal particles. However as shown in this study there are striking similarities between *of course* and the Swedish modal particle *ju* although *ju* can be assumed to be more grammaticalized. Other uses of *of course* can be described as discourse markers namely if they have a connective function. On the basis of the data from this study we can assume that the distinction between discourse marker and modal particle can be made in many languages. On the other hand, languages may differ in the frequencies with which discourse markers and modal particles are found. In this respect there is a difference between English (or French; cf. Schoonjans, this volume) and typical modal particle languages like German or Swedish. Moreover modal particles may have language-specific properties in addition to more general or universal ones.

Formal properties such as position in the clause may for example be more or less important depending on the language. Translations are an important key to finding out more about the relation between discourse markers and modal particles. However they also reflect the fact that there may be ambiguity and fuzzy boundaries between categories. The present study suggests that the distinction between discourse markers and modal particles can be investigated also on the basis of a language which is not usually associated with modal particles. It is clear that the problems of categorization need to be studied on the basis of many different languages. Contrastive studies (combined with diachronic studies) may result in a better description of the relations between (modal) adverbs, discourse markers and modal particles.

Primary sources

English sources:

AT Anne Tyler. *The accidental tourist.* New York 1985.
FF Frederick Forsyth. *The fourth protocol.*London 1984.
FW Fay Weldon, *The heart of the country.* London 1984.
RD Robertson Davies. *What's bred in the bone.* Harmondsworth 1985.
RR Ruth Rendell. *Kissing the gunner's daughter.* London 1992.

Swedish sources:

ARP Allan Rune Pettersson. *Frankenstein faster- igen.* Stockholm 1999.
CE Christina Engfors (ed.). *E.G. Asplund* Stockholm 1990.
EGAH Europaparlamentets överläggningar. Strasbourg and Brussels 1998–1999 (Per Gahrton).
EISC Europaparlamentets överläggnngar. Strasbourg and Brussels 1998–1999 (Inger Schörling).
GT Göran Tunström *Juloratoriet.* Stockholm 1983.
PE Per-Olof Enquist. *Nedstörtad ängel.* Stockholm 1986.
SC Stig Claesson. *Vem älskar Yngve Frej?* Stockholm 1968.
TR Torsten Rinman Rederiet Göteborg 1990.

Acknowledgement

I have profited from reading Steven Schoonjan's article in this volume. His comments on my own article have been of great help in revising this article.

References

Aijmer, Karin. 1997. "*I think*– an English Modal Particle." In *Modality in Germanic Languages. Historical and Comparative Perspectives*, ed. by Toril Swan, and Olaf J. Westvik, 1–47. Berlin: Mouton de Gruyter.

Aijmer, Karin. 2009. "Does English Have Modal Particles?" In *Corpus Linguistics: Refinements and Reassessments*, ed. by Antoinete Renouf, and Andrew Kehoe, 111–130. Amsterdam and New York: Rodopi.

Aijmer, Karin, and Anne-Marie Simon-Vandenbergen. 2003. "The Discourse Particle *well* and its Equivalents in Swedish and Dutch." *Linguistics* 41–6: 1123–1161.

Aijmer, Karin, Ad Foolen, and Anne-Marie Simon-Vandenbergen. 2006. "Pragmatic Markers in Translation: A Methodological Proposal." *Approaches to Discourse Particles,* ed. by Kerstin Fischer. 101–114. Amsterdam: Elsevier.

Altenberg, Bengt, and Karin Aijmer. 2000. "The English-Swedish Parallel Corpus: A Resource for Contrastive Research and Translation Studies." In *Corpus Linguistics and Linguistic Theory. Papers from the 20th International Conference on English Language Research on Computerized Corpora (ICAME 20) Freiburg im Breisgau 1999,* ed. by Christian Mair, and Marianne Hundt, 15–33. Amsterdam & Philadelphia: Rodopi.

Bertuccelli Papi, Marcella. 1997. "Implicitness." In *Handbook of Pragmatics*, ed. by Jef Verschueren, Jan-Ola Östman, Jan Blommaert, and Chris Bulcaen, 1–29. Amsterdam: John Benjamins.

Diewald, Gabriele. 2006. "Discourse Particles and Modal Particles as Grammatical Elements." In *Approaches to Discourse Particles,* ed. by Kerstin Fischer, 403–425. Amsterdam: Elsevier.

Dyvik, Helge. 1998. "A Translational Basis for Semantics." In *Corpora and Cross-linguistic Research: Theory, Methods, and Case Studies* ed. by Stig Johansson, and Signe Oksefjell, 51–86. Amsterdam: Rodopi.

Dyvik, Helge. 1999. "On the Complexity of Translation." In *Out of Corpora: Studies in Honour of Stig Johansson,* ed. by Hilde Hasselgård, and Signe Oksefjell, 215–230. Amsterdam: Rodopi.

Fischer, Kerstin. 2007. "Grounding and Common Ground: Modal Particles and their Translation Equivalents." In *Lexical Markers and Common Grounds,* ed. by Anita Fetzer, and Kerstin Fischer, 47–66. Amsterdam: Elsevier.

Fraser, Bruce. 1996. "Pragmatic markers." *Pragmatics* (6)2: 167–190.

Hasselgård, Hilde. 2006. "'Not now'– On Non-Correspondence between the Cognate Adverbs *Now* and *Nå*." In *Pragmatic Markersin Contrast,* ed. by Karin Aijmer, and Anne-Marie Simon-Vandenbergen. 93–113. Amsterdam: Elsevier.

Holmes, Janet. 1988. "*Of course*, A Pragmatic Particle in New Zealand Women's and Men's Speech." *Australian Journal of Linguistics* 2: 49–74.

Hoye, Leo. 1997. *Adverbs and Modality in English*. London and New York: Longman.

Lambrecht, Knud. 1994. *Information Structure and Sentence Form. Topic, Focus, and the Mental Representations of Discourse Referents*. Cambridge: Cambridge University Press.

Lewis, Diana. 1998. "From Modal Adverbial to Discourse Connective: Some Rhetorical Effects in Present-Day English." In *Pragmatics in 1998: Selected Papers from the 6th International Pragmatics Conference.* Vol. 2., ed. by Jef Verschueren. 363–375. Antwerp: International Pragmatics Association.

Lewis, Diana M. 2003. "Rhetorical Motivations for the Emergence of Discourse Particles, with Special Reference to English *of course*." In *Particles,* ed by Ton van der Wouden, Ad Foolen, and Piet Van de Craen, Special issue of *Belgian Journal of Linguistics* 16: 79–91.

The Longman Dictionary of Contemporary English. 1995 [1978] [LDOCE].

Quirk, Randolph, Sidney Greenbaum, Geoffrey Leech, and Jan Svartvik. 1985. *A Comprehensive Grammar of the English Language.* London: Longman.

Rühlemann, Christoph. 2007. *Conversation in Context.* London and New York: Continuum.

Schiffrin, Deborah. 1987. *Discourse Markers.* Cambridge: Cambridge University Press.

Simon-Vandenbergen, Anne-Marie, and Karin Aijmer. 2002/2003. "The Expectation Marker *of course*." *Languages in Contrast* 4 (1): 13–43.

Simon-Vandenbergen, Anne-Marie, Peter R. White, and Karin Aijmer. 2007. "Presupposition and 'Taking-For-Granted' in Mass Communicated Political Argument: An Illustration From British, Flemish and Swedish Political Colloquy." *Political Discourse in the Media,* ed. by Anita Fetzer, and Gerda Lauerbach. 31–74. Amsterdam/Philadelphia: John Benjamins.

Thompson, Geoff, and Jianglin Zhou. 2000. "Evaluation and Organization In Text: The Structuring Role of Evaluative Disjuncts." In *Evaluation in Text. Authorial Stance and the Construction of Discourse,* ed. by Susan Hunston, and Geoff Thompson. 121–141. Oxford: Oxford University Press.

Traugott Closs, Elizabeth. 2007. "Discourse Markers, Modal Particles, and Contrastive Analysis, Synchronic and Diachronic." *Catalan Journal of Linguistics* 6 (Special issue: Contrastive Perspectives on Discourse Markers, ed. by Maria Josep Cuenca.): 139–157.

Vaskó, Ildiko, and Thorstein Fretheim. 1997. "Some Central Pragmatic Functions of the Norwegian Particles *altså* and nemlig." In *Modality in Germanic Languages. Historical and Comparative Perspectives*, ed. by Toril Swan, and Olaf J. Westvik, 233–292. Berlin: Mouton de Gruyter.

Waltereit, Richard, and Ulrich Detges. 2007. "Different Functions, Different Histories. Modal Particles and Discourse Markers from a Diachronic Point Of View." *Catalan Journal of Linguistics* 6 (Special issue: Contrastive perspectives on Discourse Markers, ed. by Maria Josep Cuenca.): 61–80.

Modal particles, discourse markers, and adverbs with *lt*-suffix in Estonian

Annika Valdmets
University of Tartu

This paper discusses a series of invariable Estonian adverbs with an *lt*-suffix and attempts to account for them within the framework of grammaticalization. This study investigates the functions of the forms *loomulikult* 'naturally; of course', *ilmselt* 'visibly; apparently', *tegelikult* 'in reality; actually', and *lihtsalt* 'simply; just' from the 1890s to 2000s. Excerpts from Estonian fiction and newspaper texts demonstrate the use of identical word forms as autosemantic items (adverbs) as well as synsemantic items (pragmatic markers). The paper suggests that the category of pragmatic markers can be further divided into two subcategories, modal particles and discourse markers. Several criteria that support the classification into subcategories will be outlined.[1]

1. Introduction

Two main issues will be discussed in this chapter within the broader frame of the grammaticalization of adverbs. First, the general theory of pragmatic markers will be introduced in the context of four Estonian adverbs ending in *-lt*. Similar expressions have been the subject of recent studies in different languages. The words studied in this paper behave similarly to the corresponding units in other world languages in that they are multifunctional (see Brinton 1996; Simon-Vandenbergen and Aijmer 2007) and have a tendency to grammaticalize (Hopper and Traugott 2003; Heine and Narrog 2010), displaying generalization in meaning content, occurrence in and spread into new contexts, loss in morphosyntactic properties, and loss of phonetic substance. The *lt*-suffix in Estonian can in many cases be compared to the English *ly*-suffix (see, e.g., Traugott and Dasher 2002 or Lenk 1998 for *actually, incidentally* etc.). Additionally, it may correspond to

---

1. I am grateful to Leelo Keevallik, Külli Habicht, Bert Cornillie, Djuddah Leijen, and two anonymous reviewers for their useful comments and fruitful discussions covering various aspects of this paper.

differently formed but similarly functioning items such as *of course* (see, e.g., Simon-Vandenbergen and Aijmer 2007). Second, it will be examined whether these expressions ending in *-lt* can be defined as belonging to the word class of pragmatic markers, and whether a boundary between modal particle (MP) and discourse marker (DM) uses for the items under examination can be drawn. In languages with strict word order the distinction between MPs and DMs is often made on the basis of the position of the item in the clause. Yet, Estonian has a relatively free word order, which is an additional complicating factor. This makes the sub-categorization of pragmatic items in Estonian quite challenging (see the discussion in Traugott 2007).

All four words discussed in this paper (*loomulikult, ilmselt, tegelikult, lihtsalt*) may function as a) adverbs, b) MPs, and c) DMs, and therefore all of these words belong simultaneously to three different categories. The three different uses are shown schematically in Figure 1 and exemplified in example (1) below (see Fraser 2006; Aijmer this volume).

(1) a.   *Tüdruku juukse-d on   loomulikult lokkis.*
          girl.GEN hair-PL   be.3PL   naturally   curly
          'The girl's hair is naturally curly.'

     b.   *Sa või-d   loomulikult auto-t   laena-ta.*
          you may-2SG   certainly   car-PRT   borrow-INF
          'You may certainly borrow the car.'

     c.   *Ta   luba-s   õhtusöögi-ks suppi   teh-a.*
          (s)he   promise-PST.3SG   dinner-TR   soup.PRT   make-INF
          Loomulikult, kui   koju   jõud-si-me,
          of_course   when   home.ILL arrive-PST-1PL
          pid-i-me   ise süü-a   tege-ma.
          have_to-PST-1PL   self eat-INF make-SUP
          '(S)he promised to make soup for dinner. Of course, when we got home, we had to cook by ourselves.'

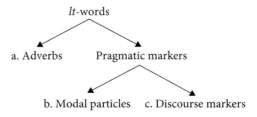

Figure 1. *lt*-words in Estonian functioning as adverbs, MPs, and DMs

In the current functional approach, only written edited sources of Estonian are investigated, but it is taken for granted that the use of pragmatic markers in written language is driven by colloquial Estonian. The material selected for analysis (journalistic and fictional texts) originates from the Corpus of Estonian Literary Language (CELL) and from the Balanced Corpus of Estonian (BCE).

The material presented in this article is gathered from the newer literary Estonian (starting from the 1890s). The Corpus of Old Literary Estonian does not contain any entries of the words studied here in the form that are used today (see also Valdmets and Habicht 2013, 207). *loomulikult* makes a first appearance in corpora texts in 1900s (7 sentences), *ilmselt* in 1930s (12 sentences), *tegelikult* in 1890s (3 sentences), and *lihtsalt* in 1890s (13 sentences). All of these words are derivations form an adjectival source and the *lt*-suffix is added to the genitive form of the adjective. The stems themselves are present in the older literature but may carry a different meaning.[2]

It is not clear why there is no trace of these *lt*-adverbs in the corpus of the earlier written language and unfortunately the gathering of the oral data from Estonian dialects started later. Based on the data available it can be stated that the words investigated here have come to the language quite recently. More generally, if we look at the group of *lt*-adverbs as a whole then it is possible to say that the widespread use of these words started due to the intentional and official enrichment of Estonian which took place in the beginning of 20th century. Thus, these *lt*-words are fascinating because of their extremely rapid development; these words were a part of the formal register but have nevertheless changed fast during the last century. Also, their overall token frequency in corpora has grown into hundreds of examples (for *tegelikult* and *loomulikult* see Valdmets 2011). All of the four words investigated here are from the first appearances in the corpora used as adverbs. Nevertheless, it is possible to follow in CELL, how the pragmatic function arose soon after the first uses or grew side by side with the adverbial function.

While determining the meaning of a particular word under investigation, the explanations from the Concise Dictionary of Estonian (CDE) and Prescriptive Dictionary of Estonian (PDE) were used.

---

2.   While going through the biggest old dictionaries that are written on Estonian language before the 20th century, I have found that the first dictionary that has traces of all of the four words is F. J. Wiedemann's "Ehstnish-Deutsches Wörterbuch" from 1869 (here, I have used the 3. edition from 1923 which is unchanged edition from the second print in 1893). It gives the following forms: *ilmne:ilmse* (adj; p. 117); *loomulik:loomuliku*; *loomuline:loomulize* (adj; p. 529); *lihtus:lihtsa* (adj) and, *lihtsaste, lihtsalt=lihtjas* (adv; p. 498), *tegeline:tegelize* (adj; p. 1138) (Wiedemann 1923). This means that the only exact written form in older dictionaries is *lihtsalt*. If we take a look to the old stems then the stem that date even further back is *ilm-* (*ilm*, Göseken 1660 (Kingisepp *et al.* 2010); *ilmsi, ilmsiks sama*, Thor Helle 1732 and Hupel 1780).

2.   Definition of pragmatic markers

Pragmatic markers are a diffuse group of items which can be defined as signals that have indexical, rather than propositional effects (Aijmer; Diewald this volume). The grammaticalized units studied here are considered a subgroup of pragmatic markers (Fraser 1996) which usually function as MPs but may, in some instances, also be classified as DMs. Hence, it is suggested that MPs and DMs form a bigger group of pragmatic markers.[3] The term *pragmatic marker* is used here as applied by Brinton (1996, 29–30); the term *marker* is used in favor of other possible terms like *word* or *particle* because it covers both single words and pragmatic phrases. Later, while talking about *MPs*, I will turn back to the single-word notion, as the items under investigation consist of no more than one word.

Pragmatic markers are items that appear more often in speech than in written discourse. In written or formal discourse, they are often seen as redundant "fillers" that occur frequently and can be left out of a sentence because they do not offer much to the truth conditional meaning of the clause (Brinton 1996, 33; Schourup 1999, 234; see also Bybee 2007). The meaning of these units may be hard to define, yet they are not meaningless items (for a discussion about traditional approaches, see Brinton 1996, Section 1.1.1.). The distinction between two categories of pragmatic markers, i.e., MPs and DMs is not always obvious. Traugott (2007, 141) explains that there are two possible ways of separating the group of MPs from DMs: first, on the basis of formal and discourse functional criteria, and second, by recognizing that MPs appear clause-internally while DMs do not.

In many languages, studied both contrastively (Cinque 1999) as well as within their own limits (Ernst 1984), the position of the specific item in a text is determining the difference in function. In English, for example, manner adverbs usually appear in the right margin of the clause, cooperating with the verb-phrase. If the item acquires a new function as an epistemic particle, it can move more freely while adding some kind of emphasis to the truth value of the proposition. In contrast to the previous two, a DM appears outside the clause (Traugott and Dasher 2002, 158–159). More precise explanations will be presented in the following sections.

2.1   Modal particles

MPs express the speaker's or writer's view on how true or certain the proposition expressed by the utterance is. Most of them carry epistemic modality; some of

---

3.   Some authors propose alternative definitions, e.g., Waltereit (2001, 1392) addresses MPs as a specific class of discourse particles.

them may be seen as evidential markers (but see the definition of *MPs* from other authors in this volume). Epistemic and evidential modality is often handled together since they may not differ in a larger sense (Hakulinen *et al.* 2004, 1518; Palmer 2001, 8; but see Cornillie 2009). Evidentiality is an indication of the nature of evidence (the source) for a given proposition. A fine line exists between those two domains, so some of the particles carrying epistemic modality share some characteristics with the evidential domain. For example, *loomulikult* 'of course' can, in some instances, have evidential properties. Additionally, these items may be used as emphatic and emphasizing words; the notion of *intensity* (Labov 1984) is hereby relevant (see, e.g., *loomulikult* in example (b)).[4] MPs may also carry other functions such adversativity or hedging[5] (e.g., *tegelikult* 'actually' in sentence (14)). In this paper, epistemic and evidential modalities are not henceforth divided since the notion of evidentiality is not common for all of the *lt*-words. Yet, different features of the studied items are handled under subsections, in case the example sentences represent a specific function.

Estonian MPs are traditionally treated as modal items that move freely in a clause and that are facultative in a text. The absence of an MP in a clause does not make the clause ungrammatical but can cause a situation where the notion of the text is unclear. In addition to textual functions, MPs play an important role on an interpersonal level: expressing the speaker's or writer's subjective stand and, in a dialogue, creating a sense of intimacy between the speaker and the listener (Brinton 1996, 35–40; for a discussion on *(inter)subjectivity* see Davidse *et al.* 2010). Modal/epistemic particles are metatextual, i.e., they add some kind of comment to the text. Moreover, they are deictic items that indicate the speaker's or writer's metatextual attitude while trying to guide the addressee towards the same stance. (Traugott 1999, 181) In spite of the different criteria presented for the analysis of MPs or pragmatic markers, it is hard to define the meaning of these grammatical items. Also, they may not be easily translatable to other languages (Brinton 1996, 33–34). However, for the sake of clarity, I have attempted to translate all of the *lt*-suffix items studied in this paper.

2.2   Discourse markers

DMs are the other subclass of pragmatic markers (Fraser 1988). They are considered to be words that give us clues about the structure of the discourse (Redeker 1990). Brinton (2010, 285–286) has listed the main features of a DM: DMs are

---

4.   For *intensity markers*, see, e.g., Quirk *et al.* 1985.

5.   Hedges delimit the strength of the utterance and are largely seen as part of epistemic modality (see, e.g., Holmes 1984).

phonologically "short" words that usually appear clause-initially. Additionally, they are syntactically independent items that can form an intonational unit by themselves in spoken discourse. DMs are frequent items that can be stylistically marked.

Since one of the main functions of DMs is connecting pieces of discourse, many authors refer to DMs as *discourse connectives*. Schiffrin (1987, 31) sees them as "sequentially dependent elements which bracket elements of talk; the beginning of one unit is the end of another". DMs show how the present sentence or utterance is related to the nearby discourse and help the speaker to produce a coherent discourse. Traugott and Dasher (2002, 155) explain that two sentences that are in the scope of a DM need not be adjacent but these sentences must have an apparent relationship in terms of condition, topic shift, elaboration, contrast, justification among other things. Schourup (1999, 234) argues that these elements are syntactically loosely related to the clause and are used to relate one utterance to the immediately following utterance. Even though it is said that DMs lack semantic meaning, he explains how items with similar semantic field are not interchangeable in the same context: their "communicative effects" may be very different (Schourup 1999, 242–243). These kinds of items may have procedural meaning which emerges in a specific context (*ibid.*, 244ff).

DMs structure the discourse, but they are not the only linguistic expressions that do so. Many other lexical items have the same function but do not qualify as DMs. In her study, Lenk (1998, 50) shows that some structuring phrases in English (like *in other words*, *summing up*, *as a result*) are only used to express a structuring function in a text or utterance and do not have any other functions. However, DMs have a pragmatic meaning, but can often also have an original lexical meaning. Importantly, these meanings do not overlap in the speech context, i.e., "they do not express the propositional meaning of their homonyms at the same time" (Lenk 1998, 51). In Estonian, similar structuring words are used, e.g., *teiste sõnadega* 'in other words'. Some of them even have an *lt*-suffix, e.g., *kokkuvõtvalt* 'in a nutshell'. Still, words of this kind only have a structural function in discourse; they do not carry other functions that are characteristic of the category of pragmatic markers.

Many of the DMs tend to hold a specific position in the clause, usually either as the first or last element. The left or right periphery depends on the word order of a specific language. In English, the left margin is dominant (Traugott and Dasher 2002, 156). If the item does not hold the initial position within the unit, its primary function is probably something else than to structure the discourse (Lenk 1998, 51). In Estonian, DMs tend to appear sentence-initially. In Japanese, by contrast, both the left and the right periphery are possible for DMs. In Greek, DMs occupy the second position in the clause (Traugott and Dasher 2002, 156).

3. The multifunctionality of *lt*-words

To explain the multifunctionality of adverbs and pragmatic markers, I have to recourse to the concept of grammaticalization. Etymologically, the adverbial items under scrutiny originate from adjectives: the adjective stem is used with the adverbial suffix -*lt*. In Estonian, -*lt* is a productive adverbial suffix expressing manner or degree and it is semantically transparent for present day speakers, unlike the pragmatic marker uses that are not so transparent anymore. In all instances studied here, the pragmatic markers are polysemous.[6] The phenomenon of different readings coexisting in a language has been termed *layering* (Hopper 1991, 22). There is a historically earlier form/meaning unit A (manner adverb) and a grammaticalized unit B (pragmatic marker). Brinton (2010, 302) explains that DMs do not always represent prototypical cases of grammaticalization but they do undergo usual morphosyntactic and semantic changes that can be considered from the point of view of grammaticalization. These central changes are also the reason for choosing grammaticalization as the framework of the present paper.

3.1 From adverb to modal particle/discourse marker

The *lt*-words studied in the present paper are used in three different ways in Estonian: a. manner adverbs, b. MPs, and c. DMs. The latter two also form a bigger group of pragmatic markers. Manner adverbs with *lt*-ending often grammaticalize. Their grammaticalization involves the generalization in meaning content, spread into new contexts, loss of morphosyntactic properties, and loss of phonetic substance. The items gradually acquire new pragmatic functions and witness layered uses as adverbs and pragmatic markers. There are some semantic-pragmatic tendencies that describe the unidirectional change of these words (Traugott and Dasher 2002, 40, 281) which also apply to the change of items studied in the article:

a. truth-conditional > non-truth-conditional
b. content > content/procedural > procedural
c. non-subjective > subjective > intersubjective
d. scope within the proposition > scope over the proposition > scope over the discourse

---

6. Not all of the authors agree on this matter. Some researchers assume homonymy (Abraham 1991, 207, 236–237; Östman 1982, 153ff), where every particle has a grammatical homonym which belongs to some other category while having a clear propositional content. Here, polysemy is suggested because of the etymological base: words studied in this article have the same origin.

The adverb, which specifies the verb, loses its characteristics as a full content word and develops into a pragmatic marker, hence turns into a procedural item. The changing word no more contributes to the truth-conditional content. Instead, the scope broadens over the proposition and later, over larger chunks of discourse.

It is important to keep in mind that regardless of the general trend of moving from adverbial to pragmatic use, the extent of grammaticalization in these words varies considerably from word to word. All of the already grammaticalized units studied here can be characterized by changes on the following levels (Valdmets and Habicht 2013):

a. phonetic level: the units are moving towards phonetic simplification/shortening (in unedited usage);
b. morphologic level: the units are becoming invariable, morphologically undividable, moving towards a closed word-class;
c. syntactic level: the units are losing the strong grammatical relations with the rest of the sentence, and are now moving freely;
d. semantic level: the items are becoming lexically difficult to define, they cannot be subject to a content question;
e. pragmatic level: the items are becoming context-dependent and possibly (inter)subjective.

The three most important levels for explaining this kind of grammaticalization are the phonetic, the semantic, and the syntactic level. This article will first focus on the syntax and the semantics of the words. If an item functions as an adverb, no phonetic reduction is possible. Phonetic simplification and shortening only happen when the item is used as a pragmatic marker. Phonetic reduction not only happens in spoken language; it can also be found in unedited written texts (in the Internet forums etc.): *tegelikult* > *tegelt, teglt, tglt* etc. Most of the pragmatic markers presumably occur first in the spoken language and then find their way to the written discourse.

The semantic change of items studied in this article shows how their concrete meaning is fading while at the same time a more abstract one is emerging. Adverbs are easy to define (e.g., in a bilingual dictionary, as they usually have a corresponding match in another language) and can be subject to a substantial question such as *how?* Pragmatic markers, on the other hand, are words that are difficult to define, i.e., they have an abstract or fuzzy meaning and cannot be subject to a substantial question. Yet, the transition between the two semantic stages is not clear-cut. Heine (2002, 86) proposes that semantic changes happen in four stages where a linguistic item acquires a new grammatical meaning (initial stage > bridging context > switch context > conventionalization). In the bridging context a new meaning of an item emerges in some contexts. What's more, it is possible to claim that the words studied here have reached to the switch context, defined by Heine (2002, 86) as a stage where the source meaning is backgrounded and the new meaning is incompatible with the initial meaning. Nevertheless, in case where the item has already reached to the switch context stage then in some contexts some of the relics from the initial stage meaning may remain (*ibid.*, 98). Since this kind of parallel use of adverbs and pragmatic markers has lasted for decades, it is not foreseeable when the initial stage of *lt*-words will fade and final conventionalization will take place.

In the case of *lt*-items, the syntactic changes happen gradually. Adverbs have strong grammatical relations with the rest of the clause. They are part of the syntactic structure and they interact with verbs as adverbials. As full-content words, they can take a modifier themselves. Moving forward, MPs and DMs can still have some grammatical relations with the sentence. They can be seen as part of the syntactic structure. This may be seen as a transition stage. Syntactically, at this point, DMs still have the ability to move the verb to the second position in the clause, and MPs function as modifiers while having a fixed position next to the main word. DMs are, at this stage, bound to the sentential level. In the last stage, only syntactically unbound pragmatic markers are present. This means that syntactically, MPs and DMs do not have grammatical relations with the sentence. At this point, these items occur outside of the syntactic structure or are, hence, only loosely attached to it.

3.1.1   *About grammatical relations inside the clause*

While talking about the development of the items studied here, the syntactic behavior of a usual sentence in a SVO- (subject-verb-object) language should be described. Aijmer (1997, 4) introduces an example from Swedish where the distinction between speech-act adverbial (here, pragmatic marker) use of a phrase *ärligt talat* 'frankly spoken, frankly' is distinguished from other adverbial usages with the help of the word-order test. Since Swedish is a verb-second (V2) language, the use of an adverb in the beginning of the clause causes a subject-verb inversion, whereas, interestingly, the use of a grammaticalized item does not. Although Estonian is also considered to be V2-language (Erelt *et al.* 1993), its word order is rather free (especially when it comes to the position of the verb in relation to its modifiers). Thus, Estonian differs from other languages that have a more rigid word order. In Estonian, the V2-rule almost always applies for affirmative declarative sentences. But the position of words and phrases in Estonian does not always depend on grammatical relations in the sentence. Rather, the word-order in Estonian specifies the theme and the rheme in a sentence. The theme is placed at the beginning of the sentence, whereas the rheme, which carries the newest and most important information, is to be found at the end of the sentence. It is also noted that sometimes pragmatic markers emphasize the important information in the sentence (Erelt *et al.* 1993, 191–194; Erelt *et al.* 2000, 405–407). In this case, the part of the sentence that they modify does not have to be in the end. This kind of syntactic flexibility creates a situation in which language users do not always follow the main SVO-structure. Nevertheless, Estonian in most cases follows the V2-word-order (which is also the normatively recommended order) and thus acts roughly as Aijmer states for Swedish: if an item affects the word-order in a clause it still has at least some grammatical relations with it and thus cannot be seen as fully developed into a pragmatic marker.

4.   The four words in focus

4.1   Loomulikult

The adverb *loomulikult* originates from the adjective *loomulik* 'natural' (GEN *loomuliku*). As a full content adverbial, taking context into account, it can be translated as 'naturally', 'truly', 'really', 'sincerely'. Once it turns into a pragmatic unit, the sense of this item is more or less synonymous and functionally similar to English words *of course, surely, certainly*. The item *loomulikult* first appears in CELL in the 1900s. This particular word form has no occurrences in corpus texts from earlier times. The adverbial use of the word has receded during the last century and the form is increasingly used as a pragmatic marker. However, *loomulikult* as an adverb is still in use. In the example (2), *loomulikult* is part of the syntactic structure of the sentence. *loomulikult* has a modifier *väga* 'very' which intensifies the adverb. The last position in this kind of sentence also indicates the adverbial use because of the easily detectable sentence structure. The word under inspection is also semantically easily definable.

> (2)   *Ta   võta-b   teispoolsus-t,   vaimu-de*
> (s)he take-3SG other_side-PRT ghost-GEN.PL
> *maailma   väga   <u>loomulikult</u>.*
> world.PRT very naturally
> '(S)he takes the other side, the world of ghosts, very naturally.'
> (CELL, ML 28/03/2002)

The Estonian sentence structure allows *loomulikult* to appear also in sentence-initial position. The adverb *loomulikult* at the beginning of the clause causes subject-verb inversion and places the verb to the second position. This kind of inversion is also noticeable in contexts where the semantics of *loomulikult* has already shifted from an adverbial use towards a pragmatic use but where syntactically it is still appropriate to define the item as an adverb. This kind of situation occurs in the example (3). The example shows two sentences of the text to demonstrate the semantic shift of the word.

(3) *Niipea   kui uks   avane-b,   alga-b*
     As_soon as   door open-3SG begin-3SG
     "võidujooks" teise-le   korruse-le registratuuri.
     race   second-ALL floor-ALL reception.ILL
     Loomulikult võida-vad need, ke-l
     of_course   win-3PL   those who-ADE
     on   väleda-ma-d   jala-d.
     be.3SG nimble-COMP-PL foot-PL
     'As soon as the door opens, the "race" to the second floor reception begins. Of course the winners are those who have nimbler feet.'

                                              (CELL, AJA1950\ol0021)

In sentence (3), *loomulikult* cannot be interpreted as an adverb anymore; the item has gained a new pragmatic function. Here, it emphasizes the proposition. Nevertheless, the second position of verb and the third position of subject indicate that the development is still on-going (*loomulikult* is pulling the verb to be on the second position, see also Aijmer 1997). Hence, in sentence (3), *loomulikult* is not yet a fully functioning DM, rather an item on its way from an adverb to a DM.

Once the item no longer strictly belongs to the syntactic structure of the clause and its semantic field has changed, the item is grammaticalized and may be allocated to the "core" of the pragmatic markers. *loomulikult* may then function either as an MP or a DM: it is only loosely attached to the syntactic structure of the sentence and it is moving freely within the clause. In sentence (4), *loomulikult* is an MP and in (5), a DM.

Sentence (4) is an example where the MP can move freely and, without a context, may be placed anywhere within the clause: *loomulikult* may obtain sentence initial, final, or central position, and still maintain the same pragmatic function. If *loomulikult* is omitted, the proposition and the clause structure will stay the same. This particle adds modal nuance to the clause. Without the word *loomulikult*, this clause would state the fact that the solution for the situation is being looked for; *loomulikult* adds a nuance by saying that this kind of action is an obvious thing to do. It does not link back to the previous sentence; rather, it functions as an intensifier on the clause level, it emphasizes the proposition.

(4) *Olukorra-st   otsi-takse   loomulikult väljapääsu.*
     situation-ELA search-PRS.PASS of_course way_out.PRT
     'A way out of the situation is of course being searched for.'

(CELL, AJA1980\tat003)

If in the example (4) the modality of *loomulikult* is obvious, then in (5), the modal function is less important and *loomulikult* carries primarily a discourse function. In example (5), *loomulikult* is a DM that has no grammatical relations with the rest of the sentence that it initiates. It creates a connection between the two sentences while being separated with a comma. A comma is not always a requisite for a DM of a written text but a punctuation mark helps to spot the discourse function. In the first sentence of example (5), the writer conveys information about rejecting all attempts of approach (by young men). The second sentence begins with *loomulikult* where the item qualifies as a DM. This DM links back to what is said while connecting the first sentence with the second. It is an item with a procedural function that elaborates the point of view of the writer; first, something is stated (*I ward off all attempts of approach*), but then, *loomulikult* indicates that the second sentence is not valid on certain circumstances (*should a young man come my way who instantly throws me off then...*).

(5) *See on   täiesti   loogiline, aga*
     this be.3SG completely logical   but
     ma tõrju-n   lähenemiskatse-d   tagasi.
     I   ward_off-1SG attempt_of_approach-PL back
     Loomulikult, kui mu   tee-le   pea-ks
     of_course   if   I.GEN way-ALL must-COND.3SG
     sattu-ma   noormees, kes mu   pea
     happen-SUP young_man who I.GEN head.GEN
     hoobilt segi   löö-b,   siis on   lähedase-ma-d
     instantly messy strike-3SG then be.3PL close-COMP-PL
     suhte-d   võimaliku-d, aga /.../.
     relationship-PL possible-PL but
     'This is completely logical but I ward off all attempts of approach. Of course, should a young man come my way who instantly throws me off balance then a closer relationship is possible but /.../.'

(CELL, KR 19/11/2002)

In sum, *loomulikult* is a word that is used with different functions. During the last one hundred years the item has been mainly used as a pragmatic marker (Valdmets 2011). Nevertheless, adverbial uses are still present and language users acknowledge its function as a content word.

4.2   Ilmselt

The word *ilmselt* has the same stem with the adjective *ilmne* (GEN *ilmse*) which carries the meaning 'apparent', 'visible', 'evident'. The adverbial use has evolved from the adjectival one; the adverb *ilmselt* can be translated as *apparently, obviously, evidently,* or *demonstrably* and appears first in the corpus of the 1930s. In its pragmatic form, the word obtains an epistemic function and can be translated as *probably*. Up to this day, the form *ilmselt* is still in use both as an adverb and as a pragmatic marker and these uses are fixed in dictionaries. However, the share of adverbial use of *ilmselt* is declining, as it is being replaced with other lexically transparent words. In contrast, the pragmatic use has been on the rise the past few decades. In earlier texts, adverbial use is clearly present, as in example (6).

(6)   *Vankriratta-d vaju-sid   pehme-i-sse, veniva   pori-ga*
      cartwheel-PL sink-PST.3PL soft-PL-ILL viscous.GEN dirt-COM
      täitu-nud   roobas-te-sse, tee   muutu-s
      fill-PTCP.PST rut-PL-ILL   road turn-PST.3SG
      ilmselt   läbipääsmatu-ks.
      obviously impassable-TR
      'Cartwheels sank to the ruts filled with soft viscid dirt; the road turned obviously impassable.'   (CELL, AJA1950\ilu0012)

As the other words studied in this paper, *ilmselt* can be found in a context where it is used as a pragmatic item while still having some connections with the adverbial content. In example (7), *ilmselt* causes subject-verb inversion and thus may be seen as an adverb. But on the other hand, the semantic content has already shifted. The text deals with the North Korean nuclear program and talks about how the negotiations will probably start the week after. In example (7), semantically, *ilmselt* cannot be interpreted as a full content word anymore.

(7)   *Läbirääkimis-te   katkemise   põhjuse-ks ol-i*
      negotiation-GEN.PL discontinuation.GEN reason-TR be-PST.3SG
      Põhja-Korea   tuumaprogramm. Ilmselt   alusta-takse
      North_Korea.GEN nuclear_program probably start-PRS.PASS
      läbirääkimis-i   tuleva-l nädala-l.
      negotiation-PRT.PL next-ADE week-ADE
      'The reason for discontinuing the negotiations was the North Korean nuclear program. Probably the negotiations will start next week.'
                              (CELL, AJAE1990\stak0310)

In example (8), *ilmselt* functions as an epistemic MP. It is operating within the clause while adding modality to the proposition. Here, the writer is speculating that the government will probably make an announcement in the week to come but expresses that this is not absolutely certain. This epistemic particle is carrying the emphasis that something is highly probable (unlike with the MP *loomulikult* which asserts something with near certainty).

(8)   *Täpse-d   tormikahju-d   tee-b   valitsus   teatava-ks*
      exact-PL storm_damage-PL make-3SG government certain-TR
      ilmselt   järgmise   nädala   istungi-l.
      probably next.GEN week.GEN session-ADE
      'The government will probably announce the exact storm damages during
      next week's session.'   (CELL, EPL, 24/01/2005)

In examples (9) and (10), *ilmselt* is a DM. It does not function on the clausal level anymore; rather, it connects two discourse units (sentences). It still has some marginal modal properties but additionally it is a discourse connector. *ilmselt* is now outside the syntactic structure and may be omitted more easily.

(9)   *Tema-le   on   kõik   igav.   Ilmselt   ta*
      (s)he-ALL be.3SG everything boring probably (s)he
      ei   taju   sisemis-i   pinge-i-d
      NEG feel-CONNEG internal-PRT.PL tension-PL-PRT
      kuumaksköe-tud   õhu-s.
      heat-PTCP.PST.PASS air-INE
      'For him/her, everything is boring. Probably (s)he does not feel the internal tensions in the heated air.'   (CELL, ILU1990\ilu0190)

(10) *Tassitäis peedimehu,   mille   krooni-ks kaks musta*
      cupful   beet_juice.PRT what.GEN crown-TR two black.PRT
      ploomi,   on   hapu ja   jääkülm pealegi.   Ilmselt
      plum.PRT be.3SG sour and ice-cold furthermore probably
      kuuma-l suvepäeva-l   ole-ks   supi-l   teine minek.
      hot-ADE summer_day-ADE be-COND.3SG soup-ADE other going
      'A cupful of beet juice that is crowned by two black plums, is sour, and furthermore, ice-cold. Probably on a hot summer day, the soup would be a hit.'   (CELL, EPL 19/03/2005)

In examples (9) and (10), *ilmselt* is added to the discourse to connect two sentences. If *ilmselt* were omitted, the discourse would still make sense and the sentences would not need any re-arrangement. Both examples consist of two sentences. In the first sentence, something is claimed or stated. The second sentence, starting with *ilmselt*, expands the idea that was presented in the first sentence.

Those examples contain a DM that carries a concessive nuance: in addition to what is previously said, something else should be considered.

In sum, *ilmselt* as a pragmatic marker is widely spread and frequently found in Estonian corpora. It seems like the adverbial use is eroding and language users do not apprehend the lexical content of the initial adverbial use anymore.

4.3   Tegelikult

tegelikult in its primary use is a manner adverb that belongs to an open word-class with other highly productive *lt*-adverbs in Estonian. In corpora, the word in this lexical form appears first in the 1890s, being used only as an adverb. The adverbial use has remained strong in present-day Estonian, although the word has gradually developed other functions. The adverbial *tegelikult* (developed from adjective *tegelik*, GEN *tegeliku* 'real', 'actual') constitutes a lexical set with *in reality, in action, in practice, existing as a fact*.

In examples (11) and (12), *tegelikult* is used as an adverbial and has strong grammatical relations with the rest of the sentence. The adverb is part of the syntactic structure of the clause and therefore cannot be omitted without changing the meaning of the sentence. It can get a modifier itself, as exemplified in (12) – a word like *ka* 'also'. *tegelikult* is saying something about the reality of the situation. In example (11), *tegelikult* contrasts reality with what only seems real.

(11)   *Põhjusmõttelikult ol-d-i   selle-ga*
       in_principle   be-PASS-PST it-COM
       nõuu-s,   aga tegelikult oll-a   wõimata   praegu
       agreement-INE but in_reality be-INF impossible now
       selle-le soowi-le wastu   tull-a.
       it-ALL wish-ALL against come-INF
       'In principle, everyone agreed on this, but in reality, it is impossible to comply with this wish now.'   (CELL, AJA1900\aja0228)

(12)   *Kas ole-d   ka   tegelikult nii*
       Q   be-2SG also in_reality so
       enesekindel,   kui paista-d?
       self-confident as   seem-2SG
       'Are you actually as self-confident as you seem?'
                                         (CELL, Kroonika 12/01/2001)

In example (13), by contrast, *tegelikult* functions semantically as a pragmatic marker but syntactically it is still related to the sentence and thus analyzable as an adverbial. *tegelikult* in (13) generalizes the statement in the previous sentence (and thus has a function that may be peculiar to a DM) but still causes the subject-verb inversion. As an evolving item, *tegelikult* has acquired the ability to connect two sentences in a discourse but it is still part of the syntactic structure of the clause.

(13) *Selle-ga tõenda-takse,   et   kelle-l-gi   p-ole*
      it-COM confirm-PRS.PASS that someone-ADE-CL NEG-be.3SG
      jõudu   seadus-t vastu   võtt-a.
      strength.PRT law-PRT against take-INF
      Tegelikult p-ole   muude-tud   projekti
      actually   NEG-be.3SG change-PTCP.PST.PASS project.GEN
      kehtestamise-ks kunagi jõudu   ol-nud.
      validation-TR   never strength.PRT be-PTCP.PST
      'With this, it is confirmed that no one has the strength to adopt the law.
      Actually, there has never been strength to validate the changed project.'
      (CELL, AJAE1980\tat0518)

tegelikult appears first as an MP and sentence modifier in the corpus in the 1910s. The word carries epistemic stress which is backed up with an adversative function. The latter has clearly developed from the adverbial use of the word because while expressing a commitment to what is said, it is also used to evoke opposition, create adversativity. In general, as a MP, its main functions are to interfere, to repair, to hedge, to intensify, or to comment.

    In example (14), *tegelikult* shows the attitude of the writer towards the proposition. The MP here either hedges the declaration or creates opposition. Either way, it gives modal emphasis to the sentence.

(14) *Humoristi-d on   tegelikult kõige sünge-ma-d*
      humorist-PL be.3PL actually most grim-COMP-PL
      inimese-d   ja   huumor kui žanr kirjanduse-s   kõige raske-m.
      human-3PL and humor as   genre literature-INE most hard-COMP
      'Humorists are actually the grimmest of people and humor as a genre is
      the hardest in literature.'   (CELL, ILU1970\ilu0117)

In example (15), *tegelikult* modifies what is said with the proposition. It can be also interpreted as expressing someone's opinion while trying to create a common ground. Sentence (15) is a rather tricky and exceptional example since the pragmatic marker is placed at the end of the clause and basically out of the syntactic structure of the sentence (*Hea ja hingeline inimene on Koorberg, tegelikult*). Usually, the elements of the sentence would be the other way around (e.g., *Tegelikult, Koorberg on hea ja hingeline inimene*). This latter kind of word order would also make sense while considering the theme and rheme of the sentence: the text is about closing down a newspaper that was edited by Koorberg and about how upset he was about it. This means that the theme could have been *Koorberg*. If we turn the original sentence around and even start the sentence with *tegelikult* (*Tegelikult, Koorberg on hea ja hingeline inimene*), then *tegelikult* could be interpreted as a DM: it summarizes on the basis of evidence in prior discourse but does not belong to the syntactic structure of the sentence.

(15)   *Koorberg oll-a   pisara-gi   poeta-nud.*
       Koorberg be-INF tear.GEN-CL shed-PTCP.PST
       Ikkagi   peaaegu et   elutöö   ja   oma
       after_all almost   that life's_work and own
       laps, alguse-st   lõpu-ni   teh-tud...
       child beginning-ELA end-TER do-PTCP.PST.PASS
       Hea ja   hingeline inimene on
       good and   soulful   person be.3SG
       Koorberg, tegelikult.
       Koorberg actually
       'Koorberg had apparently even shed a tear. After all, it was almost his life's work and his own child, from the beginning to the end. Koorberg is actually a good and soulful person.'   (CELL, EPL 03/02/2000)

Nevertheless, a more typical instance of *tegelikult* as a DM is shown in example (16). The scope of the DM is different than the one of the MP: it does not function on the clause level; rather, it signals a shift in the discourse. Even though the clause-initial position does not always directly indicate the DM function (e.g., the case of an emphatic answer), the position of *tegelikult* at the beginning of the sentence most often implies it.

(16)   *Üldjoontes ma tea-n,   mis ta   teg-i,*
       in_general I   know-1SG what (s)he do-PST.3SG
       nii või-n   selle-st ka   kirjuta-da. Tegelikult
       so can-1SG it-ELA   also write-INF   actually
       ma või-ksi-n   tema   tegevus-t   jätka-ta.
       I   can-COND-1SG (s)he.GEN function-PRT proceed-INF
       'In general, I know what (s)he did, so I can also write about it. Actually, I could continue with his/her work.'   (CELL, ILU1990\ilu0660)

In example (16), *tegelikult* is a DM that points backwards to the text while linking the discourse: it links what has been said to what will be said. In this example, it adds something that has been said while stating something more precisely: not even that there is knowledge to write about someone's work, there is actually potential to continue with the work.

In sum, *tegelikult* is a word that has all three different variants coexisting in Estonian: while the pragmatic functions are emerging, the adverbial use is still present and this kind of tendency seems to continue to this day (Valdmets 2011).

4.4   Lihtsalt

CDE states that *lihtsalt* as an adverb comes from an adjective *lihtne* (GEN *lihtsa*) which means 'easy', 'simple', 'plain', 'ordinary'. The adjective *lihtne* modifies the main word by stating that something is *not complicated*. The adverb *lihtsalt* may be found in corpora since the 1890s and it carries the same notion as the adjective: *lihtsalt* means 'simply', 'plainly', 'easily', as in example (17). Here, *lihtsalt* is cooperating with the verb *selgitama* 'to explain' and answers the question *how?*.

(17)   *Statistika selgita-b*   *lihtsalt ja*   *selgelt,*
       statistics explain-3SG simply and clearly
       et   *sina min-d peta-d.*
       that you I-PRT cheat-2SG
       'Statistics explains simply and clearly that you are cheating on me.'
                                          (CELL, TAPO\tapo015)

lihtsalt is an interesting item due to its close similarity to the English *simply*, which can also function both as an adverb and as a pragmatic marker. Therefore, the form *simply* is used in all of the examples presented below. In some of the contexts, other synonyms, such as *just*, are more convenient but *simply* is also feasible. Example (18) represents the situation where *lihtsalt* is still grammaticalizing. The word form is part of the clause and, as in example (17), cooperating with the verb. But the full content of the word is lost; *lihtsalt* in (18) may not be considered as an adverb since it does not have the semantic properties of a manner adverb. These two sentences talk about a woman who showed no resistance to physical violence. In the second sentence of example (18), starting with *lihtsalt*, the subject of the sentence is omitted. The presumed subject of the sentence is still obvious, since it appears from the preceding context.

(18)   *Naine vist*   *vastupanu*   *ei*   *avalda-nud-ki.*
       woman probably resistance.PRT NEG express-PTCP.PST-CL
       Lihtsalt seis-is   *ja*   *hoid-is*   *käs-i*   *näo*   *ees.*
       simply stand-PST.3SG and hold-PST.3SG hand-PRT.PL face.GEN in_front
       'The woman didn't even show any resistance. She just stood there and held her hands in front of her face.' (BCE, Samarüütel 2003, daydream nation)

PDE marks *lihtsalt* (as a pragmatic item) as an unstressed intensifying or delimiting word. Unlike in (18), the use presented (19) is already pragmatic. The second position in the sentence points out that *lihtsalt* cannot be merely adverbial, but rather is an MP. As an MP it may move freely inside the clause, while the sentence would still have the usual composition. In example (19), *lihtsalt* is adding certainty to the declaration *I can't see this old man*.

(19)   *Ma lihtsalt ei   näe   se-da   vanamees-t.*
         I   simply NEG see-CONNEG this-PRT old_man-PRT
         'I simply cannot see this old man.'   (BCE, Tangsoo 2004, Valguse vari)

In some contexts, *lihtsalt* may express an emphatic reaction, justification, or a supporting argument, as in (20) where the notion of intensity is present. In sentences like this one, *lihtsalt* can carry a critical nuance. In (20), it is used in a denigrating context and as an MP it is intensifying the proposition. In Estonian, *lihtsalt* as a particle is quite common in negative sentences and in the second position, as exemplified in (19) and (20). In (20), it is put to a sentence that should justify the thing that was said previously.

(20)   *ta-lle   p-ole   vist   mi-da-gi*
         (s)he-ALL NEG-be.3SG probably anything-PRT-CL
         selge-ks ka   võimalik teh-a.   Ta
         clear-TR also possible do-INF (s)he
         lihtsalt ei   saa   aru.
         simply NEG get.CONNEG mind.PRT
         '/.../ it's probably not possible to make it clear to him/her. (S)he just doesn't get it.'   (BCE, Tangsoo 2004, Valguse vari)

In the example (21), *lihtsalt* is a DM. As with other DMs analyzed in this article, it also has the same main function: to concretize the thing that is said while making coherence in the discourse more salient, while creating semantically a more precise connection. In (21), the author is describing someone's feelings. *lihtsalt* starts the second sentence where the previous utterance is elaborated on: the writer makes a statement that gives evidence for the prior statement. In the example (22), the DM connects two sentences while starting the second sentence which gives a summary to the previous text.

(21)   *Ta   p-ol-nud   veel neljakümnene-gi,*
         (s)he NEG-be-PTCP.PST yet forty_years_old-CL
         kuid tund-is,   et   hakka-b vana-ks jää-ma.
         but feel-PST.3SG that start-3SG old-TR become-SUP
         Lihtsalt rõõm ol-i   kadu-nud.
         simply joy   be-PST.3SG disappear-PTCP.PST
         '(S)he wasn't even forty but started to feel old. Simply the joy had disappeared.'   (BCE, Biin 1997, Kõik, mida pole)

(22) *Ja   kõige hulle-m,   needsama-d sinise   märgi-ga*
      and most bad-COMP the_same-PL blue.GEN mark-COM
      mehe-d tikku-si-d   igale_poole: kõrwa-le,
      man-PL intrude-PST-PL *everywhere* side-ALL
      selja   taha,   kukla-sse. Lihtsalt, see ol-i
      back.GEN behind nape-ILL simply   it be-PST.3SG
      üks möll,   mille-st   ükski   enam aru   ei   saa-nud.
      one turmoil that-ELA anybody more mind.PRT NEG get-PTCP.PST
      'And what is worse, the same men with the blue mark forced themselves
      everywhere: to the side, behind our back and nape. To be honest, it was
      such turmoil that nobody could understand a thing.'   (ILU1910\ilu0057)

In sum, *lihtsalt* is a word that in previous decade s has been increasingly used as a
pragmatic marker rather than as an adverb. Nevertheless, the adverbial function is
still visible and it is highly likely that different layers continue to coexist in the near
future (differently, e.g., from the word *ilmselt*, that has largely omitted its use as a
full content word).

4.5   In a nutshell

In the preceding paragraphs, I have analyzed the use of four words in Estonian to
explain how the adverbs with *lt*-suffix grammaticalize in Estonian. These four
items were chosen to represent a much larger group of similar words that have the
same kind of development path. *loomulikult, ilmselt, tegelikult,* and *lihtsalt* are polysemous forms with different co-existing functions. The four words may be used
as adverbs, MPs, or DMs, according to the context.

   Below, paths of development of adverbs grammaticalizing to pragmatic markers are listed. These processes describe the evolution of the words analyzed in this
article and *inter alia* contain overall observations about these four items in
Estonian.

Phonetically,

a. not phonetically shortened > may have phonetic simplification and/or short-
    ening
    Morphologically,
b. open word-class > closed word-class
c. can get a negative prefix > cannot get a negative prefix

Syntactically,

d. grammatical relations with the sentence > no grammatical relations with the
    rest of the sentence

e. part of the syntactic structure > outside the syntactic structure or loosely connected with it

f. can get a modifier > cannot get a modifier

Semantically,

g. full content, concrete meaning > abstract, fuzzy meaning

h. can be subject to a substantial question > cannot be subject to a substantial question

Pragmatically,

i. independent from the context > context-dependent

j. does contribute to the propositional content > does not contribute to the propositional content

Overall,

k. unproblematic occurrence in edited texts > less frequent in edited texts

While general criteria may sometimes be confusing, some easy tests help to determine the actual affiliation to a specific word class. These tests are neither obligatory nor exclusively applicable. Yet, they may provide a useful starting point. These tests are about questioning, intensifying, "prefixing", and omitting. Firstly, can the item under investigation be subject to a content question? If one can ask a question *how?* or *how much?* about the item, it is most likely an adverb of manner or degree. One cannot ask such a question about a pragmatic marker. Secondly, can the item take a modifier? It is possible to intensify an adverb but adding a modifier to an MP or a DM is generally not possible. Thirdly, can the item get a negative prefix? If yes, it is likely to be an adverb (e.g., *loomulikult* 'naturally' *vs. ebaloomulikult* 'unnaturally'). This means that only full content words may get a negative prefix; pragmatic marker is a fossilized form. And finally, may the item be omitted from the clause without changing the propositional meaning of the sentence? One cannot omit an adverb since it carries full content and functions as an adverbial.

All of those criteria discussed above help to determine what kind of function an item represents in a text. The question how to distinguish between MPs and DMs was discussed in the preceding subsections. To summarize, the distinction between MPs and DMs can be made on the basis of differences concerning the scope, as well as the syntactic and the pragmatic level. The scope of MPs is smaller than that of DMs. MPs function on a clausal level while DMs have scope over the discourse or at least over larger chunks of text. MPs modify the sentence and therefore have narrower scope, while DMs link back to what is previously written. As shown in Subsections 4.1.–4.4., DMs are connective units between two sentences. DMs are mainly placed at the beginning of a sentence; MPs are usually in the middle field, even if the left or right periphery is not rigidly held apart in Estonian. The syntactic level is tightly connected to the scope: MPs function on a clause level; DMs are mainly seen working outside the clause. Pragmatically, MPs carry modality (primarily epistemic modality); the modality of DMs is rather marginal in a discourse. Nevertheless, both of them may show some kind of attitude of the writer or add a nuance to what is expressed in the text. Finally, MPs as well as DMs may be (inter)subjective, procedural items, which as grammaticalized words do not change the usual word order of a sentence.

5.   Conclusion

In this article, Estonian adverbs with an *lt*-suffix and their MP and DM uses were investigated in the framework of grammaticalization. It was argued that adverbs have a tendency to evolve into pragmatic markers. The group of pragmatic markers can be divided into two: MPs and DMs. This paper showed firstly how these words have developed, and secondly, how to distinguish and appoint different uses of *lt*-words. These two goals were achieved theoretically by embedding the analysis in the literature as well as empirically by using Estonian corpus data.

Lt-words in Estonian are multifunctional items that obtain their nuance in a concrete context. In this paper, all of the four words analyzed have their initial/dictionary function as an adverb. However, over the course of time they have come to be used more and more as MPs or DMs. The data gathered from the Corpus of Estonian Literary Language and from the Balanced Corpus of Estonian showed that since the end of the 19th century, these Estonian words have been undergoing grammaticalization. As an adverb, *loomulikult* 'naturally', *ilmselt* 'visibly', *tegelikult* 'in reality' and *lihtsalt* 'simply' are content words that have all of the characteristics of a typical adverb: primarily it shows that the item has grammatical relations with the clause and it carries a concrete meaning. As MPs or DMs, *loomulikult* 'of course, certainly', *ilmselt* 'probably', *tegelikult* 'actually' and *lihtsalt* 'just' have lost their previous function and they are now semantically abstract items that have only a marginal grammatical relation with the clause. Additionally, as grammaticalized units, they are used with a different purpose in a sentence. *loomulikult, ilmselt, tegelikult,* and *lihtsalt* are undergoing grammaticalization and they are likely to continue the evolution from adverbs to MPs or DMs.

As for the prospects for further research, the general trends of grammaticalization observed here could be applied to other adverbs that may show the same kinds of nuances of development. For example, Estonian also has another group of manner adverbs ending in *-sti*. It is probable that some of the words with *sti*-suffix behave similarly, as they are also used as DMs and MPs. Of course, the investigation does not have to stay within the limits of one language and parallels between languages may be drawn.

Abbreviations used in glossing

1	first person	INF	infinitive
2	second person	NEG	negation
3	third person	PRT	partitive
ADE	adessive	PASS	passive
ALL	allative	PL	plural
CL	clitic	PRS	present
COMP	comparative	PST	past
COND	conditional	PTCP	participle
CONNEG	connegative form	Q	question marker
ELA	elative	SG	singular
GEN	genitive	SUP	supine
ILL	illative	TER	terminative
INE	inessive	TR	translative

References

Abraham, Werner. 1991. "Discourse Particles in German: How Does Their Illocutive Force Come About?" In *Discourse Particles: Descriptive and Theoretical Investigations on the Logical, Syntactic, and Pragmatic Properties of Discourse Particles in German*, ed. by Werner Abraham, 203–252. Amsterdam/Philadelphia: John Benjamins Publishing Company.

Aijmer, Karin. 1997. "*I think* – An English Modal Particle." In *Modality in Germanic Languages. Historical and Comparative Perspectives*, ed. by Toril Swan, and Olaf Jansen Westvik, 1–47. New York: Mouton De Gruyter.

Brinton, Laurel J. 1996. *Pragmatic Markers in English. Grammaticalization and Discourse Functions*. Berlin/New York: Mouton de Gruyter.

Brinton, Laurel J. 2010. "Discourse Markers." In *Historical Pragmatics*, ed. by Andreas H. Jucker, and Irma Taavitsainen, 285–314. Berlin/New York: De Gruyter Mouton.

Bybee, Joan L. 2007. *Frequency of Use and the Organization of Language*. New York: Oxford University Press.

Cinque, Guglielmo. 1999. *Adverbs and Functional Heads: A Cross-linguistic Perspective*. Oxford: Oxford University Press.

Cornillie, Bert. 2009. "Evidentiality and Epistemic Modality: On the Close Relationship of Two Different Categories." In *Evidentiality in Language and Cognition. Special Issue of Functions of Language 16: 1*, ed. by Lena Ekberg, and Carita Paradis, 44–62. Amsterdam/Philadelphia: John Benjamins Publishing Company.

Davidse, Kristin, Lieven Vandelanotte, and Hubert Cuyckens (eds). 2010. *Subjectification, Inter-subjectification and Grammaticalization*. Berlin/New York: De Gruyter Mouton.

Erelt, Mati, Reet Kasik, Helle Metslang, Henno Rajandi, Kristiina Ross, Henn Saari, Kaja Tael, and Silvi Vare. 1993. *Eesti keele grammatika II. Süntaks. Lisa: kiri* [*Estonian Grammar* II. Syntax. Appendix: Written Language]. Tallinn: Eesti Teaduste Akadeemia Keele ja Kirjanduse Instituut.

Erelt, Mati, Tiiu Erelt, and Kristiina Ross. 2000. *Eesti keele käsiraamat* [Handbook of Estonian Language]. Second, revised edition. Tallinn: Eesti Keele Sihtasutus.

Ernst, Thomas Boyden. 1984. *Towards an Integrated Theory of Adverb Position in English*. Indiana University Linguistics Club.

Fraser, Bruce. 1988. "Types of English Discourse Markers." *Acta Linguistica Hungarica* 38: 19–22.

Fraser, Bruce. 1996. "Pragmatic Markers." *Pragmatics* 6 (2): 167–190.

Fraser, Bruce. 2006. "Towards a Theory of Discourse Markers." In *Approaches to Discourse Particles*, ed. by Kerstin Fischer, 189–204. Amsterdam: Elsevier.

Hakulinen, Auli, Maria Vilkuna, Riitta Korhonen, Vesa Koivisto, Tarja Riitta Heinonen, and Irja Alho. 2004. *Iso suomen kielioppi* [The Large Grammar of Finnish]. Helsinki: Suomalaisen Kirjallisuuden Seura.

Heine, Bernd. 2002. "On the Role of Context in Grammaticalization." In *New Reflections on Grammaticalization*, ed. by Ilse Wischer, and Gabriele Diewald, 83–101. Amsterdam/Philadelphia: Benjamins.

Heine, Bernd, and Heiko Narrog. 2010. "Grammaticalization and Linguistic Analysis." In *The Oxford Handbook of Linguistic Analysis,* ed. by Bernd Heine, and Heiko Narrog, 401–423. New York: Oxford University Press.

Holmes, Janet. 1984. "Hedging Your Bets and Sitting on the Fence: Some Evidence for Hedges as Support Structures." *Te Reo* 27: 47–62.

Hopper, Paul J. 1991. "On Some Principles of Grammaticalization." In *Approaches to Grammaticalization, vol. I. Focus on Theoretical and Methodological Issues,* ed. by Elizabeth Closs Traugott, and Bernd Heine, 17–35. Amsterdam/Philadelphia: John Benjamins Publishing Company.

Hopper, Paul J., and Elizabeth Closs Traugott. 2003. *Grammaticalization*. Second edition. Cambridge: Cambridge University Press.

Hupel, August Wilhelm. 1780. *Ehstnische Sprachlehre für beide Hauptdialekte, den revalschen und dörptschen, nebst einem vollständigen Wörterbuch*. Riga: Johann Friedrich Hartknoch.

Kingisepp, Valve-Liivi, Kristel Ress, Kai Tafenau. 2010. *Heinrich Gösekeni grammatika ja sõnastik 350* [The Grammar and Dictionary of Heinrich Göseken 350]. Tartu: Tartu Ülikooli eesti ja üldkeeleteaduse instituut.

Labov, William. 1984. "Intensity." In *Georgetown University Round Table on Languages and Linguistics*, ed. by Deborah Schiffrin, 40–70. Washington D.C.: Georgetown University Press.

Lenk, Uta. 1998. *Marking Discourse Coherence. Functions of Discourse Markers in Spoken English*. Tübingen: Gunter Narr Verlag.

Östman, Jan-Ola. 1982. "The Symbiotic Relationship Between Pragmatic Particles and Impromptu Speech." In Impromptu Speech: A Symposium, ed. by Nils Erik Enkvist, 147–177. Turku, Finland: Åbo Akademi.

Palmer, Frank Robert. 2001. *Mood and Modality*. Second edition. Cambridge: Cambridge University Press.

Quirk, Randolph, Sidney Greenbaum, Geoffrey Leech, Jan Svartvik, and David Crystal. 1985. *A Comprehensive Grammar of the English Language*. London: Longman.

Redeker, Gisela. 1990. "Ideational and Pragmatic Markers of Discourse Structure." *Journal of Pragmatics* 14: 367–381.

Schiffrin, Deborah. 1987. *Discourse Markers*. Cambridge: Cambridge University Press.

Schourup, Lawrence. 1999. "Discourse Markers." *Lingua* 107: 227–265.

Simon-Vandenbergen, Anne-Marie, and Karin Aijmer. 2007. *The Semantic Field of Modal Certainty. A Corpus-Based Study of English Adverbs*. Berlin–New York: Mouton de Gruyter.

Thor Helle, Anton. 1732. *Kurtzgefaszte Anweisung Zur Ehstnischen Sprache*. Halle: Stephan Orban.

Traugott, Elizabeth Closs. 1999. "The Rhetoric of Counter-Expectation in Semantic Change: A Study in Subjectification." In *Historical Semantics and Cognition,* ed. by Andreas Blank, and Peter Koch, 177–196. Berlin/New York: Mouton de Gruyter.

Traugott, Elizabeth Closs. 2007. "Discourse Markers, Modal Particles, and Contrastive Analysis, Synchronic and Diachronic." *Catalan Journal of Linguistics* 6: 139–157.

Traugott, Elizabeth Closs, and Richard B. Dasher. 2002. *Regularity in Semantic Change*. Cambridge: Cambridge University Press.

Valdmets, Annika. 2011. "Kahe eesti kirjakeele modaalpartikli arengust viimase sadakonna aasta jooksul [On the Development of Two MPs of Written Estonian over the Last Century]." *Keel ja Kirjandus* 10: 764–776.

Valdmets, Annika, and Külli Habicht. 2013. "Episteemilistest modaalpartiklitest eesti kirjakeeles [About Epistemic Modal Particles in Estonian]." In *Teoreetilisest kecleteadusest Eestis keeleteadus Eestis III. Special issue of Journal of Estonian and Finno-Ugric Linguistics JEFUL 4–1,* ed. by Ilona Tragel, Ann Veismann, and Piret Piiroja, 205–222. Tartu: TÜ Kirjastus.

Waltereit, Richard. 2001. "Modal Particles and Their Functional Equivalents: A Speech-Act-Theoretic Approach." *Journal of Pragmatics* 33: 1391–1417.

Wiedemann, Ferdinand Johann. 1923. *Estnisch-deutsches Wörterbuch: mit einer Karte Eestis*. Third unchanged edition. Tartu: Eesti Kirjanduse Selts.

Modal particles: Problems in defining a category*

Steven Schoonjans
KU Leuven/FWO-Vlaanderen

This contribution addresses the problems of defining and delineating the category of modal particles and determining its relation to other word classes. The paper first presents the most important points of discussion, mainly at the form level, and subsequently attempts to come to grips with this apparently problematic situation by referring to the notions of prototypicality, granularity, and conceptualization. Rather than fully resolving the categorial problem, these notions serve as a tool to better understand discussion and how it should be approached. The argumentation is primarily based on the situation in German, but a brief comparison to French is included.

1. Introduction

In the last decades, modal particles (MPs) have constituted the topic of a significant body of linguistic studies. Nevertheless, there is no general agreement about the definition of this category:

> Die Termini *Partikel* und *Modalpartikel* müssen in jeder linguistischen Arbeit sowie in Nachschlagewerken stets neu definiert werden, da bislang noch keine verbindliche Abgrenzung gegenüber anderen Wortklassen existiert. (Bastert 1985, 31)
> ('The terms *particle* and *modal particle* have to be defined time and again in every linguistic writing and in reference works, as so far, no stringent delineation against other word classes exists.' – my translation, S.S.)

This quote focuses on the relation with other word classes. The lack of agreement at this level is closely related to the fact that scholars disagree on what counts as a MP. Although Bastert (l.c.) already hinted at this problem nearly 30 years ago, it is still of topical interest today, as Moroni (2010, 3) indicates:

---

* Many thanks to Kurt Feyaerts, Geert Brône, the editors of the volume, and two anonymous reviewers for useful comments on previous versions of this chapter.

> In der Forschung herrscht Uneinigkeit darüber, welche Lexeme zur Gruppe der
> Modalpartikeln zu zählen sind. Dies liegt daran, dass je nach Ansatz unterschiedliche
> Eigenschaften als Kriterien für die Abgrenzung dieser Gruppe festgelegt werden.
> ('In the research community, there is disagreement about which lexemes are modal
> particles. This is due to the fact that, depending on the framework, different features
> have been put forward as criteria to delineate this group.' – my translation, S.S.)

Precisely this problem of defining the category 'modal particle' constitutes the
topic of the present contribution. In the next section (§2), an overview of the most
important points of discussion will be offered. In a next step (§3), the key notions
of prototypicality, granularity, and conceptualization, which will serve as a gate-
way into the definitional problem, will be introduced. These concepts may not
fully resolve the problem, but at least, they allow to come to grips with it better.
This theory will then be applied to the central issue of this book, the relationship
of MPs and discourse markers, in Section 4. Finally, in a brief discussion of French
(§5), it will be shown that the situation described in Sections 2–4 is not typical of
German alone: languages such as French do at least show striking similarities.

2.   German modal particles: Problems in defining a category

As mentioned in the introductory section, the definition of 'MP' in German is a
highly debated topic. In the following, an overview of the most important issues
will be offered, taking first (§2.1) an internal perspective (what are MPs?), before
turning to the external perspective (how does the category of MPs relate to other
categories?) in §2.2.

2.1   Internal definition

The internal definition is a description of a category as such, without referring to
other categories. This includes two dimensions: the intension, i.e. the typical features of the category, and the extension, i.e. the category members (cf. Geeraerts
1986, 157). As Moroni's quote above shows, these two dimensions are closely related, and discussions situated at one level (intension or extension) bring about
discussions at the other level.

2.1.1   *Intensional definition*
As a starting point for the discussion of the intensional definition, it may be useful
to get an overview of the features typically ascribed to MPs. The following list is
based on the overviews in Thurmair (1989), Autenrieth (2002), and Diewald
(2007, this volume):

a. uninflected;
b. unstressed;
c. cannot be negated or intensified;
d. can be combined, but not coordinated;
e. no constituent or clause value;
f. syntactically and prosodically/graphically integrated into the clause;[1]
g. in the middle field;
h. scope over the entire clause;
i. used especially in colloquial speech;
j. homophones in other categories.

This list of features strongly resembles a classical definition in terms of necessary and sufficient criteria, as Diewald (this volume) suggests. It seems legitimate indeed to assume that prototypical members of the MP category show all these features, and some of these features are really uncontroversial. That MPs do not show inflection, for instance, has not been questioned so far. Quite the contrary: the fact that they are called 'modal *particles*' is an indication of this, as particles are normally uninflected. The same holds for their not having constituent or clause value. However, for most other features, counterexamples can be found. In some cases, these have already been hinted at in the literature, while others have remained largely unnoticed so far.

Unstressedness is an interesting case in point. The traditional claim is that MPs cannot be stressed at all (e.g. Bublitz 1978), but some scholars state that a few particles can be stressed under certain circumstances (e.g. Thurmair 1989), and still others think that it is normal for MPs to have a stressed form (e.g. Ikoma 2007). The most extensively discussed particle in this respect is *ja*. It is generally accepted that this particle normally bears stress when used in orders, as in (1), where it brings about an increase of the illocutionary force.[2]

---

1.   The notion of 'syntactic integration' is somewhat problematic, as it may indicate that an element is part of the syntactic structure in that it forms (part of) a constituent or is syntactically governed by another element. This is not the case for MPs. Therefore, the editors proposed to refer to the topological phrase structure as presented by Gerdes and Kahane (2007), and hence to speak of topological integration and positional constraints. However, MPs are not as constrained topologically as is sometimes claimed (cp. infra). Furthermore, this is not actually what is meant here with 'syntactic integration'. The notion is used here solely to refer to the surface level, at which MPs do not stand out from the rest of the clause: they cannot, for instance, be inserted as a parenthesis or made more prominent by means of a cleft structure.

2.   More detailed analyses of stressed *JA* are offered by Thurmair (1989), Meibauer (2003), and Gutzmann (2010), among others.

(1)   Und lassen Sie sich hier *JA* nicht mehr blicken!   (Thurmair 1989, 109)
      'And don't you *JA* dare to show up here again!'

Similarly, *nur* and *bloß* can be stressed in orders without their MP status being questioned. More disagreement exists about particles like *denn*, *doch*, and *schon*. Several scholars, including Meibauer (1994), Abraham (2000), and Ikoma (2007), claim that they are also MPs if they are stressed, whereas others (e.g. Thurmair 1989) think that the stressed variants are adverbs or focus particles, not MPs.

Another problematic feature is the restriction of MPs to the middle field, i.e. the part of the sentence between the finite verb and any non-finite verb forms or (in subordinate clauses) between the subordinator and the verbal group.[3] One may question the appropriateness of field structure theory for the study of spoken language (in which MPs are mostly found), as in spoken language, it does not seem to be uncommon to bend the traditional field distribution rules, but even when a division into fields is possible, it seems that the feature of middle field positioning is at best a strong tendency, not an absolute rule.

This is illustrated by Imo's (2008) analysis of evidence-marking *halt*, a prototypical MP of German according to Thurmair (1989). Of the 296 occurrences Imo analyzes, 14 can be situated in the front field (i.e. before the finite verb) or in the back field (also sometimes called 'end field', i.e. after the non-finite verb), as in (2):

(2)   –   Die Autos müssen andersrum fahren.
      –   Ah ja, da hat's gekracht *halt*. Ist einer so gefahren wie du.[4]
      '–   The cars have to drive the other way.
      –   Oh yes, there's been a crash *halt*. Someone has been driving like you.'

In this case, one may indeed refer to the fact that in colloquial speech, the field distribution rules are not always followed: as Imo (2011a) shows, it is not abnormal to have certain elements (including MPs) in the back field in spontaneous speech which do not belong there according to traditional grammars. However, there are also cases where the particle occurs in the front field. A typical example, mentioned by e.g. Thurmair (1989), Ormelius-Sandblom (1997), and Abraham (2010), is the use of MPs after a question word, as in (3):

(3)   Warum, warum *nur* ist immer alles so furchtbar für mich?

                                                    (F. Zorn, *Mars*, p. 160)
      'Why, why *nur* is everything always so terrible for me?'

---

3.   A somewhat more detailed overview of the German sentence structure is offered by Fischer and Alm (this volume).

4.   The example is taken from a transcript in Imo (2008, 143), but has been adapted to more conventional writing for the ease of the reader.

Admittedly this is not very frequent either: in literary texts reproducing spontaneous speech, only 2,23% of the particles in question word questions actually take this front-field position (Schoonjans submitted-a). It cannot be excluded that the figures are somewhat higher for true spontaneous speech, but whatever the case, it is clear that middle field positioning is not an exceptionless rule.

Thurmair (1989, 27) hints at another exception: MPs within a noun phrase or a prepositional phrase. This is apparently overlooked by many scholars, but it does occur:

(4) Dieser *ja* leider viel zu früh verstorbene Komponist hat uns eine Reihe von großartigen Werken überlassen. (Thurmair l.c.)
     'This composer, who *ja* unfortunately passed away far too early [literally: 'This *ja* unfortunately far too early died composer'], has left a series of magnificent works.'

(5) Ich meine "echte" Valuetitel, sowas wie coca-cola, altria, ihr wisst schon... nur mit *halt* recht hoher Divrendite etc.[5]
     'I mean "real" value titles, something like Coca Cola, Altria, you know... just with *halt* quite elevated dividend proceeds etc.'

In these cases, the field the particle figures in depends on where the constituent containing it is placed. In (4), for instance, this is the front field, simply because the noun phrase containing *ja* is in the front field. It thus seems that these examples are not real exceptions to the middle field tendency, but should be analyzed separately. They do, however, show that another typical feature of MPs may be questioned as well: the clause scope (feature *h* in the list above). In these cases, it seems that the particles have scope just over the constituent they occur in, not over the entire sentence. In (4), for instance, *ja* marks that the hearer will agree that the composer passed away too early, but not necessarily that s/he agrees on his having created a series of magnificent works. Hence, this feature turns out not to apply to all particle attestations either (see also Hentschel 1983, 50).

The discussion of the syntactic position does not end here, however. It is clear that MPs can occur outside of the middle field, yet none of the previously mentioned particles can occur sentence-initially. There are, however, scholars (e.g. Helbig 1988) who assume that certain elements which can occur sentence-initially count as MPs as well, whereas others classify them as 'situative particles' (e.g. Hentschel and Weydt 2002) or as adverbs (e.g. Thurmair 1989, Meibauer 1994). A typical example is *schließlich* (6), which is similar to English *after all*; others include *allerdings, immerhin, jedenfalls,* and the like.

---

5.   <http://www.wallstreet-online.de/diskussion/1119309-201-210/dividenden-riesen> (20-10-2011).

(6)   Im Grunde ist es nur eine verkappte Entschuldigung. *Schließlich* habe ich
      sie lebend nicht mehr gesehen.
                          (H.G.F. Schneeweiß, *Was nun, Prometheus?*, p. 68)
      'It actually is just an excuse in disguise. *Schließlich* I haven't seen here alive
      anymore.'

For most other features, potential counterexamples seem to have passed largely
unnoticed so far. One example is the claim that MPs cannot be intensified. As
shown by Schoonjans (submitted-c), obviousness-marking *einfach* does have an
intensified variant, *ganz einfach*:

(7)   Er spielt die Rolle eines Mannes *ganz einfach* besser als ein wirklicher
      Mann.   (R.F. Schütt, *Auch der Eskimo klebt an seiner Eisscholle*, p. 25)
      'He plays the male role *ganz einfach* better than a real man.'

A similar remark can be made for the non-coordinatability of MPs. Again, *einfach*
is a case in point, as this particle is regularly combined with *schlicht* by means of
und ('and'). *Schlicht* is admittedly not a typical element on MP lists, but Autenrieth
(2002, 64–88) shows that it at least strongly resembles typical MPs.

(8)   Die Faktoren, die bei einer solchen Schätzung berücksichtigt werden
      müssen, sind *schlicht und einfach* nicht objektivierbar.[6]
      'The factors to take into account for such an estimate can *schlicht und
      einfach* not be objectified.'

One could object that this is not actually a coordination of MPs, but a coordination of adverbs which as a whole has acquired MP(-like) status, next to the simple
form *einfach*. The same holds for *ganz einfach*. In that case, the question arises
whether these complex units can be considered as MPs. This issue cannot be re-
solved within the scope of the present paper, but it should be clear that there is
room for additional discussion.

   There are, however, other cases of coordinated MPs which cannot be fully explained by referring to their diachrony. An example is the coordination of the
near-synonymous particles *halt* and *eben*, as in (9). Such occurrences are rare, and
several natives of German indicate that they sound odd to them, but they do
occur.

(9)   Ja, es ist *halt und eben* schon so, dass die Society krank ist, nicht?[7]
      'Yes, it is *halt und eben* the case that the society is ill, isn't it?'

---

6.   Source: COSMAS II (database from the Institut für Deutsche Sprache in Mannheim),
corpus *rei*.

7.   <http://derstandard.at/3367476/Halbleere-Events-halbvolle-Glaeser> (01-12-2011).

Finally, although it is generally assumed that MPs cannot be negated, they do sometimes fall under the scope of negation:

(10)   Das ändert sich *doch nicht einfach* über Nacht?[8]
       'That does *doch nicht einfach* change over night?'

(11)   Aber wenn hier bereits ein Kind vorhanden ist, muss der Ehegatte (vorausgesetzt, es ist sein Kind) *doch nicht sowieso* für das Kind sorgen?[9]
       'But if there is already a child, the husband (supposing, it is his child) does *doch nicht sowieso* have to take care of the child?'

Strikingly, the particle is in both cases preceded by *doch nicht*, which seems to act as a negative counterpart of the simple particle *doch* (the function of which is to indicate that an affirmative answer is expected), rather than as a simple succession of *doch* and a negation. Precisely this seems to explain why it is possible to have another particle under the scope of the negation. Again, my goal is not to resolve the problem, but to show that there is room for discussion.

Summing up, most of the features which are typically ascribed to MPs can to some extent be subject to discussion. This does not make these features useless, however, as they are still required for the definition of the prototype of a MP (cf. §3.1), but it should be clear that there is more to it.

2.1.2   *Extensional definition*

The discussions at the intensional level have repercussions for the extensional definition as well. Some examples have been mentioned already: can the stressed forms of *denn*, *doch*, and *schon*, larger units like *ganz einfach* and *schlicht und einfach*, or forms like *immerhin* be categorized as MPs? But even disregarding these dubious cases, scholars do not agree on which elements count as MPs. A comparison of how many MPs are distinguished makes this clear. Franck (1980), for instance, lists 14 MPs, whereas Krivonosov (1977) thinks there are no less than 24 MPs in German. This debate is illustrated in Table 1, which gives an overview of 21 lexemes that are regularly listed as MPs, and indicates whether they are mentioned by ten scholars who offer a 'closed' enumeration of MPs. Strikingly, only eight forms (*bloß*, *denn*, *doch*, *eben*, *ja*, *mal*, *nur*, *schon*) are mentioned in all publications referred to in the table. The discussion of which forms count as MPs is thus not restricted to typical borderline cases like the ones mentioned above, but also affects more traditional elements such as *etwa*, which is not included by e.g. Moroni (2005; 2010), although it cannot be related directly to a defining feature which is itself subject to discussion.

---

8.   <http://www.netmoms.de/fragen/detail/das-aendert-sich-doch-nicht-einfach-ueber-nacht-15571266> (01-12-2011).

9.   <http://www.austrianlaw.at/forum/viewtopic.php?f=16&t=2188> (01-12-2012).

Table 1. The modal particles listed by different scholars

	Hartmann (1975)	Krivonosov (1977)	Bublitz (1978)	Franck (1980)	Hentschel (1986)	Thurmair (1989)	Szulc-Brzozowska (2002)	Kürschner (⁴2003)	Engel (2004)	Moroni (2005)	Moroni (2010)
aber	+	+	+		+	+	+	+	+	+	+
auch		+	+	+	+	+	+	+	+	+	+
bloß	+	+	+	+	+	+	+	+	+	+	+
denn	+	+	+	+	+	+	+	+	+	+	+
doch	+	+	+	+	+	+	+	+	+	+	+
eben	+	+	+	+	+	+	+	+	+	+	+
eh						+				+	
eigentlich			+	+	+	+	+	+	+	+	+
einfach	+	+		+	+	+	+	+	+	+	+
etwa	+	+	+	+	+	+	+	+	+		
erst		+			+		+	+			
halt	+	+		+	+	+	+	+	+	+	+
ja	+	+	+	+	+	+	+	+	+	+	+
mal	+	+	+	+	+	+	+	+	+	+	+
nicht		+				+			+	+	
nur	+	+	+	+	+	+	+	+	+	+	+
ruhig	+		+	+	+	+	+	+	+	+	+
schon	+	+	+	+	+	+	+	+	+	+	+
sowieso						+				+	
vielleicht	+		+		+	+	+	+	+	+	+
wohl	+		+		+	+	+	+	+	+	+

2.2   External definition

Given the disagreement on the internal definition of 'MP', it is not surprising that there is discussion at the external level as well, as it is precisely a category's intensional definition that differentiates it from other categories and determines its position in the linguistic system. A few issues of this kind have been hinted at above, e.g. the distinction between MPs on the one hand and adverbs and situative particles on the other.

However, the discussion stretches even further. There is, for instance, no general agreement on how many different kinds of 'particles in the strict sense' (i.e. uninflected forms which are not prepositions, conjunctions, or adverbs, cf. e.g. Möllering 2001) there are in German: Möllering (2001) distinguishes six different particle types, whereas Kürschner (⁴2003) proposes seven types, and Hentschel and Weydt (1990) list eight kinds of particles. On the other hand, not all scholars consider MPs to be 'particles in the strict sense' as defined above: a frequent alternative view is that MPs are actually a particular kind of adverb (e.g. Cardinaletti 2007; 2011).

The discussion even raises a more fundamental question: is there a word class 'modal particle' at all? Most of the above-mentioned scholars do think there is, but Thurmair (1989) considers 'MP' as a potential function of words belonging to a general class of particles. In the same vein, Rüttenauer (1983) claims that MPs are simply a loose group of forms which also fulfill other functions. It thus turns out that there is no full agreement (yet) regarding the position MPs take in the linguistic system.

3.   Coming to grips with the issues

So far, I have mainly given an overview of issues in delimiting the category of MPs. These issues are not unimportant for the study of MPs, as the position taken can have major repercussions for the analysis. The central theme of this volume, the relationship between MPs and discourse markers, is one such issue which is closely related to matters of definition: the way this relationship is conceived influences the conceptualization of the individual categories, and vice-versa. Therefore, in order to determine the nature of this relationship, it is important to tackle the definition issues.

Precisely this is the goal of the present section. Referring to the cognitive-linguistic notions of prototypicality (§3.1), granularity (§3.2), and conceptualization (§3.3), it will be shown how the definition issues can be handled. This is not to say that all discussions will receive a final answer. Quite the contrary: the goal is to come to a better view of MPs and how they relate to discourse markers despite the disagreements. The discussion will be illustrated with relevant examples, but as it is situated primarily at a meta-level (in that it talks about analyses and discussions), it will mainly exhibit a theoretical slant.

3.1   Prototypicality[10]

The idea that linguistic categories are prototypically structured is not new as such (e.g. Company Company 2002, Taylor ²1995, and Weber 2010), and the claim that

---

10.   For a more elaborate introduction to prototypicality in linguistics: see e.g. Geeraerts et al. (1994), Geeraerts (1997), and Taylor (²1995).

the MP category is in that position has already been made by Thurmair (1989), albeit not in these terms. Indeed, as the definitory issues described in Section 2 have shown, it is hard to offer an Aristotelian definition of the notion 'MP' in terms of necessary and sufficient conditions. Being confronted with such problems, scholars in different domains have recurred to protype theory, and as will be shown in the following, this is an interesting starting point for coming to grips with the definitory issues in the case of MPs as well.

Prototypicality plays at both type and token level. The two are partly linked, as type prototypicality typically follows from token prototypicality. Tokens showing all typical features of MPs are more prototypical instantiations of the MP category than those which do not. Compare, for instance, (12a), which is a slightly modified version of example (2), with the construed variant (12b), which contains a more prototypical (middle field) use of *halt*:

(12)   a.   Ah ja, da hat's gekracht *halt*.
       b.   Ah ja, da hat's *halt* gekracht.

As these examples show, not all instantiations (tokens) of the same particle (type) need to be equally prototypical MPs. This distribution of tokens is also what determines to what extent a type is a prototypical category member: the more tokens of a type are prototypical instantiations of a category, the more prototypical a member of that category the type is.

As a second example, take the case of *glaub(e)*, a particle which has originated from the CTMP form *glaube ich* 'I believe' and is used mainly in the South-West of the German-speaking area.[11] Imo (2006) states that *glaub(e)* is situated "between" three categories (MP, modal adverb, and matrix clause): it shows clear similarities with typical members of each of these categories, but differs from them in important respects as well (e.g.: more variation at scope level than MPs, cannot answer a question on its own unlike modal adverbs, cannot be negated unlike a matrix clause – see Schoonjans 2012b for a more elaborate discussion). In other words, the type *glaub(e)* is not a prototypical member of any of the three categories.

(13)   Da hab ich *glaub* sogar bedient.   (Imo 2006, 270)
       'I *glaub* even served there.'

As I have shown elsewhere (Schoonjans 2012b), however, *glaub(e)* seems to be closer to the prototype of a MP than to the prototypes of the other two categories. This is because the majority of the instantiations of *glaub(e)* resemble a MP more

---

11.   The meaning nuances *glaub(e)* can convey are rather diverse, but a basic meaning aspect seems to be the expression of uncertainty about or reduced commitment to the content of the utterance (cp. Schoonjans 2012a).

than a modal adverb or a matrix clause. There admittedly are attestations of *glaub(e)* which do not show all features of MPs and hence are not prototypical MP attestations themselves. Therefore, the type *glaub(e)* is not a prototypical MP either. However, the tokens which can be analyzed as prototypical instantiations of the category of MPs (i.e. which show all features of prototypical MPs) are more numerous than those which cannot. Therefore, *glaub(e)* as a type is still closer to the prototype of the MP category than to the prototype of the other categories.

The role of prototypicality for the present discussion is somewhat more complex, however. The reason is that MPs have developed through processes of grammaticalization.[12] Precisely this is one of the reasons for the difficulty of delineating the category of MPs, as it is hard to determine at which point a form is sufficiently grammaticalized to be said to have developed a prototypical MP use (cf. Diewald this volume, p. 13 of manuscript).

Eigentlich is an interesting example in this respect. In recent literature, it is generally accepted that *eigentlich* is a MP, but some thirty years ago, this was still subject to discussion. Kohrt (1988), for instance, claimed that *eigentlich* is not a MP, but just has adverb status, whereas Oppenrieder and Thurmair (1989), in a reaction to Kohrt's paper, argued that two uses of *eigentlich* (adverb and MP) have to be distinguished.[13] Looking at the arguments put forward by both parties, it seems that they were just arguing whether *eigentlich* was sufficiently grammaticalized to call it a MP, as they mainly refer to the dialectics of desemanticization and retention, and of decategorialization and structural persistence (Breban 2009), hence to typical features of grammaticalization, albeit not in these terms.

A complicating factor is the fact that in processes of grammaticalization, the source form often pursues its life next to the new uses developing from it. This is the case with most MPs, including *eigentlich*, which has developed precisely from the adverbial use of this form. The fact that for Kohrt, *eigentlich* is not a MP, may well be due to its already being a prototypical adverb: he seems to judge the existing prototype sufficiently strong not to assume a new one, unlike Oppenrieder and Thurmair. The fact that *eigentlich* already was an established member of another category thus seems to influence the positions in the debate.

It should be clear that a particular linguistic element can be a member of different categories at the same time. Consider the (construed) dialogue in (14):

---

12. Some scholars (e.g. Molnár 2008) disagree, but for the present argumentation, it is assumed (following e.g. Abraham 2000, Autenrieth 2002, as well as Diewald 2007 and in this volume) that the development of MPs is a case of grammaticalization, although possibly not a prototypical one. However, perceiving the process differently does not undermine the reasoning, as long as it is seen as a gradual development.

13. None of the authors mentions the adjectival use of *eigentlich*.

(14)   – Sag mal, wie heißt dein Bruder *eigentlich*?
        – *Eigentlich* heißt er Johann, aber ich nenne ihn meist Hansi.
        – Und glaubst du, dass ich ihn auch Hansi nennen darf, oder soll ich
          seinen *eigentlichen* Namen verwenden?
        '– Hey, what's your brother's name *eigentlich*?
        – *Eigentlich*, he's called Johann, but I usually call him Hansi.
        – And do you think I can call him Hansi as well, or should I use his
          eigentlich-ACC name?'

This dialogue contains three uses of *eigentlich*: first as a MP (marking that the
speaker passes on to a new theme, cf. Thurmair 1989, 176–177), second as an adverb ('actually, in reality'), and third as an adjective ('actual, real'). It may not be
the most central member of the adjective and adverb categories, as it cannot
be intensified (**sehr eigentlich*) and lacks a comparative and superlative form
(**sein eigentlicherer/eigentlichster Name*), but still it is at least a rather prototypical
member of each of the three categories.

This need not be a problem in itself: as Geeraerts et al. (1994, 57–58) indicate,
a prototype can be undecided at a certain point. This may hold for the 'category'
feature of *eigentlich*, prototypical *eigentlich* being either an adjective, an adverb, or
a MP. Thus, if the tokens of a type are prototypical instantiations of different categories, than the type itself can also be a prototypical member of different categories (and, as a consequence, different categories can share prototypical members).[14]
Similarly, the 'category' feature of *glaub(e)* is undecided, as this form falls between
three categories (with 'MP' however being the stronger candidate), and prototypical *glaub(e)* itself is not a prototypical member of any category (although some of
its tokens are prototypical instantiations of the category of MPs).

Summing up, it has been argued that the MP category has a prototypical structure with fuzzy boundaries towards other categories. Each particular type is to a
higher or lower degree a prototypical member of this category, and can at the same
time be a prototypical member of different categories. Furthermore, each type
itself has more and less prototypical instantiations (e.g. postponed *halt*, as in (12a),
is not just a non-prototypical instantiation of the MP category, but also of the type
halt, which is prototypically used in the typical MP position, i.e. the middle
field).

---

14. This implies that the relation between the different uses is seen as a case of either heterosemy or polysemy, not of homonymy, as some scholars (e.g. Hentschel and Weydt 2002) claim.
Given the diachronic relationship between the uses, and given the existence of ambiguous cases
precisely because one use has developed from the other (without context, the first *eigentlich* in
(14) could also be interpreted as an adverb), the homonymy analysis is not followed here
(cp. Diewald 2007, 125).

That a category is prototypically structured is not astonishing as such, but it should be clear that this is an important factor in understanding some of the discussions about the definition of 'MP'. Considering this category as prototypical is a plausible analysis, yet only few scholars (apart from Thurmair 1989) have made reference to such an analysis, although some of the questions as to whether a particular linguistic element is a MP or not actually come down to the question to what extent it is a (more or less prototypical) MP.

As a final remark, note that this analysis in terms of prototypicality fits in with the distinction Diewald (2007; this volume) makes between a core group and a peripheral group of MPs, just that the prototypicality analysis does not draw such a strict borderline between core and periphery.[15] The particles Diewald (this volume) lists as core group members are indeed all closer to the prototype, and note that in the more recent works mentioned in Table 1 above, all core particles except for *etwa* are accepted as MPs. In other words, their classification as a MP is less subject to discussion than is the case for more peripheral elements such as *erst*. Diewald herself (this volume) indicates that the list of features she offers, and which closely resembles the list given in §2.1.1 above, "is generally acknowledged (with some discussion about single notoriously problematic points) as relevant and sufficient criteria for classifying MPs." This is true for what she calls the core group. Indeed, except for the case of unstressedness, the discussion is not so much about whether prototypical instantiations of MPs show these features, but rather about the status of the cases which deviate from this pattern: can we consider them as MPs, and if so, to what extent does it make the violated features problematic? In other words, Diewald's main goal is to define the prototype (which is the aim of traditional definitions), while admitting that there are less prototypical cases, whereas my goal is to hint precisely at the points at which non-prototypical cases may deviate from the prototype, and to frame the discussion by referring to notions such as prototypicality.

3.2   Granularity

Prototypicality is not the entire story, however. Imo (2011b) introduces another notion which is, in my view, of major importance for the discussion of the relation between the categories of MPs and discourse markers: granularity. Strictly

---

15.   In fact, an analysis in terms of prototypicality continua may be preferable to a neat distinction for two reasons: on the one hand, it has been shown that typical core members such as *halt* can deviate from the prototype as well, and on the other hand, some peripheral elements may be closer to the prototype than others.

speaking, granularity has two dimensions, which I call vertical and horizontal.[16] Vertical granularity is related to the generality or specificity of the categories, whereas horizontal granularity relates to the preciseness of the category demarcation. For the discussion of the relation between MPs and discourse markers, mainly vertical granularity is at stake. Therefore, and because most issues of horizontal granularity are closely related to issues of prototypicality dealt with above, the discussion of the latter will be rather brief.

The notion of prototypicality implies that categories have fuzzy boundaries and show overlap, hence that there are transition zones between categories. This is illustrated in Figure 1: the category of MPs shares some features with other categories, including modal adverbs, situative particles, and discourse particles, for instance the fact of being uninflected, and hence overlaps with them.

At this level, (horizontal) granularity affects the question of where a category ends. How much variation does the prototype allow? How many features of the prototype must a form show to be a (proto)typical instantiation of a category? In other words: where is the borderline between prototypical and less prototypical instantiations, or between non-prototypical instantiations and forms which are not (i.e. not even non-prototypical) instantiations of a category? How broad is the transition zone or the overlap zone? These are all issues regarding the edges of the prototypes and the question of how fuzzy these edges are.

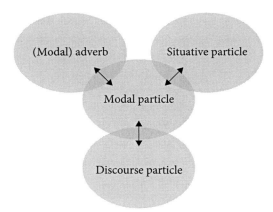

Figure 1. MPs overlapping with other categories[17]

---

16. Imo (2011b) does not make this distinction explicitly and mainly focuses on horizontal granularity.

17. This drawing is somewhat simplified: the MP category may overlap with even more categories, some categories may show more overlap than others, the other categories are likely to show some overlap as well, and the ellipses are clearly delineated although they represent categories with fuzzy boundaries.

Vertical granularity, on the other hand, pertains to the number of categories that are distinguished, and thus to their generality or specificity. As an example, note that in the top-left ellipse in Figure 1, the qualification *modal* is bracketed, a sign of its somehow being optional. This is related to the question whether different types of adverbs (modal, temporal, local...) have to be distinguished. For some analyses, it may be useful to make the difference, whereas in other studies, the difference may be of lesser importance. It thus mainly depends on the goals and the level of detail of the analysis whether the distinction between modal and e.g. temporal or local adverbs is relevant, and hence whether it should be made or not.

For the external definition of MPs, vertical granularity seems to be an important factor in understanding the different views. The main principle of vertical granularity is that the number of categories to be distinguished (and hence their degree of specificity or generality) depends on the goals of the study. If the differences between categories (say, between the different kinds of adverbs) are of lesser importance for the analysis, it may be justified to start off from one more general adverb category, whereas if the differences do matter, referring to the subcategories may be a more suited approach.

The case of the different types of adverbs is a traditional one: the different adverb types are subclasses of the adverb category. A similar point can be made for the different kinds of particles as subclasses of the more general category of 'particles in the strict sense' (cf. §2.2). However, depending on which similarities and differences are at stake, or are considered more important or more salient, different groupings of more specific categories under one more general heading may be possible. This seems to explain the different positions MPs have received in the linguistic system: it is possible to depart from traditional taxonomies and put together, for instance, MPs and modal adverbs under the heading of uninflected modalizing elements.

Recall in this respect that some scholars, including Cardinaletti (2007), consider MPs as a particular subclass of adverbs. This is not too strange a claim as such, given that both categories consist of uninflected elements only, for instance, and the function of MPs is at least highly similar to that of modal adverbs. The fact that Cardinaletti considers MPs to be a particular subclass implies that she is aware of the fact that they are to some extent different from what she calls 'strong adverbs', but she still thinks the similarities are significant enough to add MPs to the class of adverbs.[18] This is represented in Figure 2: MPs are grouped together with modal adverbs (and other kinds of adverbs, which are not shown in the drawing) to constitute together the group of adverbs.

---

18. In a later paper (Cardinaletti 2011), she nuances the need of seeing MPs as a particular subclass and simply classifies them as weak adverbs. However, the fact that these can be opposed to so-called strong adverbs implies that there is some distinction.

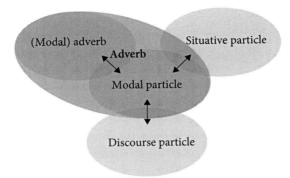

Figure 2. MPs as a subclass of adverbs

The discussion whether so-called situative particles like *allerdings* and *immerhin* are MPs (see §2.1.2) is similar. Situative particles and traditional MPs share an important range of features, the most notable exception being that situative particles can be used in clause-initial position, unlike MPs. As counterexamples can be found to most other features of MPs, one may question the use of creating a separate category for situative particles. Especially if the distinction between situative particles and traditional MPs is not too important for the analysis, it may be justified to group them together in one category, as in Figure 3.

It thus turns out that prototypicality is not the entire explanation of the debate on the definition of the notion of 'modal particle': the level of granularity plays an important role as well, in that depending on the perspective taken and on the relative importance or salience of the defining features, different higher-level groupings can be envisaged.

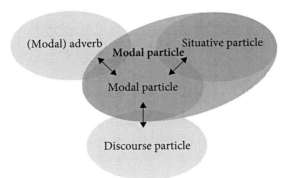

Figure 3. Situative particles as a subclass of MPs

3.3 Conceptualization

Next to prototypicality and granularity, a third notion comes into play: conceptualization. Just as people have concepts such as DOG, CHAIR, or YELLOW, so too do linguists have a concept MODAL PARTICLE, i.e. the concept which is at the basis of the category of MPs. Describing the category of MPs actually comes down to defining the concept MODAL PARTICLE. An important aspect of the notion of 'concept(ualization)' is that it is a "dynamic activity of embodied minds interacting with their environment" (Langacker 2010, 33): our concepts are shaped (in part) by our personal experiences with and observations of instantiations of the concept at stake.

Conceptualization, as understood in this paper, is precisely the process of shaping the concepts and relating the observed phenomena to them. Although categories may to some extent be pre-established (there have been attempts to define the notion of 'MP' before), actual experience still plays a role (cf. Langacker's quote). It is through this experience that we (partly unconsciously) get a feeling of which defining features may be more important or more salient than others, and what the extension of a category is. Finding out what is a salient defining feature or a prominent category member comes down to determining what is considered as such.

An important word here is 'considered': this comes down to subjective interpretation. Since personal experience is an important shaping factor for concepts, these concepts may differ across humans, i.e. the intension and extension of a concept need not be identical to all people (Portner 2005, 8–9). This makes conceptualization an individual process: people may conceptualize phenomena differently because they are working with non-identical concepts, or because they conceive of the relations of the phenomena to the concepts differently. Hence, what drives conceptualization is to a considerable extent personal experience and personal interpretation.[19]

Differences in conceptualization of linguistic phenomena are not exceptional, as Weber (2010) indicates. Such differences in conceptualization may lead to different classification proposals. Therefore, no way of categorizing the phenomena is by definition better or more correct than the other (although they may not appear to be equally suited for a particular analysis[20]), as no conceptualization is better or worse *per se*: it is just a different way of seeing things.

---

19. That people do share concepts (albeit non-identical ones) is a result of social convergence. Here lies an interesting parallel to the dialectics of the individual and the social in the functioning of language (Weber 2010): each individual has its own language system with its own categories, shaped to a major extent by personal experience with language, but still communication is possible because of social convergence.

20. Cp. Jacobs's (2011, 346) claim that the viability of a classification depends on what one wants to do with it; see also Diewald (this volume).

The conceptualization issue plays a role in the case of MPs. It should be clear from the discussion in §2 that there are indeed different views on the concept MODAL PARTICLE. These differences are found at each of the three levels of definition distinguished above, and each time, conceptualization may play a role. At the intensional level, it is one of the factors determining which features are considered salient enough to be included in the definition, and to what extent they have to be absolute (i.e. exceptionless) (cf. Schoonjans 2011, 157). As an illustration, recall that for some scholars, MPs cannot be stressed, whereas others think that some or even all MPs do have a stressed variant. At the external level, determining which categories can be united in one superordinate category is a matter of conceptualization as well, as this also depends on which features are considered more salient than others and on how the relation between the concepts is conceived. Take for instance the classification of MPs as adverbs. Cardinaletti (2007) ranges the MPs among the adverbs because she conceptualizes MPs as adverbs, i.e. she considers the features that unite MPs with adverbs (uninflected, modal meaning...) to be more salient than those which differentiate them (unlike MPs, most adverbs can occur sentence-initially, for instance).

Finally, at the extensional level, conceptualization comes into play when determining the classification of less prototypical tokens (and thus also of less prototypical types). In this case, the amount of defining criteria met normally steers the classification. In the case of postponed *halt* (example (12a)), for instance, it is clear that we are dealing with a (non-prototypical) MP instantiation. A MP does not normally occur in the back field, but since the topological tendencies seem to show exceptions and since this is the only deviation from the MP prototype, it seems legitimate to argue that *halt* is a MP even in (12a).

In other cases, however, the deviation from the basic pattern is bigger, and the amount of criteria met may not be decisive. In those cases, the salience of the features comes into play. Consider, for instance, the following example of *glaub(e)*:

(16)   Aber auch hier gibt's Hürden. Zum Beispiel musst du die Bude schon *(glaube)* 1 Jahr haben, um Anspruch zu haben usw.[21]
'But there are hurdles here as well. For instance, you need to have the booth for *(glaube)* one year already to have a claim and so on.'

In this example, it is harder to classify *glaub(e)* as a MP than in more common cases like (13), taken up again as (17) below:

(17)   Da hab ich *glaub* sogar bedient.

First of all, unlike typical MPs, *glaube* is not integrated in (16), as it is bracketed. Furthermore, although it is used in the middle field, it does not take a usual MP

---

21.   <http://www.mediengestalter.info/forum/45/bab-beantragung-41072-1.htm> (18-02-2010).

position, which is related to the fact that it only scopes over the following adverbial ('one year'), not over the entire clause. Whether such attestations can be considered as (non-prototypical) MPs is a matter of horizontal granularity, but it also depends on how salient the MP features met are thought to be when compared to the features which are not met. In case one considers the scope relations and the degree of integration as more salient, one may be less inclined to think of *glaube* in this case as a MP but rather as an adverb, because in these respects, it is more like other, typical adverbs such as *ungefähr* ('approximately').

That some features are more salient than others is generally agreed upon in prototypicality theory (Geeraerts et al. 1994, 89), but which features are the more salient ones is a matter of conceptualization.[22] Thus, depending on how a phenomenon is conceptualized, different features may be more or less salient, and this may lead to different classifications. Hence, it is not just the aims of the study that determine which features are most relevant, but also the way the analyst handles and interprets the data.

As a final example, consider the aforementioned case of *eigentlich*. To Kohrt (1988), *eigentlich* is an adverb, not a MP, whereas Oppenrieder and Thurmair (1989) think it can be used both as an adverb and as a MP. This is because they conceive of the phenomena in different ways: in Kohrt's view, the 'MP-like' attestations of *eigentlich* are still so similar to the adverbial attestations that there is no need to distinguish them (and thus, he only considers *eigentlich* to be a prototypical adverb, adverb being the 'older' category), whereas according to Oppenrieder and Thurmair, the differences between both uses are striking enough to distinguish two category uses. Hence, Kohrt and Oppenrieder and Thurmair propose different analyses, just because they conceptualize the phenomena differently.[23]

4. Discourse markers and modal particles: Two sides of the same coin?

So far, it has been shown that the definition of 'MP' is subject to discussion, and that this discussion can be related to notions like prototypicality, granularity, and conceptualization. These notions do not resolve the problem, but at least they allow us to handle it, and to deal with issues like the relationship between MPs and discourse markers (DMs) despite the lack of definition. It is important to note, in

---

22. Although other factors such as frequency and markedness play a role as well.

23. Note that Diewald (this volume) also hints at conceptualization in this respect, albeit without using this term, when she writes: "With view to peripheral members, it is clear that their status as grammaticalizing elements [...] makes it self-evident that there must be different judgements on the degree of development of single items by different researchers."

this respect, that the situation is not very different in the case of DMs, for which there is no unanimity either at either one of the three levels of definition. However, in the case of DMs, several scholars (Fischer 2006, Fraser 1999, Imo 2012, and Schourup 1999, among others) have already commented upon the issue. Therefore, and since the focus is mainly on MPs in the present paper, the definition of DMs will not be discussed in detail here.

The debate is not just restricted to the definitory level, however: like with MPs, several terms have been used to refer to this category, sometimes interchangeably, sometimes implying (subtle or less subtle) differences. Examples include 'discourse markers', 'discourse particles', 'pragmatic markers', 'discourse operators', and so forth. Still, no matter which term is used or how the category is defined, it is clear that it encompasses a rather heterogeneous group of elements fulfilling equally heterogeneous functions (Fischer 2006, 5).

Given this heterogeneity, the question whether MPs are a subclass of DMs seems justified. Several features that are recurrently mentioned in DM descriptions do indeed apply to MPs as well: connectivity (cf. the <KONNEX> function Thurmair 1989 ascribes to some MPs, i.e. the ability of relating a turn to a preceding one), optionality, non-propositional meaning, and so on. Still, a considerable number of scholars do not seem to take this position. A simple look at the different contributions to this volume reveals that there is huge variation in how the MP-DM relation is conceived. Two important explaining factors seem to be differences in the level of vertical granularity and the terminological chaos.

A case in point is the term 'discourse particle' (DP). Several scholars use this term as a (near-)synonym of 'DM' (e.g. Hansen 1998). However, as Schourup (1999, 229) notes, a difficulty with 'DP' is "the competing use of this term in recent years to refer specifically to scalar and modal particles as a group." There are indeed scholars who use the term 'DP' to refer just to MPs, e.g. Bayer and Obenauer (2011). However, as Schourup (l.c.) indicates, none of these smaller groups (MPs, scalar particles, DPs in this restricted sense) "is coextensive (or perhaps even overlapping) with the DM category as typically described."

But even if this particular use of 'DP' as a synonym of 'MP' is not taken into account, the discussion remains: how do MPs relate to DMs? It seems that the notion of vertical granularity can be helpful in tackling the problem, and in coping with the different views. All figures in the present paper contained an ellipse for DPs, but with no indication of how it is conceived. In the drawings, it refers to anything which may be considered as a DM and which does not fall under any other of the categories discussed above (MPs, situative particles, conjunctions...).[24] There is

---

24. Note that 'DP' may perhaps not be the most appropriate term, as not all DMs are necessarily particles, i.e. uninflected words (cp. Schourup 1999, 229).

some overlap with the MP ellipse, in that MPs and DPs (can) share some features and members[25], but neither one is thought to encompass the other category.

The core idea of vertical granularity was that, if the similarities are more important than the differences, it may be justified to put together several categories in one superordinate category. It seems that this is what several scholars who consider MPs as a subtype of DMs do (e.g. Stede and Schmitz 2000): on the basis of the similarities with DPs, they group MPs and DPs in one category. This is illustrated in Figure 4: the category of DMs consists of the categories MP and DP. (Note that this distinction between DPs and DMs, one being a subtype of the other, is made here just for convenience, to be able to refer to both groupings by means of different terms; this is not a generalized way of seeing the relation between those terms.)

The main point in the issue of grasping the notion of 'DM' and determining its relationship with MPs thus seems to be terminological: about a dozen terms have been created to refer to these kinds of linguistic elements, but they are often used in non-corresponding ways and at different levels of granularity. In this respect, the issue of whether MPs are DMs is highly similar to the issue of whether situative particles are MPs (see §3.2): the same term is used at two levels of granularity, i.e. in a more general or a more specific way, either including or excluding the other category, but the level of granularity is neither specified nor justified most of the time. As a consequence, the same terms are used for partly different concepts, and precisely this seems to be an important factor in explaining the discussions at the external level: the terminological identity hides conceptual differences which have repercussions on the relation to other categories.

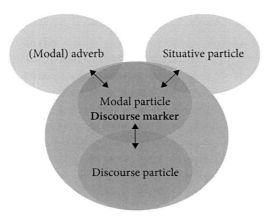

Figure 4. MPs as a subclass of DMs

---

25.   An example is *ja*, which can function as a hesitation marker and which in this use is a DP for several scholars.

5.   Comparison with French

So far, the discussion was mainly based on the situation in German. A logical next step is to ask to what extent the situation in other languages is similar, or whether categories such as DM and MP are necessarily language-bound. This is an important question if one wants to study the relationship between MPs and DMs, which is the central goal of this volume: if the categories themselves are language-specific, then so is their mutual relationship. Hence, for the relationship between MPs and DMs to be cross-linguistically valid, one first has to make sure that the categories to be related are also found cross-linguistically; otherwise the relationship between the categories will differ across languages and can at most be compared, not generalized.

The goal of the present section is precisely to address this issue of cross-linguistic validity of the category descriptions. Two questions are at order here. First, one has to ask whether other languages have a category of MPs similar to the German one. If this is the case, we need to address how it relates to other categories (adverbs, DPs...), and to what extent this corresponds to the situation in German. Since MPs are often thought to be a typically German(ic) phenomenon, this discussion will be illustrated by referring to a non-Germanic language: French.

5.1   Modal particles in other languages

The question whether the category description of MPs given for German can simply be extended to other languages has to receive a negative answer, for the simple reason that all word classes are language-specific (Haspelmath 2010, 345). However, this does not mean that cross-linguistic comparison (and potentially generalization) is excluded as such; it only implies that category descriptions which hold for one particular language cannot be generalized just like that across languages. In other words, there may well be "a" category of MPs in other languages; one should just be reluctant in assuming that it is the same category with the same intensional and external definition (cf. Haspelmath 2010, 350).[26]

The question then remains if other languages have a category that corresponds to the MP category in German. Cuenca (this volume), for instance, indicates that Catalan is generally thought not to have many prototypical MPs, if at all, and Aijmer (this volume) raises the question whether English forms such as *of course* can be considered as MPs.

---

26. Note that Diewald (this volume) also indicates that category features may vary across languages.

As for French, there is some discussion about the existence of a MP category
as well. Examples of MP candidates include *donc, quand même, seulement*, and
tout de même, as in (18–20).

(18)   Mais je ne peux *tout de même* pas les faire coincer?
       (B. Clavel, *Malataverne*, p. 120)
       'But I can't *tout de même* make them get caught?'

(19)   Asseyez-vous *donc*, Messieurs! (H. Bazin, *La Mort du petit cheval*, p. 145)
       'Take *donc* a seat, gentlemen!'

(20)   Si j'avais *seulement* pu le consulter avant de rencontrer Reslaut!
       (C. Mauriac, *La Marquise sortit à cinq heures*, p. 175)
       'If *seulement* I could have consulted him before meeting Reslaut!'

Looking back at the list of features of German MPs, it seems that most of them do
also apply to the French particles. These elements cannot be inflected, negated, or
intensified, they do not have constituent value, and they scope over the entire
clause. Furthermore, their function is highly similar to that of German particles
like *doch* (18–19) and *bloß* (20) (indicating that a positive answer is expected in
(18), increasing the illocutionary force in (19–20)).

Still, scholars like Abraham (1988) and Waltereit (2006) claim that French
cannot have MPs for topological reasons: German MPs are restricted to the middle
field, whereas Romance languages do not have a middle field. Both parts of this
reasoning turn out to be problematic, however: it has been shown above (§2.1.1)
that German MPs can occur outside of the middle field, and at least in (18) and
(20), it is clear that the French particles are placed between the finite and non-
finite verb forms, hence in the middle field. Although the middle field tendency is
admittedly somewhat weaker in French (but note that French generally has a less
expanded middle field than German), the middle field seems to be the prototypical position for MPs in French as well.[27] Furthermore, one may wonder if this
difference in strength of the topological tendencies is sufficient to say that French
does not have MPs, if the categories are language-specific: French does not have
the German MP category, but it has a corresponding word class. It thus seems that
one can agree with Söll (1974), Fónagy (1995), and Hansen (1998), among others,
and claim that French does have MPs just like German (cf. Schoonjans submitted-
b). The categories are not identical, but at least the same typical intensional features are at stake.

---

27.   In the data presented in Schoonjans (submitted-a), if the middle field is clearly marked
(i.e. if the clause contains a finite and a non-finite verb), 73.19% of the particles occur in the
middle field, as opposed to 99.46% in German.

5.2   Prototypicality, granularity, and conceptualization in other languages

The existence of "a" category of MPs in other languages does not necessarily imply that the situation is fully comparable to German: one could imagine a well-delineated and neatly defined class of MPs in those other languages. However, Aijmer (this volume) and Cuenca (this volume) suggest for English and Catalan respectively that the MP category is not so neatly distinguishable from other word classes.

It seems that the categories are not entirely discrete in French either. This can be illustrated with the case of *seulement*, which, just like its German counterpart *nur*, can be used both as a DP and as a MP (next to its use as a focus particle). Both of these interpretations are possible in (21), taken from a discussion board about a computer game.

(21)   Tu le tiens a distance en le blessant a la même occasion. *Seulement* ne te laisse pas prendre! Ce boss one shot en attaque de mêlée donc fais attention.[28]
'You keep him at a distance and injure him at the same time. *Seulement* don't get caught! This one-shot boss attacks massively so be careful.'

Another example is the use of *tout de même* in (22). *Tout de même* is somewhat ambiguous here: it can be interpreted both as an adverb (meaning 'nevertheless') and as a MP (similar to German *doch*).

(22)   – Je suis venu vous dire au revoir.
– Eh bien, au revoir! Buvez *tout de même* un dernier verre, nous savons vivre, après tout.   (A. Camus, *Requiem pour une nonne*, p. 832)
'– I have come to say good bye.
– Well, good bye! Drink *tout de même* one final glass, we know how to live, after all.'

This example is similar to the case of German *eigentlich*, discussed above. In both cases, the use as a MP has developed from the adverbial use, and scholars disagree on whether the MP use has to be distinguished from the adverbial use. Jacques Moeschler (p.c.), for instance, claims that *tout de même* cannot be a MP because its contrastive meaning aspect is still too strong. This is an argument referring to the retention in grammaticalization processes, and is highly similar to Kohrt's arguments for *eigentlich*. Again, the degree of grammaticalization and the existence of an older use as a prototypical adverb seems to influence the discussion.

---

28.   <http://jd-forum.fr.perfectworld.eu/showthread.php?t=302641> (04-01-2012).

We can thus conclude that in French as well, there is a category of MPs which has a prototypical structure and fuzzy boundaries, and which furthermore overlaps with categories like adverbs and DPs, just like its German counterpart. The prototypicality is shown by the fact that most, but not all, French MP tokens occur in the middle field, as indicated in the previous section, and the fuzzy boundaries become obvious when looking at the examples just mentioned (*seulement* and *tout de même*). Furthermore, issues of granularity and conceptualization play a role as well, as can be seen from the fact that there is discussion on whether these forms are MPs or not. What is more, the discussion goes beyond the level of MPs: as Léard (1996) shows, opinions about the status of a class of particles and about its structure and position in the linguistic system vary.

It thus turns out that the description in Sections 2–4 above does not only hold for German. At least French, and probably several other languages as well, show a situation which is highly similar: there is a category of MPs which strongly resembles the German one, and for its definition (both internal and external), notions like prototypicality, granularity, and conceptualization may be helpful.

6.   Summary and conclusions

The present contribution discussed the problem of defining the notion of 'modal particle' in German. The discussion focused on three levels of definition: the intensional level (typical features), the extensional level (category members), and the external level (position in the linguistic system), with special attention being paid to the central issue of this volume: how do MPs relate to DMs?

The starting point was the observation that, despite the significant body of literature on MPs, there still is no full agreement on the definition of this category. The goal was not to try to resolve this problem and come up with one final solution; rather, the aim was to get an overview of the points of discussion at the different levels of definition, and to try to come to grips with the discussion, i.e. to understand why is there so much disagreement, and if (and how) it is possible to work with this category nevertheless.

The answer was found in three cognitive-linguistic notions: prototypicality, granularity, and conceptualization. That these notions can be applied to lexical categories is not a new claim in itself. So far, however, they have hardly been called upon when dealing with MPs, although they seem to be useful in trying to cope with the definition debate. Indeed, this category turns out to be prototypically structured, to have fuzzy boundaries and to show overlap with other categories (e.g. adverbs, DPs...). Whether a form is a MP thus depends on the level of horizontal granularity, i.e. on the amount of variation the prototype may show and to the extent a form may deviate from the prototype to still be a (non-prototypical) member of the category. This is where conceptualization comes in: how the category is conceived partly determines which features are thought to be more important or more salient, and this may have an impact on the structure of the prototype and the level of horizontal granularity chosen.

As for the relation with other categories, important notions are vertical granularity and (again) conceptualization. Depending on the aims and level of detail of an analysis, the level of vertical granularity may differ, in that it may be more appropriate to work with more specific or more general categories. Which groupings are at order depends on which similarities or differences are judged more important or more relevant, and this depends itself on the aims of the study and on the conceptualization of the phenomena. This turns out to be an important factor in the debate on the MP-DM relationship, together with the terminological confusion and the lack of a clear definition.

It has been shown as well that these problems are not just restricted to German. That they are most apparent for German is due to the fact that German is the language *par excellence* to study MPs, but they are not significantly smaller in other languages, as has been shown for French. The situation as described in the main part of this paper (§2–4) may be typical for German, but other languages do at least show striking similarities.

It should be clear that notions like prototypicality, granularity, and conceptualization cannot bring the answer to the discussion, but they can help to better understand the debate. Still the reported issues should not prevent us from studying the linguistic elements in question. The terminological confusion does not make (reporting on) the research easier, but does not exclude it either, as long as it is clearly indicated how the terms are used. Further empirical analysis leads to an even better understanding of how language functions in this domain, which may eventually result in more terminological transparency and agreement on the definitions and the mutual relations of the categories. At least for the time being, however, it seems that notions of prototypicality, granularity, and conceptualization can be helpful in tackling the definitory issues.

References

Abraham, Werner. 1988. "Vorbemerkungen zur Modalpartikelsyntax im Deutschen." *Linguistische Berichte* 118: 443–465.

Abraham, Werner. 2000. "Modal particles in German: Word Classification and Legacy beyond Grammaticalisation." In *Approaches to the Typology of Word Classes*, ed. by Petra Maria Vogel, and Bernard Comrie, 321–350. Berlin: de Gruyter.

Abraham, Werner. 2010. "Diskurspartikel zwischen Modalität, Modus und Fremdbewusstseins-abgleich." In *40 Jahre Partikelforschung*, ed. by Theo Harden, and Elke Hentschel, 33–78. Tübingen: Stauffenburg.

Autenrieth, Tanja. 2002. *Heterosemie und Grammatikalisierung bei Modalpartikeln*. Tübingen: Niemeyer.

Bastert, Ulrike. 1985. *Modalpartikel und Lexikographie*. Tübingen: Niemeyer.

Bayer, Josef, and Hans-Georg Obenauer. 2011. "Discourse Particles, Clause Structure, and Question Types." *The Linguistic Review* 28 (4): 449–491.

Breban, Tine. 2009. "Structural Persistence: A Case Based on the Grammaticalization of English Adjectives of Difference." *English Language and Linguistics* 13 (1): 77–96.

Bublitz, Wolfram. 1978. *Ausdrucksweisen der Sprechereinstellung im Deutschen und Englischen*. Tübingen: Niemeyer.

Cardinaletti, Anna. 2007. "Für eine syntaktische Analyse von Modalpartikeln." In *Gesprochene Sprache – Partikeln*, ed. by Eva-Maria Thüne, and Franca Ortu, 89–101. Frankfurt: Lang.

Cardinaletti, Anna. 2011. "German and Italian Modal Particles and Clause Structure." *The Linguistic Review* 28 (4): 493–531.

Company Company, Concepción. 2002 "Grammaticalization and Category Weakness." In *New Reflections on Grammaticalization*, ed. by Ilse Wischer, and Gabriele Diewald, 201–215. Amsterdam: Benjamins.

Diewald, Gabriele. 1997. *Grammatikalisierung. Eine Einführung im Sein und Werden grammatischer Formen*. Tübingen: Niemeyer.

Diewald, Gabriele. 2007. "Abtönungspartikel." In *Handbuch der deutschen Wortarten*, ed. by Ludger Hoffmann, 117–141. Berlin: de Gruyter.

Engel, Ulrich. 2004. *Deutsche Grammatik. Neubearbeitung*. München: Iudicium.

Fischer, Kerstin. 2006. "Towards an Understanding of the Spectrum of Approaches to Discourse Particles: Introduction to the Volume." In *Approaches to Discourse Particles*, ed. by Kerstin Fischer, 1–20. Amsterdam: Elsevier.

Fónagy, Ivan. 1995. "Figement et mouvement. Changements lexicaux en cours dans le français contemporain." *Revue Romane* 30 (2): 163–204.

Franck, Dorothea. 1980. *Grammatik und Konversation*. Königstein: Scriptor.

Fraser, Bruce. 1999. "What Are Discourse Markers?" *Journal of Pragmatics* 31 (7): 931–952.

Geeraerts, Dirk. 1986. *Woordbetekenis. Een overzicht van de lexicale semantiek*. Leuven: Acco.

Geeraerts, Dirk. 1997. *Diachronic Prototype Semantics*. Oxford: Clarendon.

Geeraerts, Dirk et al. 1994. *The Structure of Lexical Variation: Meaning, Naming, and Context*. Berlin: de Gruyter.

Gerdes, Kim, and Sylvain Kahane. 2007. "Phrasing It Differently." In *Selected Lexical and Grammatical Issues in the Meaning-Text Theory*, ed. by Leo Wanner, 297–335. Amsterdam: Benjamins.

Gutzmann, Daniel. 2010. "Betonte Modalpartikeln und Verumfokus." In *40 Jahre Partikelforschung*, ed. by Theo Harden, and Elke Hentschel, 119–138. Tübingen: Stauffenburg.

Hansen, Maj-Britt Mosegaard. 1998. *The Function of Discourse Particles*. Amsterdam: Benjamins.

Hartmann, Dietrich. 1975. "Zur Semantik von Satzpartikeln und zu ihren Funktionen in Texten." In *Beiträge zur Grammatik und Pragmatik*, ed. by Veronika Ehrich, and Peter Finke, 233–252. Kronberg: Scriptor.

Haspelmath, Martin. 2010. "Framework-free Grammatical Theory." In *The Oxford Handbook of Linguistic Analysis*, ed. by Bernd Heine, and Heiko Narrog, 341–365. Oxford: Oxford University Press.

Helbig, Gerhard. 1988. *Lexikon deutscher Partikeln*. Leipzig: Enzyklopädie.

Hentschel, Elke. 1983. "Partikeln und Wortstellung." In *Partikeln und Interaktion*, ed. by Harald Weydt, 46–53. Tübingen: Niemeyer.

Hentschel, Elke. 1986. *Funktion und Geschichte deutscher Partikeln*. Tübingen: Niemeyer.

Hentschel, Elke, and Harald Weydt. 1990. *Handbuch der deutschen Grammatik*. Berlin: de Gruyter.

Hentschel, Elke, and Harald Weydt. 2002. "Die Wortart ‚Partikel'." In *Lexikologie: Internationales Handbuch zur Natur und Struktur von Wörtern und Wortschätzen*, ed. by D. Alan Cruse et al., 646–653. Berlin: de Gruyter.

Ikoma, Miki. 2007. *Prosodische Eigenschaften der deutschen Modalpartikeln*. Hamburg: Kovač.

Imo, Wolfgang. 2006. "'Da hat des kleine *glaub* irgendwas angestellt' – ein *construct* ohne *construction?*" In *Konstruktionen in der Interaktion*, ed. by Susanne Günthner, and Wolfgang Imo, 263–290. Berlin: de Gruyter.

Imo, Wolfgang. 2008. "Individuelle Konstrukte oder Vorboten einer neuen Konstruktion? Stellungsvarianten der Modalpartikel *halt* im Vor- und Nachfeld." In *Konstruktionsgrammatik II: Von der Konstruktion zur Grammatik*, ed. by Anatol Stefanowitsch, and Kerstin Fischer, 135–155. Tübingen: Stauffenburg.

Imo, Wolfgang. 2011a. "Ad-hoc-Produktion oder Konstruktion? Verfestigungstendenzen bei Inkrement-Strukturen im gesprochenen Deutsch." In *Konstruktionsgrammatik III: Aktuelle Fragen und Lösungsansätze*, ed. by Alexander Lasch, and Alexander Ziem, 239–254. Tübingen: Stauffenburg.

Imo, Wolfgang. 2011b. "Die Grenzen von Konstruktionen. Versuch einer granularen Neubestimmung des Konstruktionsbegriffs der Construction Grammar." In *Sprachliches Wissen zwischen Lexikon und Grammatik*, ed. by Stefan Engelberg et al., 113–147. Berlin: de Gruyter.

Imo, Wolfgang. 2012. "Wortart Diskursmarker?" In *Nicht-flektierende Wortarten*, ed. by Björn Rothstein, 48–88. Berlin: de Gruyter.

Jacobs, Joachim. 2011. "Grammatik ohne Wörter?" In *Sprachliches Wissen zwischen Lexikon und Grammatik*, ed. by Stefan Engelberg et al., 345–372. Berlin: de Gruyter.

Kohrt, Manfred. 1988. "Eigentlich, das ‚Eigentliche' und das ‚Nicht-Eigentliche'. Zum Gebrauch einer sogenannten ‚Abtönungspartikel'." *Deutsche Sprache* 16: 103–130.

Krivonosov, Aleksej T. 1977. "Die Wechselbeziehungen der modalen Partikeln zu anderen Wortklassen im Deutschen. Zum Problem der wechselseitigen Durchlässigkeit der Wortklassen." *Sprachwissenschaft* 2: 349–367.

Kürschner, Wilfried. ⁴2003 (1989). *Grammatisches Kompendium*. Tubingen: Francke.

Langacker, Ronald W. 2010. "Conceptualization, Symbolization, and Grammar." *International Journal of Cognitive Linguistics* 1 (1): 31–63.

Léard, Jean-Marcel. 1996. "*Ti/-tu, est-ce que, qu'est-ce que, ce que, hé que, don*: des particules de modalisation en français?" *Revue québécoise de linguistique* 24 (2): 107–124.

Meibauer, Jörg. 1994. *Modaler Kontrast und konzeptuelle Verschiebung*. Tübingen: Niemeyer.

Meibauer, Jörg. 2003. "Auf dem JA-Markt." In *Satz und Illokution. Band 2*, Inger Rosengren (ed.), 127–149. Tübingen: Niemeyer.

Möllering, Martina. 2001. "Teaching German Modal Particles: A Corpus-based Approach." *Language Learning & Technology* 5 (3): 130–151.

Molnár, Anna. 2008. "Pragmatische Sprachphänomene und das Grammatikalisierungskonzept." *Argumentum* 4: 280–289.

Moroni, Manuela Caterina. 2005. "Zur syntaktischen Distribution der Modalpartikeln im Deutschen." *Linguistica e Filologia* 20: 7–30.

Moroni, Manuela Caterina. 2010. *Modalpartikeln zwischen Syntax, Prosodie und Informationsstruktur.* Frankfurt: Lang.

Oppenrieder, Wilhelm, and Maria Thurmair. 1989. "Kategorie und Funktion einer Partikel, oder: Was ist eigentlich ,eigentlich' EIGENTLICH? Eine Replik auf M. Kohrt." *Deutsche Sprache* 17: 26–39.

Ormelius-Sandblom, Elisabet. 1997. *Die Modalpartikeln ja, doch und schon.* Stockholm: Almqvist & Wiksell.

Portner, Paul H. 2005. *What Is Meaning?* Malden: Blackwell.

Rüttenauer, Martin. 1983. "Zum Bedeutungswandel bei Modalpartikeln." In *Allgemeine Sprachwissenschaft, Sprachtypologie und Textlinguistik*, ed. by Manfred Faust et al., 143–148. Tübingen: Narr.

Schoonjans, Steven. 2011. "Rezension zu: Tilo Weber, Lexikon und Grammatik in Interaktion. Lexikalische Kategorisierungsprozesse im Deutschen. Berlin: Walter de Gruyter, 2010." *Gesprächsforschung OZS* 12: 155–168.

Schoonjans, Steven. 2012a. "The Particulization of German Complement-taking Mental Predicates." *Journal of Pragmatics* 44 (6–7): 776–797.

Schoonjans, Steven. 2012b. "Aus *Verba sentiendi* hervorgegangene Partikeln im Deutschen: Formen, die zwischen den Stühlen sitzen?" *Muttersprache* 122 (3): 177–193.

Schoonjans, Steven. [submitted-a]. "Topologie contrastive des particules de démodulation: comparaison de l'allemand et du français." [submitted to: *Akten der 7. internationalen Arbeitstagung ,Romanisch-deutscher und innerromanischer Sprachvergleich'*, ed. by Eva Lavric and Wolfgang Poeckl. Frankfurt: Lang].

Schoonjans, Steven. [submitted-b]. "Oui, il y a des particules de démodulation en français." [submitted to *CogniTextes*].

Schoonjans, Steven. [submitted-c]. "Zur Kombinierbarkeit, Koordinierbarkeit und Modifizierbarkeit von Modalpartikeln." [Submitted to *SKY Journal of Linguistics*]

Schourup, Lawrence. 1999. "Discourse Markers." *Lingua* 107: 227–265.

Stede, Manfred, and Birte Smitz. 2000. "Discourse Particles and Discourse Functions." *Machine Translation* 15 (1–2): 125–147.

Szulc-Brzozowska, Magdalena. 2002. *Deutsche und polnische Modalpartikeln und ihre Aquivalenzbeziehungen.* Lublin: Towarzystwo Naukowe KUL.

Söll, Ludwig. 1974. *Gesprochenes und geschriebenes Französisch.* Berlin: Schmidt.

Taylor, John R. ²1995 [1989]. *Linguistic Categorization.* Oxford: Clarendon.

Thurmair, Maria. 1989. *Modalpartikeln und ihre Kombinationen.* Tübingen: Niemeyer.

Waltereit, Richard. 2006. *Abtönung.* Tübingen: Niemeyer.

Weber, Tilo. 2010. *Lexikon und Grammatik in Interaktion.* Berlin: de Gruyter.

From TAM to discourse

The role of information status
in North-Western Italian *già* 'already'

Mario Squartini
Università di Torino

This study investigates some discursive uses of the North-Western Italian adverb *già* 'already', which cumulates the Italian interjectional function with the interrogative use typical of the French cognate *déjà*. While as an interjection *già* acquires the metadiscursive functions of a proper discourse marker, the interrogative use shares formal and functional properties with modal particles. The analysis will show that, apart from their morphosyntactic differences, these uses are interconnected by their common functional interpretation as pragmatic markers of 'given' information ('backchecking' in the interrogative use and 'confirmativity' in interjections). A comparative assessment of Italian and French data contributes to clarifying what features modal particles and discourse markers have in common but also where they morphosyntactically diverge.

1. The discursive uses of Romance phasal adverbs

The development of discursive uses in French temporal-aspectual adverbs (*déjà* 'already', *encore* 'still') has been comprehensively elucidated by Hansen (2002, 2008), who also capitalized on the import of these data in distinguishing between propositional meanings of phasal adverbs in a temporal-aspectual dimension (van der Auwera 1998) and 'context-level' uses of the same forms in different discursive domains including their functions as pragmatic markers, connectives and focus particles. More recent works by Bazzanella et al. (2005, 2007) and Hansen and Strudsholm (2008) have proposed a wider comparative perspective in which other Romance languages have been taken into account, highlighting the extremely varied array of discursive uses that can be covered by Romance T(emporal)-A(spectual)-M(odal) markers and especially by the descendants of Latin *iam* 'already'. As well as showing that these uses go well beyond those detected by Kroon and Risselada (2002) and Rosén (2009, 342, 348) for the Latin ancestor *iam*, a detailed intra-Romance comparison turns out to be particularly intriguing if one considers that the discursive uses of 'already' are extremely diverse across the Romance area and, in some cases, the distribution of different uses seems to be mutually exclusive (Hansen and Strudsholm 2008), ultimately suggesting possible internal partitions within the extensive domain of discourse-pragmatic functions. Moreover, as emphasized by Bazzanella et al. (2005), a comparison based on a richer array of languages in which regional varieties are also taken into account might produce results that, being more fine-grained, are also more interestingly problematic in distinguishing various discursive uses. In a similar vein, the principal aim of this article will be to pursue this comparison further by also taking into account the discursive functions of *già* 'already' in a regional variety of Italian (the one spoken in the North-West of Italy). Not only will this empirical enrichment provide a more varied picture than the one offered by the Romance languages investigated so far, but it will also contribute to the debate on the functional/formal distinctions between Discourse Markers (DM) and Modal Particles (MP) along similar lines as those followed in other chapters of this volume. It will be claimed that North-Western Italian *già* occurs in discursive functions in which it behaves as a MP, not differently from other Romance forms having this use (Hansen 1998, Coniglio 2008, Detges and Waltereit 2009). Conversely, the same form will also be described in other interactional uses in which it typically covers the function of a DM, the latter notion being defined not only in the extended sense admitted by Bazzanella (1995, 2006),[1] but also in the narrower delimitation squarely proposed by Diewald (2006, this volume) and Detges and Waltereit (2009). The intention of what follows is to emphasize the extent to which a Romance comparative perspective taking into account parametric variations among similar phenomena in sister languages including their regional varieties may be illuminating in disentangling the complex bundle of functional and formal features characterizing the boundary between DMs and MPs (in a similar comparative perspective see Lauwers et al. (2012) and Detges and Waltereit (2009) on Spanish and French cognate adverbs *bien* 'well').

In comparison with other chapters of this book, the analysis that follows will put particular emphasis on the role of information structure ('given'/'new' information, shared knowledge) as a common feature on which the whole functional behaviour of the pragmatic markers[2] under scrutiny is based. Following Chafe

---

1.   Bazzanella (2006, 2009) intends 'discourse markers' as a macro-category which also includes "modalizers, such as hedges and boosters", thus considering modal particles as a subtype of 'discourse markers' (cf. especially Bazzanella 2006, 463, fn. 22).

2.   Following Fraser (1996) I will use the label 'pragmatic markers' in referring to the general macrocategory including DMs as well as MPs.

(1987) and Lambrecht (1994), information structure will be intended here as a discursive dimension having to do with the degree of activation that the propositional content of an utterance acquires in the informational flow governing textual progression. In particular, the mechanism of backchecking, whose connection to MPs has already been underlined by Waltereit (2001), will be further elaborated within more general principles of information structure as a possible common ground among the various interactional uses of North-Western Italian *già* described here.

Section 1.1. sets the general comparative scene by providing selected examples of the major discursive uses of Romance 'already' that will be dealt with in more detail in the rest of this work. The following two sections constitute the bulk of the empirical analysis and will be reserved to describing the relevant regional uses of Italian *già*, whose distribution will be systematically analyzed by comparing them with standard Italian *già* and, when applicable, with French *déjà*. The two main functions of *già* as a MP and as a DM will be treated separately, in Section 2 and 3 respectively, and then compared in Section 4, where the role of information structure will be emphasized.

1.1   Discursive 'already' in Romance: Interrogative and interjection

In analyzing the complex array of functions covered by French temporal-aspectual adverbs Hansen (2002, 46; 2008, 171, 213) mentions a rather "marginal" use of the phasal adverb *déjà* 'already' in direct questions (1), a phenomenon which, among others, had already been signalled by Fonagy (1982, 68) and Välikangas (2004). As described by Hansen (2002, 46; 2008, 171, 213), *déjà* functions in (1) as a speech-act modifier signalling that "the host speech act is in some sense premature when compared to what might have been expected" (it "might be paraphrased as *I already have to ask you what your name is*"):

> (1)   Quel est votre nom, *déjà*?   (Hansen 2008, 213)
>   'What's your name, ALREADY?

Further elaborating on phasal adverbs from a comparative perspective Hansen and Strudsholm (2008) include this interrogative use in a comprehensive semantic (and pragmatic) map in which the various functions of French *déjà* are compared to its Italian cognate adverb *già*. In this map (1) is described as belonging to what Hansen (2008, 213) defines ("for lack of a better term") as an "interactional" extension directly deriving from the temporal-aspectual meaning of the phasal adverb 'already' (on the diachronic process see also Buchi 2007):

> (2)   PHASAL > INTERROGATIVE

In comparing French and Italian Hansen and Strudsholm (2008) highlight the opposite distribution shown by these two languages in the pragmatic uses of *déjà/già*. While the interactional function in interrogative sentences is restricted to French *déjà*, its Italian cognate *già* has independently developed a different 'interjectional' function (Hansen and Strudsholm 2008), which Bazzanella (1995, 242) lists among Italian 'discourse markers' interpreting it as a signal of dialogic confirmation:

(3)   *Già* – confermai – ce l'abbiamo fatta   (Bazzanella 1995, 242)
      'ALREADY – I confirmed – We managed'

In Hansen and Strudsholm's (2008) semantic map this pragmatic evolution of Italian *già* is represented as a parallel extension which shares the 'interactional' nature of French *déjà* but is conceived as an independent path towards interjectional uses:

(4)   PHASAL > INTERJECTION

Further extensions of the comparative picture seem to confirm the tendency towards a mutually exclusive distribution between interjectional and interrogative uses (Bazzanella et al. 2005). In this respect, Spanish *ya* (5), which, apart from other temporal and non-temporal uses (Deloor 2011), is well attested as an interjectional "meta-discursive conversational marker" (Martín Zorraquino and Portolés 1999, 4191; cf. also Koike 1996, Delbecque and Maldonado 2011) but, like Portuguese and Sardinian (Bazzanella et al. 2005, 55, fn. 22), does not admit the French interrogative use, is relevant in confirming the tendency towards mutual exclusion between the two interactional uses under scrutiny:

(5)   A: Quiero que lo hagas ahora   (Koike 1996, 271, fn. 6)
      B: *Ya*
      'A: I want you to do it now
      B: OK'

Table 1 sums up the main features of the comparison of French, Italian and Spanish by showing the different distribution of French as opposed to the other two languages:

Table 1. Romance descendants from Latin (DE)IAM: 'interactional' functions

	French	Spanish	Italian
INTERROGATIVE	+	–	–
INTERJECTION	-	+	+

But, the neat and chiastic distribution provided by Table 1 tends to blur if one also considers North-Western Italian varieties, which have therefore attracted closer inspection with the aim of verifying formal and functional correlations between the two interactional uses presented here. After describing in detail the relevant data, the impact of North-Western Italian on the general comparative picture depicted in Table 1 will be schematized in Table 2 (Section 4 below), where the theoretical consequences in the confrontation between MPs and DMs will also be discussed.

2. Interrogative *già*

As already noticed by Välikangas (2004), speakers from the North-West of Italy, especially those from Piedmont, do not seem to conform to the distribution just shown in Table 1 as they admit *già* in an 'interrogative' use which is directly comparable to the one exemplified in (1) for French. The similarity, also observed by Bazzanella et al. (2005, 55, fn. 23), is confirmed by the following pair of examples from the web. (6) is another example of the French interrogative *déjà* presented in (1), while (7) represents the regional Italian use.[3]

> (6) Quel est *déjà* le nom de cet acteur qui se prénomme Robert et joue au côté de Marilyn Monroe dans Rivière sans retour? [from www. in a site commenting on the *mot sur le bout de la langue* 'tip of the tongue']
> 'What is ALREADY the name of that actor whose first name is Robert, who acts with Marilyn Monroe in River of No Return?' [the answer is: Robert Mitchum]
> (7) ciao come si chiama *già* la bassista di colore che suona con david bowie? mi ricordo che ho anche visitato il suo sito ma mi sono dimenticato ... [from www.]
> 'hello what's ALREADY the name of the black bassist who plays with david bowie? I can remember that I also visited her site but I forgot ...'

Both contexts in (6–7) refer to a 'tip of the tongue' situation, where the originally TAM marker 'already' does not indicate the anteriority of a state of affairs to a given reference time, as would be required by its temporal-aspectual nature. By using *déjà/già* the speaker is instead discursively qualifying the speech act (the question itself), in these cases signalling that the question might be considered as

---

3. The majority of the data analyzed here was specially collected for the purpose of the present research either by web-extractions or by taking manual records of authentic oral conversations in Piedmont. Artificial examples submitted to native speakers' judgements have also been used, especially in Section 3 when dealing with interjectional *già*.

redundant and only due to a contingent extralinguistic fact (an accidental tip of the tongue).

Obviously, examples extracted from the web cannot be attributed to a definite regional area, and the geographical boundaries of this use of Italian *già* are still poorly studied and variously interpreted. Whereas the description given in Bazzanella et al. (2005, 55) seems to imply that an interrogative *già* should not in principle be considered as exclusively 'regional', possibly extending to Italian in general, Cerruti (2009, 113–114) lists it among the regional features typically characterizing North-Western varieties, as also suggested by Välikangas (2004) and confirmed by Fedriani and Miola (in press). Interestingly, folk linguistics from the web seems to help us in suggesting a solution, as is shown by the following metalinguistic comment apparently produced by a speaker belonging to another regional area, who stigmatizes the overuse of *già* attributing it to the area of Turin, the biggest urban agglomeration in Piedmont:

(8)   si ma i torinesi che dicono *"già"* quando non c'entra un cazzo [from www.]
      'yes but those from Turin who say "già" when there is no reason whatsoever to do so'

Additional empirical research is needed to map more carefully the actual geographical extent of this phenomenon, a task which goes beyond the perspective adopted in this work. However, the metalinguistic comment in (8) shows that, despite the controversy on geographical distribution, the occurrence of interrogative *già* in Italian can still be considered as a 'regional' phenomenon which is particularly frequent in some areas (typically in the North-West and especially in 'Piedmontese Italian'),[4] while being (still?) unknown in other areas (e.g. the Central Italian varieties spoken in Tuscany, which will be used as comparing terms).[5]

---

4.   Note that 'Piedmontese Italian' is the variety of Italian spoken in a regional area in the North-West of Italy (Piedmont), which should not be confused with the substantially different local Romance vernacular directly descended from Latin ('Piedmontese dialect'). Using Maiden and Parry's (1997, 2) terminology, the variety that will be described here might be labelled as an 'Italian dialect' (i.e. a local variety of 'the standard Italian language') whereas the Piedmontese dialect belongs to the list of the 'dialects of Italy'.

5.   A detailed assessment of the geographical boundaries of this phenomenon should also take into account the fact that the North-Western area, where interrogative *già* appears to be more entrenchedly rooted, immediately borders areas where other particles occur as comparable interactional markers in direct wh-questions. This is the case of the varieties of regional Italian spoken in Liguria and Western Emilia, where *più* 'more' and *pure* 'also' occur with the same function as Piedmontese *già* (Fedriani and Miola, in press). This seems to support the hypothesis that also French *déjà* should be considered as an areal feature (Välikangas 2004) influenced the German MP *schon* along the Romance/Germanic borders (especially in French-speaking Switzerland).

Disregarding the details of the geographical distribution of these 'interrogative' uses, *déjà* and *già* will be interpreted in Section 2.1 as pragmatic markers having properties typically associated with MPs. In so doing, the morphosyntactic features of French *déjà* and regional Italian *già* will be analyzed along with their functional nature, whose connection to information structure will also be discussed.

2.1   *Già* as a MP: Formal and functional properties

In describing the interactional function of French interrogative *déjà* in (1) Hansen (2008, 213) elaborates on its role as a speech act modifier clearly suggesting an interpretation as a modalizer ("downtoner [...] of directive speech acts"), which corresponds to some characterizations of MPs as elements which "crucially refer to participants' stance toward speech acts" (Waltereit 2001, Detges and Waltereit 2009, 54). Nonetheless, Hansen (2008, 213) also insists on the extra-sentential syntactic behaviour of French interrogative *déjà* by remarking that it "is always right-detached with respect to the host utterance". In her analysis, this peripheral location is significant in confirming that *déjà* "scopes the speech act level" (Hansen 2008, 213), but, if one considers that one of the main defining features of MPs is traditionally recognized in their structural insertion within the clause (cf. Diewald 2006, 408, this volume, and previous literature on German *Abtönungspartikeln* quoted therein) periphericity might be considered as a counterargument to the interpretation of French interrogative *déjà* as a MP. It can be counter-objected that French *déjà* is not necessarily right-dislocated and can in fact be placed within the VP, as this example demonstrates:

(9)   bonjour quel est *déjà* votre niveau initial (V, IV, III?)
       'hello what's ALREADY your starting level (5, 4, 3?)'

The same holds for regional Italian *già*, which can be placed between the verb and argumental NPs:

(10) come si chiamano *già* questi pantaloni? [informal conversation, Turin[6]]
       'what's ALREADY the name of these trousers?'

(11) ma quando devono cambiare, *già*, Windows
                              (Cerruti 2009, 113 [oral corpus of regional Italian])
       'but when should they change ALREADY Windows'

---

6.   Apart from the examples extracted from the web or quoted from previous literature (Bazzanella et al. 2005, Cerruti 2009) the rest of the Western-Italian data presented in what follows was collected from every-day conversations I personally heard in Turin in January-June 2011.

In commenting (11) Cerruti (2009, 113) mentions the intonational nature of *già* as a parenthetical element (signalled by the two commas in his transcription), which might suggest an extra-sentential position. Nonetheless, a parenthetical location contrasts with the possibility of inserting *già* within the complementizer of a cleft question, where an intonational (parenthetical) breakdown would be impossible:[7]

(12)   com'è *già* che si fa a calcolare la media? [informal conversation, Turin]
       'how do you calculate
       (lit. 'how is it ALREADY that you calculate') the average mark?'

These data show that, despite being a speech act modifier, *déjà/già* can be 'topologically integrated' within the structure of the clause (Gerdes and Kahane 2007), which strengthens it as a MP. This behaviour contrasts with the interjectional use of *già* mentioned above (3), which will be more thoroughly analyzed in Section 3. While interjections constitute prosodically independent utterances at the beginning of a turn and are therefore "discourse-structurally governed" (Detges and Waltereit 2009, 45), *déjà/già* as 'MPs' can be found within the syntactic structure of the clause with different degrees of topological integration that include the right periphery but also the morphosyntactic nucleus of a cleft sentence.[8]

Apart from their morphosyntactic properties, the interpretation of interrogative *déjà/già* as MPs is also strengthened by their interactional nature. As mentioned by Hansen (2008, 213) in commenting (1), "[t]ypically, *déjà* will be used in this way in contexts where the addressee has already stated his name at some earlier point during the same speech event". A comparable description, which appears to be an analytical reformulation of what has been defined as a backchecking context (Klein 1994, Waltereit 2001), might hold for the regional Italian use of interrogative *già* (Bazzanella et al. 2005, 55, fn. 23, Cerruti 2009, 113).

In the regional Italian example in (13) the backchecking interpretation is made explicit by reference to the popularity of a song ('It is very famous') that the speaker had repeatedly tried to tune without remembering it correctly. In requesting the addressee's help the speaker assumes shared encyclopaedic knowledge, which is linguistically signalled by means of the particle *già*:

---

7.   The possibility of inserting *già* into the syntactic core of the clause is confirmed by Fedriani and Miola (in press), who nonetheless suggest that intra-syntactic location might be influenced by sociolinguistic factors, with younger speakers preferring a peripheral location of *già*.

8.   A non-peripheral location can also be found in (i), where *già* precedes the right-dislocated topical pronoun *lui* 'he':

(i)   Diego, che numero ha *già*, lui? [informal conversation, Turin]
      'What's Diego's number? (lit. Diego, what number has already, he?')

(13) e come fa *già*? che è famosissima [informal conversation, Turin]
'how does it go, ALREADY? It is very famous [the topic is a well-known melody]'

Backchecking strategies have been considered by Waltereit (2001) as a typical functional equivalent of what would be expressed by a MP in German and other Germanic languages. Significantly, in my regional Italian data a functional correlation with backchecking is confirmed by the frequent syntagmatic combination of *già* with a backchecking Imperfect, which is precisely the strategy that Waltereit (2001) considers as a Romance equivalent of Germanic MPs (cf. also Bazzanella et al. 2005, 55):

(14) come *si chiamava già* quel tizio? [informal conversation, Turin]
'what was [IMPERFECT] ALREADY the name of that guy?'

More generally, backchecking can be connected to the 'non-initial' status in the information flow that Diewald (2006, this volume) and Diewald et al. (2009, 197) consider as the basic function of MPs. The 'presuppositional' meaning inherently linked to backchecking is the functional core of interrogative *déjà/già*, which presuppose previous knowledge, thus qualifying the information requested in the interrogative speech act as <u>already</u> 'given'. Obviously, enquiring on something which is not informationally 'new' is rather unusual (we normally ask for something we don't know) but is contextually justified by the fact that the speaker has momentarily forgotten that piece of information. Even though not infrequent in everyday life, this is a pragmatically marked situation, which is iconically represented by the behaviour of French and North-Western Italian speakers, who morphosyntactically mark this type of question (*Erinnerungsfrage*, according to Franck 1980 and Välikangas 2004) by means of a MP.[9] Presupposition also justifies the combination of interrogative *già* with wh-interrogative sentences (Cerruti 2009, 113), which inherently trigger more presupposed elements than 'yes/no' questions, where an interrogative *già* is described as ungrammatical (Cerruti 2009, 113, Fedriani and Miola, in press).

Summing up the results reached so far it can be concluded that the interrogative use of *già* in North-Western Italian is characterized by the possibility of topological integration, a formal property which is coupled by a functional specialization

---

9.   Fedriani and Miola (in press) provide a typological overview of the *Erinnerungsfragepartikeln* in the languages of Europe, where, apart from showing a generalized tendency to mark the special pragmatic nature of these questions, the authors also recognize various lexical source of the particles used ('inchoative' particles as in French *déjà* and North-Western Italian *già*, 'iterative' particles as in English *again* or Belgian French *encore* and 'cumulative' particles as in Ligurian Italian *più* 'more, cf. also fn. 5).

(backchecking) connected to information status. On the basis of these discrimina-
tory features it has been argued that an interrogative *già* can be included among
Romance MPs. In the next section the results on the role of information structure
will be extended from interrogative *già* to its interjectional function, underlining the
similarities between the two uses, which will both turn out to be linked, albeit in different ways, to the marking of 'given' information. But, despite functional compara-
bility, the two uses radically differ in their syntactic and scopal properties, which will
become particularly clear in contrasting the topological integration demonstrated
above for the interrogative use with the 'holophrastic' nature of interjections, which
makes them recalcitrant to any form of structural insertion within the clause.

3.   Interjectional *già*

In introducing a comparison between the interrogative use of *già* as a MP described in Section 2 and the interjectional use that will analyzed in detail below a
preliminary proviso on the geographical distribution of the two phenomena is
needed. While the interrogative use of *già* belongs to regional features and might
be ungrammatical in some areas (see the discussion in Section 2 above), *già* used
as an interjection has no special regional flavour, thus occurring in North-Western
Italian as well as in other areas. However, regional differentiation can be detected
if one considers the possibility of reinforcing an interjectional *già* with a preposed
vowel. These vocalizations show a certain degree of variation, and, again, the
North-Western area turns out to be particularly productive in this domain having
its special form of vocalized *già* (*oh già*). A description in discursive terms is given
in a specific section (3.3).

3.1   Confirmativity

When used as an interjection (Poggi 1995) Italian *già* belongs to the list of 'pro-
sentential' particles (Bernini 1995, Ortu 2003) occupying the same paradigmatic
slot that is more generally covered by the Italian affirmative particle *sì* 'yes':

(15)   S1: Vuoi uscire?
      S2: *Sì/Già*
      'S1: Would you like to go out?
      S2: *Yes/Right*'

However, despite the fact that, as is the case in (15), *sì* and *già* may share the same
distribution, the affirmative function of *già* has a special informational nature which
makes it not freely interchangeable with *sì* 'yes'. Those who have described this

interjectional use of *già* (Bazzanella 1995, 242, Bernini 1995, 220, Poggi 1995, 415, Hansen and Strudsholm 2008, 496–497) have all emphasized the role of information structure ('given'/'new' information) in this interjection as opposed to the unmarked choice of *sì*. While the latter is the generalized form occurring in any affirmative context, *già* is a marked form, whose occurrence is limited to a more restricted set of contexts in which the relevant piece of information is not 'new', or, as Hansen and Strudsholm (2008, 497) put it, is conceived as "unsurprising". In order to grasp the different informational import of *sì* and *già* consider that in a context such as (15) *già* could only replace *sì* if the requested information ('Would you like to go out?') is contextually represented as already activated within the informational background shared by the two speakers. The requirement imposed by this contextual scenario might be fulfilled if, for instance, speaker 2 stands close to the front door with his coat on and ready to go out. In this case, inferential reasoning (Bernini 1995, 221) is activated by external evidence (the coat on), which is directly perceivable to both discourse participants and therefore considered as 'already given'. By referring to 'given' information *già* functions as a 'confirmative' marker, which confirms what is somehow already evident in the relevant context. While *sì* can be more generally defined as an 'affirmative' particle, *già* is more specifically a 'confirmative particle'. As a consequence, *già* is particularly appropriate as a reply to a positively oriented question (Hansen and Strudsholm 2008, 496–497) used as a request of confirmation (*Vuoi uscire, vero?* 'You want to go out, don't you?').

The interpretation in which the relevant information is activated by 'direct evidence' is not the only context making the occurrence of the confirmative particle *già* appropriate. Generally speaking, what triggers confirmativity is the degree of activation, which implies that, apart from the case imagined above in which the relevant information is activated by direct evidence, common world knowledge that for any number of reasons discourse participants consider as mutually shared and therefore always retrievable can always allow the construal of a confirmative situation.[10] For instance, if both speaker 1 and 2 know that speaker 2 regularly goes out for a walk at

---

10. Since the main focus here is on comparing these interjections with MPs, it might be relevant to recall that the role of 'evidentiality' including external evidence, inferences and reports of common world knowledge has also been suggested for MPs. Among the contextual factors triggering the use of German *Abtönungspartikeln* König (1991) explicitly refers to 'evidential' elements, as they can for instance be detected in the use of German *ja*. In the following pair of examples (from König 1997, 70, Waltereit 2001, 1398) the occurrence of *ja* is linked to evidence derived either from external sensory data (i) or from commonly shared sources ('As you know'):

  (i)   Dein Mantel ist *ja* ganz schmutzig!
        'But your coat is all dirty!'

 (ii)   Die Malerei war *ja* schon immer sein Hobby.
        '(*As you know*), painting has always been his hobby.'

noon and speaker 1 poses the question in (15) at 11.55 am, speaker 2 may freely interchange between *sì* and *già* as affirmative particles, thus recognizing the confirmative interpretation triggered by mutually shared information.

The crucial role played by confirmativity explains why *già* is not only an answering particle used to respond questions but it also occurs as a generalized reply to declarative statements (Bernini 1995, 221). Replacing the question in (15) with a declarative sentence would not prevent either *sì* or *già* being used as 'replying' particles:

(16) S1: È simpatico
        S2: *Sì/Già*
        'S1: He is nice
        S2: *Yes/I know*'

When occurring in replies to declarative statements confirmation of 'already' given information is the only possible value, which neutralizes the differences between *già* and *sì*. Unlike the question in (15), the declarative statement in (16) does not request S2 to provide information, and therefore the reply *sì/già* can only be intended as a confirmation elliptically echoing what S1 has just said, either because S2 already knew the relevant propositional content or because some external evidence indicates that S1's statement is correct.

Note that Italian *già*, unlike its unmarked counterpart *sì*, is primarily a phasal adverb meaning 'already', which, as interpreted by Hansen and Strudsholm (2008), 'contextually' acquires this interjectional function as a confirmative marker. The holophrastic context in (16) also admits a temporal-aspectual interpretation of 'already', but, significantly, the form used might be morphologically differentiated by integrating *già* with a prepositional element. Even though the prepositional form (*di già*) is not obligatory for a temporal-aspectual interpretation (in (17) a simple *già* might also be used), it should be stressed that the distribution of *già* and *di già* is not totally overlapping, since *di già* is restricted to a TAM reading and would not be admitted as a confirmative particle replacing a simple *già* in (15–16).

(17) S1: Vorrei uscire
        S2: *Di già?*
        'S1: I would like to go out
        S2: *Already?*'

The prepositional form *di già* in (17) parallels the diachronic evolution of French *déjà* in which the form deriving from a prepositional precursor (Latin *de* + *iam*) has replaced Old French *ja*. While French *déjà* has ousted *ja*, Italian *già* and *di già* coexist in the current synchronic stage, even though the latter is a very marked form whose occurrence, apart from the holophrastic context in (17), is either regional or obsolete. However, the specialization of current Italian *di già* as an interjectional form restricted to a temporal-aspectual interpretation with no confirmative function shows the tendency to produce formal differentiations (*già* vs. *di già*) which ultimately supports a functional partition between the grammatical domain represented by TAM marking (where both *già* and *di già* are possible) and 'context-based' uses as a confirmative interaction (which only admit *già*). The importance of formal differentiations in expressing functional distinctions will be elaborated further in the following section by analyzing those cases in which *già* is reinforced by a syntagmatic combination with other interjections, thus providing a formal differentiation of the interjectional uses of *già* with respect not only to the temporal-aspectual marker but also to the MP described in Section 2.

3.2   Syntagmatic combinations of *già* with other interjections

Apart from *sì*, *già* and an extremely varied array of lexical items (Poggi 1995), standard Italian also admits the possibility of using long as well as extra-long vowels (*ah, uh, eh, oh, aah, ooh*, etc.) as interjections. The exact list and distributions of these vocalic interjections is characterized by regional variation and submitted to restrictions of diverse nature (Poggi 1995), which will not be dealt with in detail in what follows, where, instead, I will focus on the empirical observation that some of these vocalizations also occur as preposed elements syntagmatically combined to the interjection *già* described above (*ah già* and *eh già* are commonly admitted).[11] These agglutinations appear to be syntagmatically constrained (vowels can only be preposed, postpositions being not grammatical: **già eh*) as well as paradigmatically restricted (only some vowels can be agglutinated). In this respect, geo-dialectal differences become relevant and will be described in this section, especially because they involve the regional variety under scrutiny (North-Western Italian), where the list of syntagmatic combinations includes *oh già* in addition to the agglutinated form admitted in other varieties (*ah già* and *eh già*) and described as standard forms in Poggi (1995). All in all, these agglutinated forms confirm the role of information structure as the major functional feature governing the selection of these interjections.

As described in Bernini (1995, 220–221), *eh già* and *ah già* substantially differ in several functional aspects connected to their semantic and pragmatic properties, which are also significantly linked to information structure. As noticed by Poggi (1995, 419–420), when used alone as a single interjection, *ah* is a marker of

---

11.   Agglutination of two interjections is in fact a more general phenomenon which also includes the possibility of duplicating the same interjection (*sì sì* as well as *già già* are well attested reduplication in Italian, cf. Välikangas 2000).

'new' information and this function is also transmitted to the agglutinative form *ah già*. Since *già* has the opposite value ('given' information), the potential clash between 'new' and 'given' is functionally balanced by producing a combined meaning which expresses 'sudden remembrance' of something that the speaker had accidentally forgotten and suddenly comes to his/her mind again. In this combination the 'surprise effect' is triggered by *ah* as a marker of new information,[12] while *già* maintains its stable connection to given information ('the speaker used to know that piece of information'). As a consequence of this combined meaning, *ah già* cannot as such occur as an affirmative particle in answering a question, as it is instead the case with an unvocalized *già* (see (15) above). By using *ah già* as a reply to a question (18), the request for information is not positively or negatively answered. The speaker is rather signalling that the propositional content of the question or what the propositional content might trigger as conversational implicatures were contingently forgotten. For instance S2 in (18) might indicate that, albeit planned, the idea of going out belonged to S2's previously acquired knowledge:

(18)   S1: Vuoi uscire?
       S2: *Ah già!*
       'S1: Would you like to go out?
       S2: *Oh. I forgot it!*'

Consistently with this informational function, *ah già* is appropriate as a reply to a declarative statement, whose propositional content is confirmed by suddenly remembering it:

(19)   S1: Oggi è domenica e i negozi sono chiusi
       S2: *Ah già!*
       'S1: Today is Sunday and shops are closed
       S2: *Oh. I forgot it!*'

As opposed to the function of 'sudden remembrance' characterizing *ah già*, the agglutination of *già* with a front mid vowel (*eh già*) produces a different informational function, which makes it possible as a proper answering particle:

(20)   S1: Vuoi uscire?
       S2: *Eh già!*
       'S1: Would you like to go out?
       S2: *Right!*'

---

12.   Via 'surprise' the function of these interjectional markers might be connected to mirativity, another highly controversial category (DeLancey 1997, Lazard 1999) which is also strictly related to information status. In particular, mirative markers signal the surprise produced by extraordinarily 'new' information in the speaker's unprepared mind.

As is apparent from the different English translations of *Eh già* ('Right!) and *Ah già!* ('Oh, I forgot it!') in (20) and (18) respectively, the former functions as an answering particle in confirming the propositional content of the question, while *Ah gia!* in (18) simply qualifies the propositional content of the question (or its implicatures) as information which, even though already given, was accidentally forgotten. Form this point of view, *eh già* is a substitutive form of a simple *già* described in Section 3.1 above, with which it shares the interjectional role as an answering particle expressing confirmativity.

Apparently, the only difference between the vocalized form in (20) and an unvocalized *già* in a comparable context (15) has to do with the degree of expectedness, which, like the other uses of an interjectional *già*, is ultimately connected to information status ('given information'). Native speakers tend to agree that the vocalized form *eh già* expresses a stronger degree of confirmativity in which the speaker more explicitly shows certainty in the relevant propositional content. Stronger certainty may be contextually exploited to express different degrees of expectedness from other discourse participants. In (20) the selection of *eh già* instead of *già* might signal that S2 is aware that that his/her desire to go out, albeit derivable from external evidence (e.g., the coat on) or based on shared knowledge, will possibly sound unexpected or controversial to S1. From an interactional perspective, such a contrast of expectations among discourse participants might be variedly exploited in negotiating reciprocal stances in dialogic interactions. For instance, by using the vocalized form S2 might recognize and prevent further S1's objections to something which, even though not uncontroversial, S2 considers as not under discussion. Whatever formal representation of this interactional dynamics one should eventually prefer, the basic assumption is that *ah già* and *eh già* both signal unexpectedness, but, at the same time, they require opposite orientations with respect to the discourse participants to whom unexpectedness is attributed. While *ah già* signals the speaker's sudden surprise at something that is unexpected because it was forgotten, by using *eh già* as an answering particle the speaker attributes potential surprise to the addressee, whose 'unprepared mind' is focussed in order to fulfil various interactional objectives. More research on authentic data from oral corpora would be needed to verify native speakers' intuitions on these subtle nuances, but, as will be argued in Section 3.3, the behaviour of North-Western speakers when using their local vocalized forms (*oh già*) fits well in the speaker/addressee dynamics suggested by the opposition between *ah già* and *eh già* as just described.

The bulk of the data presented here regarding the use of agglutinated forms of *già* confirms the role of information structure as the regulating notion governing the interactional use of these interjections. Taken all together, the three interjections scrutinized so far (*già* and its two vocalized variants *ah già* and *eh già*) demonstrate the existence of a paradigmatic set of interjections used to signal a varied array of contextual nuances which, albeit diverse in their possible interactional uses, are all connected to the same discourse domain, and ultimately have to do with the degree of activation of discourse referents. In all of these markers the original TAM meaning of the adverb *già* 'already' still influences their discourse uses (what is discursively 'given' *already* belongs to shared knowledge among discourse participants). Either used as sheer confirmative particles (*già, eh già*) or additionally signalling 'sudden remembrance' (*ah già*), they all refer to previously acquired ('already given') knowledge.

3.3   From confirmativity to conclusivity: North-Western Italian *oh già*

With respect to the general picture characterizing the use of vocalized interjections in standard Italian, the data provided by North-Western varieties corroborate the paradigmatic system of pragmatic markers presented above by adding a form in which *già* is reinforced by a back mid vowel (*oh già*). Even though *oh* and *già* do exist as independent interjections in standard Italian, their syntagmatic combination seems to be peculiar to the regional variety spoken in the North-West. Apart from enriching the list of combinatorial possibilities between *già* and the set of vowels independently used as interjections, North-Western *oh già* also seems to fill a functional gap within the system of vocalized forms of *già* admitted in standard Italian. As suggested above, standard Italian *ah già* and *eh già* can be opposed by measuring the degree of activation of the information marked with these interjections in which two discourse participants, as distinct deictic poles, play different roles. While *ah già* marks the speaker's unprepared mind, *eh già* focuses on the addressee's expectations as they are imagined and prevented by the speaker. The same functional distinctions characterize the use of *ah già* and *eh già* in North-Western Italian, where, however, speakers have the additional possibility of avoiding the deictic bifurcation between *ah già* and *eh già* by using *oh già*, which, interestingly, seems to neutralize any confrontation between S1 and S2 by marking information whose degree of activation is presented as equally recognized by all discourse participants. *Oh già* can be described as a neuter confirmative interjection recognizing that the speaker and the addressee share the same degree of responsibility in accepting that the relevant piece of information belongs to given information and has therefore to be trusted.

A typical context in which *oh già* occurs in the North-West is represented by the dialogue in (21), where *oh già* closes a discourse segment by confirming what S1 has just said and presenting it as shared information equally expected by both discourse participants and therefore accepted as uncontroversial.

(21) S1: Da quel dottore lì devi aspettare almeno due ore ogni volta
      S2: *Oh già!* [informal conversation, Turin]
      'S1: When you go to that doctor's, you have to wait at least two hours
            every time
      S2: Right!'

Due to its 'neuter' character as a marker of confirmative agreement among discourse participants *oh già* can interestingly be exploited in conversational dynamics, where it is reinterpreted as a marker of conclusivity. A similar function has also been detected in Spanish *ya* 'already', whose interactional 'neutrality' as a discourse regulator has been pointed out by Delbecque and Maldonado (2011, 75). Not differently from Spanish *ya* (Martín Zorraquino and Portolés 1999, 4192), by using North-Western Italian *oh già* the confirmative meaning is discursively reinterpreted as a signal that the topic is satisfactorily settled, which might have two discursive consequences: either the conversation ends (this was actually the case in the specific context, which I personally witnessed) or a new topic can be initiated.[13] In this function *oh già* typically allows a speaker to take the turn only to confirm the point made by the other speaker without maintaining it afterwards, which reinforces the conclusive nature of this marker.

When distinguishing between DMs and MPs Diewald (2006, 406, this volume) insists on the fact the former "relate items of discourse to other items of linguistically expressed discourse", this observation being rephrased by Detges and Waltereit (2009, 44) with their characterization of DMs as elements denoting a "two-place relationship". Conclusivity can be very naturally interpreted along the lines suggested by Diewald (2006, this volume) and Detges and Waltereit (2009, 44) as a relationship between different discourse chunks (S1's argument and S2's confirmative conclusion). The interpretation of *oh già!* as a DM is also confirmed by its role in turn alternation, which is undoubtedly a prototypical function connected to DMs (Detges and Waltereit 2009, 44). Even though *per se* an interjection is not a DM, by structuring discourse organization *oh già* tends to be used as a "phatic" and "receptive" regulator, which makes it possible to interpret it as a DM *stricto sensu* (Diewald 2006, Detges and Waltereit 2009, 44). Nonetheless, it should be borne in mind that *oh già* is still a prosentential particle which crucially refers

---

13. By modulating the intonational contour of the utterance it is also possible to reverse the original confirmative meaning thus expressing irony and incredulity and possibly non-confirmativity. Apart from being well attested in the corresponding Spanish DM *ya* (Martín Zorraquino and Portolés 1999, 4191, Delbecque and Maldonado 2011, 75), this 'reversive' modulation, which is also common with other particles (the Italian affirmative interjection *sì* 'yes' can also express incredulity and irony, if modulated with the appropriate intonational contour), simply confirms that confirmativity is the main function which can be contextually reversed by means of intonational modulation.

to the propositional content of S1's previous statement (Bernini 1995). The interjection is not solely shaping "the structure or form of discourse" (Detges and
Waltereit 2009, 44) and cannot therefore be totally equated to a DM. The comparison between *oh già* and the metadiscursive use of *già* that will be analyzed in
the next section will clarify this point by permitting us to measure the extent of the
transition between what is still an interjection, albeit textually exploited as a discourse regulator, and what is a proper DM.

3.4   Where interjections become DMs: metadiscursive *già*

In the analysis conducted above confirmativity has been demonstrated as the overall function encompassing various interjectional uses of *già*, while in Section 3.3 it
has been suggested how confirmativity can be textually reinterpreted as connected
to discourse regulation in which it signals topic conclusivity. However, this is not
the only possibility in extending the discursive scope of an interjection, especially if
one considers those contexts in which the interjection is not an answering particle
but a reply to a declarative statement. Quite naturally, these replies in which *già*
marks dialogic confirmativity (see (16) and (19) above) may represent bridging
contexts to metadiscursive uses in which what is confirmed is not the propositional
context of previous statements, but the structure of the dialogic exchange in itself.

A displacement from semantic content to discourse structuring is exactly what
happens with the Italian answering particle *sì* when used as a phatic signal of back
channelling (as is for instance the case when *sì* replaces the more stereotyped
Italian *pronto* 'hello' as the listener's initiating formula in answering a phone call).
As pointed out by Bernini (1995, 180–181), the metadiscursive nature of these
uses crosses the boundary between prosentential interjections, whose function is
still connected to the propositional content of the preceding utterance, and
'discourse markers' (*segnali discorsivi* 'discourse signals' in Bernini's 1995 as well as
in Bazzanella's 1995 terminology), where the link to the propositional content is
missing (in answering a phone call there is no propositional content to be confirmed). In comparing *sì* and *già* from this perspective it is interesting to observe
that the latter has not developed so far as to cover the whole range of metadiscursive functions connected to the phatic uses of *sì* (for instance, it may not be used
by the listener in answering a phone call). Nonetheless, Bernini (1995, 212) interestingly pointed out a special context (also cited by Hansen and Strudsholm 2008,
496) in which *già* occurs as a proper DM, having lost any reference to the propositional content of preceding utterances and assuming a metadiscursive function.
This is clearly the case in (22), where *già*, instead of confirming the propositional
content of what has been just said, is rather used to confirm the adequacy of the
speech act represented by the question posed by S2 (*Dove?* 'Where?').

(22) S1: Ti scriverò
      S2: Dove?
      S1: *Già*. Dove?
      'S1: I'll write to you
      S2: Where?
      S1: *You're right*. Where?'

Despite the promise to write, S1 does not know S2's address and consequently recognizes that the conversational move made by S2 is metadiscursively adequate. Interestingly, *già* keeps its original confirmative value (S1 confirms that S2's question is correct), which, however, is shifted from informational content to metadiscursive modification. In the perspective adopted here, this behaviour may be instructive in demonstrating how the retention of the original discursive function as a marker of information structure also characterizes the evolution towards metadiscursive functions. What is common to all uses of *già* considered so far is their connection to information structure which constantly refers to given information.

In order to complete the comparison between *già* and *sì*, it can be observed that while in (16) above both interjections were proven as possible, *già* being the marked form of *sì* in contexts where contextually given information can be confirmed, in (22) *sì* would not be appropriate as a substitutive form of *già*. This confirms that when used as a metadiscursive marker *già* enters a new domain where the paradigmatic correlation with the unmarked interjection *sì* no longer applies. Conversely, the metadiscursive uses typical of *sì* as a phatic marker (as, for instance, at the outset of a phone call) cannot be expressed by *già*, which indicates the tendency of these two interjectional markers to separate their distributional behaviours once they cover metadiscursive functions.

The descriptive account on the interjectional use of *già* and its vocalized forms provided in the whole of Section 3 has displayed the rich array of discursive functions covered by this marker in Italian with a special focus on the North-Western variety. In particular, its role as a pro-sentential particle of confirmativity which tends to develop towards textual conclusivity and may also lose any connection to the propositional content of preceding utterances by developing purely metadiscursive uses has shown its gradual transition towards DMs. Having concluded the descriptive analysis, we are now in a position to propose a comparative assessment of the functional and formal properties of North-Western *già* as a MP described in Section 2. This will be undertaken in the next section, where North-Western Italian data will be comprehensively reappraised by also elucidating their interplay with the behaviour of the other Romance languages mentioned throughout this work.

4.   North-Western Italian *già* between MPs and DMs

Table 2 sums up the main results of the discussion developed above by placing them into the same comparative model already presented in Table 1 (Section 1.1), from which the whole discussion was originated. As a consequence of the analysis presented in Sections 2–3 Hansen's (2008) structural labels ('interrogative' and 'interjection') have been replaced by more general functional characterizations ('MP' and 'DM', respectively) and a fourth column has been added to account for the behaviour of N(orth-)W(estern) regional Italian. Considering that the geographical distribution of the interrogative use of *già* in other varieties of Italian is still poorly investigated, which also affects a correct interpretation of the extent to which this phenomenon has extended to Italian in general (see the discussion in Section 2.1 above), the North-Western varieties, which appear to cover the area in which this phenomenon is majorly represented, are contrasted with other varieties where it does not occur. As announced in Section 2.1, Central Italian regional varieties such as those spoken in Tuscany will be taken here as representatives of this behaviour, without excluding the possibility that the same distribution might be found in other regions.

As is graphically apparent from Table 2, the main result of the comparative analysis conducted above is that in North-Western Italian, unlike the other Romance languages considered here, *già* cumulates the two functions under scrutiny (MP and DM) in one and the same form, thus also distinguishing itself from other Italian varieties, in which it is only used as a DM (prototypically represented by *già* as a metadiscursive interjection). The distribution of *già* in Central Italian only covers a subset of the functions admitted by the more extensive use of North-Western *già*. However, my aim in interpreting the data schematized in Table 2 is not simply to observe which language admits which function, but rather to point out the bifurcation between two main language types. On the one hand, some languages (actually the majority in our small sample: French, Spanish and Central Italian) show a 'privative' distribution, in which the occurrence of one of the two functions excludes the other. On the opposite side, one finds the case of North-Western Italian, in which a 'cumulative' distribution occurs. Now, the occurrence of contradictory findings (cognates that tend to bifurcate their uses in sister

Table 2.   Romance descendants from Latin (de)iam: DMs vs. MPs

	French	Spanish	Central Italian	NW Italian
MP	+	–	–	+
DM	–	+	+	+

languages, while in some languages there is one form cumulating the two uses) suggests an internally composite explanation which should not only indicate what the two interactional uses presented above have in common, but also permit us to define their differential features.

Trying to explain first the cumulative distribution found in North-Western Italian, I think that the analyses presented above do indicate a common functional feature shared by MPs and DMs which can justify why they are expressed by the same marker. In my view, this unifying feature is to be found in the common reference to information structure. Despite more specific differences, what backchecking and the different forms of confirmativity analyzed above have in common is that they all refer to given information. From this point of view, backchecking can be considered as the interrogative counterpart of what appears as a confirmative marker in a declarative sentence (see also Cerruti 2009, 113). Even though in some cases confirmativity is variedly combined with other notions, as is the case with the 'mirative' surprise expressed by the interjection *ah già* (cf also fn. 12), confirmativity is still the primary functional feature encompassing the whole spectrum of uses covered by an interactional *già*. However, what counts more in my perspective is that 'given information' not only characterizes backchecking as well as the varied list of subfunctions expressed by interjectional *già*, but it also affects its metadiscursive use as a proper DM *stricto sensu*, where confirmativity refers to discourse structure instead of denoting a contextually given propositional content. This demonstrates that becoming a DM does not require losing the original link to information structure, which ultimately retains the function of 'already' as a TAM marker.

'Information status', also labelled as 'knowledge status', has often been recognized as a grammatical category paradigmatically marked by dedicated particles in some (mostly Asian) languages (DeLancey 1986, Choi 1995). According to Choi (1995, 168) 'knowledge status' denotes "the degree to which knowledge has been integrated in the speaker's mind", which implies a basic distinction to be drawn between 'given' and 'new' information. 'Knowledge status' admits different degrees of accessibility to the information "on the part of the speaker and the listener" (Choi 1995, 169), in which the amount of information that the speaker has just acquired from the present context should also be included. Given these definitions, backchecking and the various types of confirmativity discussed above seem to smoothly accommodate within the general notion of 'information status', a grammatical category that in some of the languages where it has been detected (DeLancey 1986, Choi 1995) is also paradigmatically connected to evidentiality and mirativity.

In my opinion, recognizing a unifying notion which might cover the different uses considered above provides compelling evidence in support of a close relationship between the two pragmatic phenomena under scrutiny in this book, ultimately reinforcing the positions of those who, like Bazzanella (2006, 2009), tend to minimize the discrepancies between MPs and DMs by advocating a general solution in which the two categories belong to the same discursive tier. Nonetheless, we still need to explain why Table 2 also contains cases of privative distribution. In other words, it must be explained why Spanish, French and Central Italian keep MPs formally separate from DMs, thus appearing insensitive to the same functional principles governing North-Western Italian. In this respect, the discursive behaviour of interjections, which are holophrastically characterized by the absence of any syntactic constraints, is illuminating in demonstrating their formally different status from MPs, which, on the contrary, show syntactic restrictions. Following Diewald (2006) and Detges and Walltereit (2009), I think that, whatever functional similarity might be detected with DMs, these morphosyntactic restrictions of MPs and the scopal differences that derives from morphosyntax should not be underestimated. From this point of view DMs and MPs radically differ and it is therefore not surprising that the use of *già* as a DM (the metadiscursive *già* described in Section 3.4) derives from the interjectional use of *già*, whose non-sentential holophrasticity may acquire the extrasentential scope which is necessary to regulate and connect discourse chunks.

As a conclusion, the composite explanation extracted from Table 2 seems to suggest further elaboration connected to the main research thread proposed by our editors (*Modal particles and discourse markers: two sides of the same coin?*) By looking at North-Western Italian *già*, it might be answered that they are in fact two sides of the same coin, whose unifying feature is provided by information status. On the other hand, formal properties including morphosyntactic and scopal behaviour keep the two coins mutually exclusive. North-Western Italian data also contain specific features that might be indicative of a tendency to introduce formal differentiations among the various uses of *già*. Agglutinated vowels that can only be added to the interjection but not to interrogative *già* provide a formal differentiation between MPs and those uses of *già* that tend to develop in the functional direction of DMs.

As to the role of information status, one might additionally wonder whether this is a generalized feature whose unifying nature can be extended to other cases in which MPs and DMs show complex boundaries. Alternatively, it might be argued that the importance of information status in the case under scrutiny here is a mere epiphenomenal effect due to the original meaning of the TAM marker 'already', which intrinsically refers to 'given' information. This is an empirical issue that requires comparative data from other semantic and grammatical domains and cannot, therefore, be addressed now. However, before concluding I would like to add a final comparative point which complements the description of French *déjà* and its

North-Western Italian counterpart by showing that in a language where the overlap between MP and DM does not apply (French *déjà* as opposed to regional Italian *già* is only used as a MP and not as a DM, cf. Table 2), the role of information status is less stable and MPs tend to evolve towards more general illocutionary domains.

As summed up in Table 2, French and regional Italian share the same interrogative use. Nonetheless, upon closer inspection I have observed that the similarity between French and regional Italian only covers some of the relevant data. As its regional Italian counterpart, French *déjà* is 'typically' (Hansen 2008, 213) used as a backchecking strategy, but, while in regional Italian this is the only function of interrogative *già* as a MP, French interrogative *déjà* appears to be compatible with contexts in which the backchecking function does not apply. This is for instance the case in (23), where the speaker and the addressee have just got in touch for the first time on the net (the addressee has been enquiring about job opportunities). Lacking previous acquaintance, backchecking is not applicable. Even more explicitly the context in (24) clarifies that the addressee has not properly introduced himself (*tu commence[s] par te presenter* 'you start by introducing yourself') and therefore those addressed to him are 'real' informative questions and not backchecking questions referring to previously given information.

(23) Quelques questions: quel est déja ton dîplome et quel est ton but en voulant faire ces formations?
Ta réponse pourrait m'aider à te donner des pistes
Cordialement [from www]
'Some questions; what's ALREADY your degree and what's your goal with this education?
Your answer might help me to give you some hints
Best'

(24) Bonjour. Très bonne initiative mais je pense qu'il serait plus raisonnable que tu commence par te présenter et donner plus d'info déjà, sur ton cursus personnel au sein de ce nouveau parti. quel est déjà ton degré d'instruction? de quel écoles est tu issu? etc etc etc.
'Hello. A very good initiative but I think that it would be more reasonable that you start by introducing yourself and giving already more information, on your career in this party, what's ALREADY your level of education? what schools do you come from? etc. etc. etc.'

The interesting comparative point is that in similar contexts *già* would not be admitted even in those varieties of regional Italian where it does occur as a backchecking strategy, which shows that, if compared to its French cognate, regional Italian has a more restricted use of modal *già*.

Since backchecking is still the most 'typical' use of French interrogative *déjà* and this function is shared by the variety of regional Italian described above, it can be hypothesized with a decent degree of confidence that what we observe in (23–24) is an extension of the original backchecking function, eventually producing a French innovation which is not shared by neighbouring North-Western Italian varieties. Assuming that this French innovation is the result of pragmaticalization,[14] I think that reference to information status might be considered as an intermediate phase, followed by a subsequent stage corresponding to the current French distribution in which *déjà* is not restricted to backchecking, being instead a more general 'interrogative' marker. Evolving from backchecking to interrogative implies that the connection with information status tends to be loosened as the pragmatic evolution proceeds and *déjà* becomes more and more connected to the speech act in itself, instead of exclusively marking the degree of novelty of the requested information. When used as a generalized speech act modifier, *déjà* can be consistently considered a politeness strategy, as also hypothesized by Hansen (2008, 213), who suggests how backchecking might be reinterpreted in terms of politeness ("asking for the second time might be impolite and face-threatening"). Nonetheless, assuming a generalized interpretation via politeness cannot explain why regional Italian *già* does not extend to contexts such as (23–24). The behaviours of regional Italian and French demonstrate that we definitely need a unifying account (which might be connected to politeness) in order to explain the French extended distribution but we also need a modular interpretation that could justify the more restricted interpretation (backchecking only) in regional *già*. Due to its connections with information status, backchecking can be conceived as still being linked to the propositional content of the utterance (the degree of novelty of the propositional content)[15] and appears therefore reasonable as an intermediate stage between content-level uses and fully-fledged context level uses (Hansen 2008), the latter being anchored to the illocutionary

---

14. Well aware that, as convincingly concluded by Diewald (2011, 376), the whole debate on the boundary between pragmaticalization and grammaticalizaton ultimately relies on where one draws the dividing line between grammar and pragmatics, the choice of the term 'pragmaticalization' has been consistently selected under the assumption that in its evolutionary process the French marker *déjà* extends the role of prototypical pragmatic functions related to illocution and speech-act specifications. The data analyzed here seem to indicate that, in order to grasp the different evolutionary stages represented by French *déjà* and regional Italian *già*, a dividing line should be drawn between 'discourse grammar', which refers to information flow, and more extended 'pragmatic' modulations of illocutionary force represented by the French use of *déjà* as a speech-act downtoner (see Squartini, in press).

15. See Bazzanella (2006, 463, fn. 22) for a distinction between two different types of modalizers, those connected to social interaction and politeness and those linked to the propositional content.

domain of the speech act and more extensively compatible with questions as illocutionary types in general.[16] In a sense, backchecking and illocutionary modification of questions are both interactional dimensions which involve reference to the addressee's sphere and are therefore equally connected to intersubjectification (Traugott and Dasher 2002), but in fact they seem to represent different dimensions of intersubjectivity in the pragmatic dynamics between content and context.

5. Future research

A thorough description of the functional properties of North-Western *già* has shown to what extent DMs and MPs may derive their functional load from the same area of discourse grammar where information status and referents' activation degrees are regulated. Future research should concentrate on clarifying whether information status might be extended to other comparable pragmatic phenomena and how it is linked to principles suggested as general tenets encompassing the whole domain of MPs such as the notion of non-initial status in the information flow, which, according to Diewald (2006, this volume) and Diewald et al. (2009), characterizes MPs in general. However, it is the diachronic comparison between North-Western Italian and French suggested in the last section that especially demands more refined analyses on the pragmaticalization process of Romance 'already'. In developing this perspective Squartini (in press) pays particular attention to more thoroughly test the hypothesis of a gradual evolution from

---

16. As illocutionary modifiers, the Romance descendants of Latin *iam* tend to specialize in different illocutionary functions. As seen above, the use in direct questions is restricted to French *déjà* and North-Western Italian *già*, but French also admits a marginal use of *déjà* as a jussive marker in imperative sentences (i), which does not occur in standard and North-Western Italian. Instead, the jussive use is frequent in Spanish (ii) and Catalan (iii), where it covers various illocutionary acts including orders (ii) and permissions (iii):

    (i)   Montre-moi *déjà* ce que tu sais faire!   (Hansen 2008, 213)
         'Just show me what you can do!'

    (ii) ¡Lárgate *ya*!   (Bazzanella et al. 2005, 71)
         'Go away, now'

    (iii) *Ja* pots entrar, *ja*   (Torrent 2011, 89)
         'Right, you can come in now'

Interestingly, this list of illocutionary specializations is complemented by the behaviour of Occitan, where *ja* occurs in declarative sentences as an emphatic marker of assertiveness (Pusch 2007, 97–98), a distribution that, even though under different syntactic restrictions, can also be found in Sardinian (Bazzanella et al. 2005, 62–67, Calaresu in press).

the domain of discourse grammar, in which information status (either backchecking or confirmativity) plays a crucial role, and illocutionary modification, in which pragmatic interaction comes to the foreground.

References

Bazzanella, Carla. 1995. "I segnali discorsivi." In *Grande grammatica italiana di consultazione* 3, ed. by Lorenzo Renzi, Giampaolo Salvi, and Anna Cardinaletti, 225–257. Bologna: il Mulino.

Bazzanella, Carla. 2006. "Discourse markers in Italian: Towards a 'Compositional' Meaning." In *Approaches to discourse particles*, ed. by Kerstin Fischer, 449–464. Oxford/Amsterdam: Elsevier.

Bazzanella, Carla. 2009. "Review of Maj-Britt Mosegaard Hansen *Particles at the Semantics/ Pragmatics Interface: Synchronic and Diachronic Issues. A Study with Special Reference to the French Phasal Adverbs*, Amsterdam: Elsevier, 2008." *Journal of Pragmatics* 41 (7): 1468–1472.

Bazzanella, Carla, Cristina Bosco, Emilia Calaresu, Alessandro Garcea, Pura Guil, and Anda Radulescu. 2005. "Dal latino *iam* agli esiti nelle lingue romanze: verso una configurazione pragmatica complessiva." *Cuadernos de filología italiana* 12: 49–82.

Bazzanella, Carla, Cristina Bosco, Alessandro Garcea, Barbara Gili Fivela, Johanna Miecznikowski, and Francesca Tini Brunozzi. 2007. "Italian *allora*, French *alors*: Functions, Convergences, and Divergences." *Catalan Journal of Linguistics* 6: 9–30 [special issue *Contrastive Perspectives on Discourse Markers*, ed. by Maria Josep Cuenca].

Bernini, Giuliano. 1995. "Le profrasi." In *Grande grammatica italiana di consultazione 3*, ed. by Lorenzo Renzi, Giampaolo Salvi, and Anna Cardinaletti, 175–222. Bologna: il Mulino.

Buchi, Éva. 2007. "Approche diachronique de la (poli)pragmaticalisation de français *déjà* ("Quand le grammème est-il devenu pragmatème, déjà?")", in *Actes du XXIVᵉ Congrès International de Linguistique et de Philologie Romanes (Aberystwyth 2004)*, ed. by David A. Trotter, vol. 3, 251–264, Tübingen: Niemeyer.

Calaresu, Emilia. in press. "Modalizzazione assertiva e funzioni confermative/asseverative dell'avverbio fasale GIÀ: usi preverbali di Sardegna (sardo e italiano regionale) vs. usi olofrastici in italiano standard." In *Les variations diasystémiques et leurs interdépendances, Actes du Colloque ΔIA II (Copenhagen, November 19–21, 2012)*, ed. by Kirsten Kragh and Jan Lindschouw, Cambridge Scholars.

Cerruti, Massimo. 2009. *Strutture dell'italiano regionale. Morfosintassi di una varietà diatopica in prospettiva sociolinguistica*. Bern: Lang.

Chafe, Wallace. 1987. *Cognitive Constraints on Information Flow. Coherence and Grounding in Discourse*. Amsterdam/Philadelphia: John Benjamins.

Choi, Soonja. 1995. "The Development of Epistemic Sentence-Ending Modal Forms and Functions in Korean Children." In *Modality in Grammar and Discourse*, ed. by Joan Bybee, and Suzanne Fleischman, 165–204. Amsterdam/Philadelphia: Benjamins.

Coniglio, Marco. 2008. "Modal particles in Italian." *Working Papers in Linguistics University of Venice* 18: 91–129.

Degand, Liesbeth, and Anne-Marie Simon Vandenbergen. 2011. "Grammaticalization, prag-
    maticalization and (inter)subjectification. Methodological issues in the study of discourse
    markers.", special issue *Linguistics* 49 (2).
DeLancey, Scott. 1986. "Evidentiality and Volitionality in Tibetan." In *Evidentiality: The linguis-
    tic Coding of Epistemology*, ed. by Wallace Chafe, and Johanna Nichols, 203–213. Norwood
    (New Jersey): Ablex.
DeLancey, Scott. 1997. "Mirativity: The Grammatical Marking of Unexpected Information."
    Linguistic Typology 1: 33–52.
Delbecque, Nicole, and Ricardo Maldonado. 2011. "Spanish *ya*. A Conceptual Pragmatic
    Anchor." *Journal of Pragmatics* 43: 73–98.
Deloor, Sandrine. 2011. "Los valores temporales y no temporales del adverbio *ya*." In *Estudios de
    tiempo y espacio en la gramática española*, ed. by Elia Hernández Socas, Carsten Sinner, and
    Gerd Wotjak, 29–42, Bern: Lang.
Detges, Ulrich, and Richard Waltereit. 2009. "Diachronic Pathways and Pragmatic Strategies:
    Different Types of Pragmatic Particles from a Diachronic Point of View." In *Current Trends
    in Diachronic Semantics and Pragmatics*, ed. by Maj-Britt Mosegaard Hansen, and Jacque-
    line Visconti, 43–61. Oxford: Emerald.
Diewald, Gabriele. 2006. "Discourse Particles and Modal Particles as Grammatical Elements." In
    Approaches to Discourse Particles, ed. by Kerstin Fischer, 403–425. Oxford/Amsterdam:
    Elsevier.
Diewald, Gabriele. 2011. "Pragmaticalization (Defined) as Grammaticalization of Discourse
    Functions." *Linguistics* 49 (2): 365–390.
Diewald, Gabriele, Marijana Kresic, and Elena Smirnova. 2009. "The Grammaticalization
    channels of Evidentials and Modal Particles in German: Integration in Textual Structures as
    a Common Feature." In *Current Trends in Diachronic Semantics and Pragmatics*, ed. by
    Maj-Britt Mosegaard Hansen, and Jacqueline Visconti, 189–209. Oxford: Emerald.
Fedriani, Chiara and Emanuele Miola. in press. "French *dèjà*, Piedmontese Italian *già*: a Case of
    Contact-induced Pragmaticalization." In *Markers from Latin to the Romance Languages*, ed.
    by Chiara Ghezzi, and Piera Molinelli, Oxford University Press.
Fonagy, Ivan. 1982. *Situation et signification*. Amsterdam: Benjamins.
Franck, Dorothea. 1980. *Grammatik und Konversation*. Königstein: Scriptor-Verlag.
Fraser, Bruce. 1996. "Pragmatic Markers." *Pragmatics* 6 (2): 167–190.
Gerdes, Kim, and Sylvain Kahane. 2007. "Phrasing It Differently." In *Selected Lexical and
    Grammatical Issues in the Meaning-Text Theory. In honour of Igor Mel'čuk*, ed. by Leo
    Wanner, 297–335, Amsterdam: Benjamins.
Hansen, Maj-Britt Mosegaard. 1998. *The Function of Discourse Particles: A Study with Special
    Reference to Spoken Standard French*. Amsterdam/Philadelphia, Benjamins.
Hansen, Maj-Britt Mosegaard. 2002. "From Aspectuality to Discourse Marking: the Case of
    French *déjà* and *encore*." *Belgian Journal of Linguistics* 16: 23–51 [Special issue on *Particles*
    ed. by Ton van der Wouden, Ad Foolen, and Piet van de Craen].
Hansen, Maj-Britt Mosegaard. 2008. *Particles at the Semantics/Pragmatics Interface: Synchronic
    and Diachronic Issues. A Study with Special Reference to the French Phasal Adverbs*.
    Amsterdam etc.: Elsevier.
Hansen, Maj-Britt Mosegaard, and Erling Strudsholm. 2008. "The Semantics of Particles:
    Advantages of a Contrastive and Panchronic Approach: a Study of the Polysemy of French
    déjà and Italian *già*." *Linguistics* 46: 471–505.

Klein, Wolfgang. 1994. *Time in Language*. London/New York: Routledge.

Koike, Dale A. 1996. "Functions of the Adverbial *ya* in Spanish Narrative Discourse." *Journal of Pragmatics* 25: 267–279.

König, Ekkehard. 1991. *The Meaning of Focus Particles. A Comparative Perspective*. London/New York: Routledge.

König, Ekkehard. 1997. "Zur Bedeutung von Modalpartikeln im Deutschen: Ein Neuansatz im Rahmen der Relevanztheorie." *Germanistische Linguistik* 136: 57–75.

Kroon, Caroline, and Rodie Risselada. 2002. "Phasality, Polarity, Focality: a Feature Analysis of the Latin Particle *iam*." *Belgian Journal of Linguistics* 16: 65–78 [Special issue on *Particles* ed. by Ton van der Wouden, Ad Foolen, and Piet van de Craen].

Lambrecht, Knud. 1994. *Information Structure and Sentence Form. Topic, Focus, and the Mental Representations of Discourse Referents*. Cambridge: Cambridge University Press.

Lauwers, Peter, Gudrun Vanderbauwhede, and Stijn Verleyen (eds). 2012. Pragmatic Markers and Pragmaticalization. Lessons from false friends. Amsterdam/Philadelphia: Benjamins.

Lazard, Gilbert. 1999. "Mirativity, Evidentiality, Mediativity, or Other?" *Linguistic Typology* 3: 91–109.

Maiden, Martin, and Mair Parry. 1997. *The Dialects of Italy*. London/New York: Routledge.

Martín Zorraquino, María Antonia, and José Portolés Lázaro. 1999. "Los marcadores del discurso." In *Gramática descriptiva de la lengua española*, ed. by Ignacio Bosque, and Violeta Demonte, 4051–4214, Madrid: Espasa.

Ortu, Franca. 2003. "Wie höflich läßt sich mit Partikeln zustimmen?" In *Partikeln und Höflichkeit*, ed. by Gudrun Held, 367–382. Frankfurt: Peter Lang.

Poggi, Isabella. 1995. "Le interiezioni." In *Grande grammatica italiana di consultazione 3*, ed. by Lorenzo Renzi, Giampaolo Salvi, and Anna Cardinaletti, 403–425. Bologna: il Mulino.

Pusch, Claus. 2007. "Is there Evidence for Evidentiality in Gascony Occitan?" *Italian Journal of Linguistics/Rivista di Linguistica* 19: 91–108.

Rosén, Hannah. 2009. "Coherence, Sentence Modification, and Sentence-part Modification. The Contribution of Particles." In *New Perspectives on Historical Latin Syntax 1. Syntax of the Sentence*, ed. by Philip Baldi, and Pierluigi Cuzzolin, 317–441. Berlin: Walter de Gruyter.

Squartini, Mario. in press. "The Pragmaticalization of 'already' in Romance: from Discourse Grammar to Illocution." In *Discourse and Pragmatic Markers from Latin to the Romance Languages*, ed. by Chiara Ghezzi, and Piera Molinelli, Oxford University Press.

Torrent, Aina. 2011. "Modal Particles in Catalan." In *The Pragmatics of Catalan*, Lluís Payrató and Josep Maria Cots (eds.), 81–114, Berlin/Boston: De Gruyter Mouton.

Traugott, Elizabeth Closs, and Richard B. Dasher. 2002. *Regularity in Semantic Change*. Cambridge: Cambridge University Press.

Välikangas, Olli. 2000. "*Jà jà, jà déjà* et *già già* en français et en italien au XVIe siècle." *Neuphilologische Mitteilungen* 101: 365–374.

Välikangas, Olli. 2004. "*Wie heißt er schon? Comment s'appelle-t-il déjà?* Zur Problematik der Erinnerungsfragen." In *Etymologie, Entlehnungen und Entwicklungen. Festschrift für Jorma Koivulehto zum 70 Geburtstag*, ed. by Irma Hyvärinen, Petri Kallio, and Jarmo Korhonen, 423–437. Mémoires de la Société Néophilologique de Helsinki 63.

van der Auwera, Johan. 1998. "Phasal Adverbials." In: *Adverbial Constructions in the Languages of Europe*, ed. by Johan van der Auwera, 25–145. Berlin/New York: Mouton de Gruyter.

Waltereit, Richard. 2001. "Modal Particles and their Functional Equivalents: A Speech-Act-Theoretic Approach." *Journal of Pragmatics* 33: 1391–1417.

The fuzzy boundaries between discourse marking and modal marking

Maria Josep Cuenca
Universitat de València

1. Introduction

Discourse markers and modality markers are related in several respects. Some authors consider modal markers a type of discourse or pragmatic marker along with cohesive markers or connectives.[1] Authors such as Fitzmaurice (2004), Detges and Waltereit (2007) and Traugott (2007) have highlighted their diachronic relationship.[2] In addition, the analysis of discourse markers uncovers that some of them have a hybrid nature in that they exhibit structural (or frame) and modal (or qualifying) functions.[3]

Assuming that discourse and modal marking stand for functions than can be expressed by different categories, in this paper the classes of particles that can perform one function or the other are defined. The identification of the word classes implementing these functions is by no means trivial and its characterization can shed some light on the borderline between modal and discourse marking.

This paper aims at illustrating the fuzzy boundaries between the two functions by analyzing some particles used in oral Catalan that exhibit features typically associated with modal markers (hence MMs), and specifically modal particles (MPs), and discourse markers (hence DMs). Like MMs, the particles analyzed encode (inter)subjective values and like DMs they bracket units of talk. Nonetheless, they

---

1. See, e.g., Aijmer and Simon-Vandenbergen 2006; Norrick 2007; and also Fischer (2006), the volume "Contrastive perspectives on Pragmatic Markers" of *Catalan Journal of Linguistics* edited by Cuenca (2007), and the volume of *Journal of Pragmatics* on "Pragmatic Markers" edited by Norrick (2009).

2. From a diachronic point of view, subjectification and intersubjectification processes as described by Traugott and her associates (e.g., Traugott and Dasher 2002) often imply modal structures that evolve into connectives.

3. See, for example, Cuenca (2008), which deals with the polysemy of *well*, Marín (2005, 2007) on perception verbs grammaticalized as discourse markers, and the references cited in these works.

are not a homogeneous group. Each particle is more or less proximal to the proto-typical behavior of either modal or discourse marking.

I assume previous analyses of some Catalan particles such as *clar* (Cuenca & Marín 2012), *home/dona* (Cuenca & Torres 2008), *és que* (Marín & Cuenca 2012), *bueno/bé* (Cuenca 2008, González 2004), and markers derived from perception verbs such as *a veure, aviam, mira, escolta* (Cuenca & Marín 2001, Marín 2005, 2007), all of them polyfunctional items resulting from a grammaticalization process. Some of them will be described by considering their multiple functions and the formal and functional features defining their use as markers.

The analysis is based on an oral corpus (COC, *Corpus oral de conversa col·loquial*, Payrató and Alturo, 2002) containing spontaneous conversations among 3 or more participants. The 10 conversations (selected from 50 units of ca. 30 minutes each) last 281 minutes and include 70,493 words.

2.   Discourse markers and modal markers

As Schiffrin (1987, 2001), Fraser (1990, 1999, 2009) and Norrick (2009), among many other authors, claim, discourse markers are a set of expressions that include different word classes. The same can be said of modal markers, which include (at least) three word classes, namely, modal adverbs, interjections and modal particles.[4] The basic difference between the two kinds of markers can be determined by considering that discourse markers, at least in their more traditional definition as connective elements or items that bracket units of talk, are two position operators, i.e. units typically linking two content segments, whereas modal particles are one position operators that modify the illocution of an utterance (Fuentes 2003, 2009).

In this section, I will try to sketch my categorical proposal for discourse and modal markers, and identify the intermediate zone that will be illustrated in the following sections.

Conjunctions (e.g., *and, or, but*) can be located at the periphery of discourse marking, so that some authors may include or exclude them from this pragmatic category depending on the definition assumed. Conjunctions are linking words that indicate grammatical relationships (traditionally identified with subordination or coordination) and various propositional meanings (namely, addition, disjunction, contrast, concession, cause, consequence, condition,

---

4.   We assume that modal particles are one of the classes included in the functional category of modal markers, which also comprises interjections and modal adverbs. This proposal is developed in following sections.

purpose, comparison, time, place, manner). They typically introduce clauses in compound sentences, as in (1).[5]

(1) Congress was banking on at least 12 seats here, *but* most observers think they will be lucky to get 10.   [*Guardian*, 1989.11.08]

Although the basic function of conjunctions is to link segments inside a sentence, as in the previous example, some can also preface independent utterances as in (2):

(2) Investors were elated by the prospect of a more buoyant West German economy as Bonn provides houses and jobs for arrivals from the East. "The mood is super," a senior dealer said. *But* the prospect of economic growth rising by a further half-point during the next six months raised fears on the international currency markets of an uncontrolled expansion and increased concern about inflation throughout Europe.
                                                               [*Guardian*, 1989.11.11]

This structural possibility relates (some) conjunctions to discourse marking, since connecting at text level is what prototypical DMs do.

Another group of markers that indicate connection between two content meanings are invariable words or phrases such as *however, yet, nonetheless, consequently, as a consequence, in contrast* or *moreover*.

(3) Despite high unemployment in some areas there were large openings in sectors such as the electronics and engineering industries in the south. The gap was being filled by the arrivals. *Nonetheless*, short-term unemployment among the refugees is likely to remain high. At present, about a third of the arrivals are unemployed.
                                           [Guardian, electronic edition of 1989.11.08]

These connectives have generally been described as adverbs exhibiting a special use in discourse. But it can be argued that when used as utterance introducers they are not adverbs despite their form or their adverbial use in other contexts. In fact, not all of them correspond to adverbs *stricto sensu* (in Catalan and Spanish, for instance, most of these items are prepositional phrases formally) and they no longer behave as adverbs. On the lines of Rouchota's (1998), I have defined them as *parenthetical connectives* (see Cuenca 2006).

Parenthetical connectives are syntactically peripheral (and generally also prosodically detached) items indicating basic logico-argumentative meanings that can be grouped together in four basic types, namely, addition, disjunction,

---

5.   The English examples come from the *British National Corpus*.

contrast, and consequence. In (3), *nonetheless* makes explicit the contrastive link
– concessive, specifically – between the following sentence and the previous two.

Parenthetical connectives can combine with conjunctions, both at sentence
and at text level:

(4)   The rises, he said, were predictable, *but nonetheless* very disappointing.
[*East Anglian Daily Times*. 1993]

Parenthetical connectives are generally more varied in formal written texts than in
oral texts.

In brief, conjunctions and parenthetical connectives are two position operators that make explicit the relationship between two content units. Conjunctions
are more frequent and varied in use at sentence level and only some of them
(mainly *and* and *but*) are used at text level. Parenthetical connectives are typical
text connectives, though they can be used at sentence level on their own or following a conjunction with a similar or compatible meaning.

At the other pole of the gradient, we find modal adverbs, interjections and
modal particles. Adverbs can be identified as words or phrases that are verbal adjuncts or sentence specifiers indicating manner or modality in a broad sense. Like
in the case of conjunctions, modal adverbs also have a role on sentence structure,
so that they can be either included or excluded from modal marking considered as
a discourse mechanism.

Interjections and modal particles are more difficult to define. Interjections
implement modal and interactional meanings that according to Jakobson's functions of language can be classified into expressive, conative, phatic, metalinguistic
and representative (Cuenca 2000, 2011). They are sentence or utterance equivalents, since they can be used as a complete utterance.

(5)   a.   "*Gee*," said the actor.
[*Return of the red nose joke book*. London: Boxtree, 1991]

In the previous example *gee* stands for a whole utterance. If we retrieve the context
of appearance, its meaning becomes clearer:

(5)   b.   "There's a food company which wants someone to dress up for an ad-
vertisement as a giant slice of ham with cheese and tomato between
two halves of an enormous bun." "*Gee*," said the actor. "Sounds like a
big roll!"

Gee expresses surprise at something that the speaker doesn't like.

Since interjections have a very schematic and context-depending meaning, it
is not unusual for them to be followed by a segment that specifies it.

(6) "Ye Olde Motorway Services. Come on; yer Aunty Ashley'll buy you a coffee and a sticky bun." "*Gee*, you sure know how to show a boy a good time."
[*The Crow Road*. Banks, Iain. London: Abacus, 1993]

In these uses, interjections (specially phatic and metalinguistic ones) resemble discourse markers as the boundary between expressing a modal value and introducing an utterance becomes blurry.

Modal particles are uninflected words that specify the illocutionary type of the utterance or, generally speaking, express pragmatic meanings related to the attitude or the knowledge of speaker and hearer as regards the utterance where they appear. This is the case of *ja* in the following example in German:

(7) Udo hat ja Gerda geheiratet.
'Udo has *ja* married Gerda.'
[Jacobs 1991, 142, quoted from Waltereit 2001, 1394]

Ja modifies the assertion *Udo has married Gerda* implying that "the speaker expresses the belief that the addressee neither believes that the proposition is false nor that he/she considers the possibility of its being false in the given situation" (cf. Jacobs 1991, 146).[6] MPs, in languages like German, are integrated within the topological structure of the predication, since they occur in middle-field position, but are dispensable items.[7]

It is worth noticing that, in contrast with the previously discussed word classes, many languages do not have a clear-cut class of MPs. As Waltereit (2001) convincingly argues, the functions of German MPs can be equivalent to the effects created by lexical and morphological devices in English or Romance languages which lack such particles.

In between the modal and the connective poles, it is possible to identify a number of units that share some of the defining characteristics of both DMs and MPs.

(8) A boy called round at his girlfriend's house one evening. "Are we going out to eat?" asked the girl. "*Well*, I thought we might just eat up the road," the boy replied. "Oh, no," said the girl, "I don't think I'd like tarmac."
[*Return of the red nose joke book*. London: Boxtree, 1991]

In the previous example, *well* is a parenthetical particle that introduces a turn and announces a dispreferred answer to the previous question. It mitigates an utterance that conveys disagreement.

---

6. For a detailed account of German modal particles, see the chapters by Diewald and Schoonjans in this volume.

7. On the notion of topological integration, as a alternative to syntactic integration, see Gerdes & Kahane (2007).

Markers such as *well*, that I have called *pragmatic connectives*, are syntactically peripheral (they tend to occur in initial or pre-field position) and prosodically detached items that typically preface an utterance and combine frame and modal meanings. They are mainly used in oral texts, bracketing units of talk such as interventions, turns or units within turns and also indicating interactional meanings (e.g., agreement, disagreement, topic change or reformulation). They can combine with other connectives.

As the previous description shows, the main problem for defining categorical spaces stems from the fact that no feature seems to be a necessary and sufficient condition. A description by means of a bundle of features must be called on.

As I will try to show, pragmatic connectives, and to some extent also interjections and modal particles, occupy the intersection between modal and discourse marking. The boundaries between the classes identified in this Section are fuzzy for various reasons:

a. their defining features (invariability, parenthetical character, initial position, modal meaning and so on) are neither necessary nor sufficient to classify a particle as a modal marker or a discourse marker,
b. the same form can exhibit different morphosyntactic behaviors; most of the markers have non-particle counterparts from which they derive as a result of a grammaticalization process, and some have developed uses that can be identified with or related to different categories,[8]
c. even as a particle, a single form can develop various pragmatic functions according to factors such as its position, the units in which it occurs (type, modality, etc.) or intonation.

As for the meaning that a marker can express, a threefold classification will be assumed here: propositional, structural and modal.

a. Propositional meaning arises when connection takes place at the content-level. Propositional markers relate discourse units and indicate meanings such as addition, disjunction, contrast, concession, cause or consequence between their contents. Conjunctions and parenthetical connectives typically express propositional meanings.
b. Structural meaning is the result of a marker bracketing a unit of talk such as the text, a sequence, a turn or a unit within a turn. A structural marker indicates meanings such as start, closing, pre-closing, continuity, topic change or reformulation. Some conjunctions, parenthetical connectives and pragmatic connectives can fulfil these frame functions.

---

8.   On the polyfunctionality of adverbs that have evolved into MPs and DMs, see Aijmer (this volume).

c. Modal meanings are inherently interactional in that they put forward the attitude, knowledge or stance of the speaker with respect to what it is been said or to the hearer. Pragmatic connectives and, especially, modal markers are typical vehicles of modal meanings such as agreement, disagreement or emphasis.

It must be borne in mind that propositional and structural meaning are typically connective and that a specific marker can highlight more that one type of meaning at a time.

In the following sections, some Catalan markers indicating modal and connective functions will be characterized and their hybrid character will be discussed.

3. **Case study 1. The marker *home/dona***

The noun *home/dona* ('man/woman') is very frequently used in Catalan conversation as a solidarity marker that expresses various interactional meanings (Cuenca & Torres 2008), as illustrated in (9):[9]

(9) EUU: no saps ni obrir [una cerve]sa\   you can't even open a beer
     PUY: [ah sí\] (soroll de l'obridor)   oh, yes (sound of an opener)
     MJJ: *home*\ mira\ obrir_ obrir_ el   *home* 'man', look, opening_
     que és obrir_ una cervesa_ no se'm   opening_ opening a beer is not
     dóna bé\ (COC05, 159–170)   something I'm very good at

In (9) a man (MJJ) responds to a woman's (EUU) reproach. The use of *home* to introduce his turn softens his admission that he is not able to open a can of beer.
Home/dona is thus a polyfunctional unit:

a. As a noun, it is the head of an NP and has a referential meaning.
b. As a marker, it is parenthetical and has a procedural or intersubjective meaning. It looks like a vocative but it has lost completely its referential meaning and partially its appellative force, as we can see by the fact that in the COC corpus *home* ('man') is addressed to a woman in many examples (78 out of 133 cases).[10]

---

9. Since the examples come from informal conversation, the glosses will be quite literal. See Appendix 1 for transcription conventions.

10. The participants in the conversational corpus are 35 women and 22 men. Only one conversation is exclusively among women. As for *home*, 41 instances are used by a man addressing a woman and 37 are used by a woman addressing another woman.

3.1   Formal features

A former noun has undergone a process of grammaticalization affecting its morphology, syntactic function, position and frequency.

a. Morphology. Comparing the nominal and the marker uses, a tendency to morphological invariability can be observed: (1) the masculine is used to address men and also women while the reverse is not possible, (2) as a consequence, the feminine is less used than the masculine (only one case of *dona* '*woman*' in the corpus), (3) no plurals are used as markers, and (4) the masculine singular can be used to address a plural hearer.

b. Syntactically, *home/dona* cannot be part of a complex NP; whenever a determiner or a complement is added to the form, the marker interpretation disappears or the structure becomes ungrammatical.

c. The marker's position is completely different from ordinary nouns and partially different from vocatives. It is detached from the predicative structure and, although, like vocatives, *home/dona* can occur in final position, especially *home* tends to be sentence initial.

d. The increase in frequency of use as the items become more grammatical is evident in this case, since as a noun there are 29 instances in the corpus whereas there are 134 cases as a marker.

3.2   Functional features

The literal referential meaning ('man', 'woman') has changed to pragmatic meanings related to the hearer's involvement in the interaction and to conversation management (intersubjectification process, Traugott & Dasher 2002).[11] The different meanings can be grouped together into two types including several subtypes: attenuation (partial agreement, disagreement, assertion attenuation) and reinforcement (assertion reinforcement, command reinforcement, affirmative emphasis, negative emphasis, affirmative reversal) (see Cuenca & Torres 2008 for a detailed analysis).

In initial or left-periphery position *home* is often used to soften an utterance that indicates disagreement or partial agreement (10):

---

11.   The semantic change experienced by the noun is not unique since the selection of the conative value is one of the main pathways for the creation of discourse markers, especially those which incorporate the hearer in the discourse structure (see Lamiroy & Swiggers, 1993).

(10) PEI: lo que passa es que vosaltres sí   the point is that you can place an ad,
     que podeu posar-hi una_ un: anunci   can't you?
     (. 0.12) o no\

     RRR: (.0.26) *home*\ però si ja ho   *home* 'man', we've already told
     tenim dit a tothom\ (COC08,   everyone
     34–39), [W-W][12]

In final (or intermediate) position, *home/dona* is used to reinforce an utterance, frequently a command (11) or a polarity item, either negative or positive (12):[12]

(11) VIE: divendres_ la truquem\   we'll call her on Friday, huh?

     ALL: (.. 0.34) eh:/   uh?

     JON: al vespre truqueu\ i ja està   you call her in the evening and that's
     [*home* \]   it, *home* 'man'

     ALL: [val\] (COC10, 1252–1257),   OK
     [M-M]

(12) NIA: (.. 0.81) tu has agafat les peles/   You've taken the bucks

     MAM: (.. 0.98) {(F) sí *home* sí\}   yes, *home* 'man', yes, it doesn't
     (. 0.17) @@@@ (.0.25) no és per re   matter, does it?
     oi/ (COC06, 79–82), [W-W]

The various meanings that *home/dona* can express are related to the source meaning of the marker: a conative feature associated with the vocative. By using the marker, the addressor calls the addressee's attention to make him or her aware that what (s)he says is important. The conative feature, along with subjectivity and an interpersonal relationship of solidarity that it conveys, modifies the illocution of speech acts that can be face-threatening. As Portolés and Vázquez (2000) claim for the parallel Spanish marker, it can contribute to a compensatory strategy:

> Politeness is associated in Spanish, not only with the performance of face-satisfy-ing acts (FSAs) but also of face-threatening acts (FTAs). And the use of *hombre/mujer* seems to be associated with certain compensatory strategies which make up for the occurrence of certain threatening acts. The threat to face is reduced to a more tolerable level by adding *hombre/mujer* to the impositive formulation. (Portolés & Vázquez 2000, 224)

As the previous examples show, *home* (or *dona*) is a polyfunctional lexical item whose behavior is between that of a vocative and that of a particle. It often

---

12.   In the following examples, a final coda will be included to identify the interlocutors' gender (woman, W, man, M).

mitigates a (total or partial) disagreement or a command. Sometimes, however, it is emphatic, especially regarding a polarity item. This dual behavior can be related to the marker's position: if it is utterance initial, disagreement is more predominant (in 61 out of 67 cases of attenuation the marker in initial position) and its use is more similar to that of DMs. If it is final or non-initial, emphasis shows up (in 48 out of 53 cases of reinforcement the marker is in final position) and the vocative nuance is more prominent, enhancing the modal value. When it is isolated (12 cases), the utterance has not been completed or the use is that of an interjection, since it is sentence equivalent.

4.   Case study 2. The marker *(és) clar*

The marker *(és) clar* (lit. '(is) clear') is also very typical in Catalan conversation. It also has a literal counterpart: *clar* 'clear, fair' is primarily an adjective (inflected for gender and number: *clar, clara, clars, clares*), and as such it often combines with the verbal form *és* 'is' in a copular construction.

As an invariable and fixed form, *(és) clar* occurs in several configurations that exhibit different functions in various syntactic and pragmatic contexts, although sometimes they are very close to one another (Cuenca & Marín 2012).[13]

The adverbial use is not frequent in oral texts. As a manner adverb, *clar* modifies a verb: *veure-hi clar* ('to see clearly'), *parlar clar* ('to speak clearly').

In conversation, *clar* or *és clar* frequently act as an interjection or a marker.[14]

(13)	FAN (.. 0.35) si am(b) el meu avi ens haguéssim entès abans lo que passa que_ (.. 0.47) tant tens por de parlar-li tu com:_ [1 com ell:s] de dir-te [2 algo a tu\]	If me and my grandfather had understood each other before, but the point is that... you are afraid of talking to him and they also of telling you something
	NAA [1 sí\]	yeah
	HIL [2 fer algo per a tu\]	of doing something for you
	NAA (.. 0.39) perquè ja falta la:_	because the xx is already missing

---

13.   On the polyfunctionality of *claro* and other Spanish discourse markers derived form adjectives, see Hummel (2012).

14.   Since it is difficult to gloss the nuances introduced by the marker, we will generally translate it in the examples as 'of course'. The comments following the examples will try to establish the precise meaning in each case.

FAN (... 1.47) i *clar*\ i després representa que si:_ (.. 0.61) que si: tu vols portar la veu cantant_ llagons e- --

and *clar* ('of course'), and then it seems that if you want to take the lead then

HIL [sí\ sí\]

yeah, yeah

FAN [ets el que incòrdies] i l'aprofitat\

you're being annoying and taking advantage

HIL sí\

yeah

NAA (... 1.42) *clar* \ és que és això\

clar ('of course'), that's it

FAN (.. 0.58) i *clar* \ (... 1.03) jo ja li vaig dient al meu pare_ ja que jo:_ (. 0.23) dic_ parla-n'hi tu_ (.. 0.31) p(e)rò *clar* _ a ell també li fa cosa\ (COCO2: 1475–1496)

and *clar* ('of course'), I'm already telling my father that I_ I say: "talk to him about that", but *clar* ('of course') he's also reluctant.

The previous example exhibits different uses of *clar* as an invariable form. FAN is making his point and NAA and HIL show their agreement, by using an affirmation in the case of HIL (*sí, sí* 'yeah, yeah') and by using *clar* in the case of NAA (*Clar. És que és això* 'of course, that's it'). In this context, *clar* is a phatic interjection indicating agreement and can be defined as a stressed agreement in paradigmatic opposition with *sí*, as Pons (2003) argues and the previous examples clearly show. It signals that the speaker assumes that what (s)he says coincidences with the addressee's expectations (Chafe 1986, 270; Aijmer and Simon Vandenbergen 2004, 1791).

In the other uses in (13), the maker is added to a conjunction (*and, but*) to indicate a consequence or an antithesis presented as obvious and generally acknowledged.

(És) clar as a marker often occurs on its own introducing a turn or a move inside a turn.[15]

(14) MEC tenia gana\

he was hungry

MAT bue[no\]

well

JOJ [bue]no\

well

MAT *clar* \ ((de fons se sent un comentari de JOJ)), quan fan règim_ fan règim_ [{(@) i despúes estan morts de gana\]} (COC04 : 1305–1311)

clar ('of course'), when they're on a diet, they're really on a diet and then they're starving

---

15. *Clar que* is becoming a grammaticalized conjunction that introduces a clause indicating contrast or concession.

In (14) *clar* introduces an argument and presents it as something that is obvious and so everyone would agree on.

4.1   Formal features

(És) clar used as a marker has several distinctive features:[16]

a. Morphologically, the invariable marker *clar* can be clearly distinguished from the adjective, which is inflected for gender and number (*clar, clara, clars, clares*).
b. Syntactically, *(és) clar* does not function as either an adjective – or a copula plus an adjective – or as an adverb. It introduces an utterance or reinforces another connective mainly *and, because, but*, just as parenthetical or pragmatic connectives often do.
c. The marker's position is different from that of the adjective or manner adverb. It is detached from the predicative structure and is utterance initial.
d. Its frequency of use as a marker increases: the use of *clar* as an adjective in the corpus is only 10.8% (13 cases) of the total (120 cases). The cases in which *(és) clar* is a marker are 45% (54 cases, 20 of which the marker is combined with other connectives).

4.2   Functional features

(És) clar typically occurs in interactional contexts, such as face-to-face conversation, and adds to its host utterance illocutionary values of certainty, emphasis, agreement and shared knowledge. In some contexts, it can reinforce or up-grade the following utterance, so that it "identifies what comes next as an informative focus, introducing the relevance of that constituent" (Pons 2003, 234).

When introducing a turn, it indicates that the speaker agrees with the addressee about something that is generally known or could be generally accepted. Therefore, the utterance containing the marker is co-oriented with the previous one. For instance, in (15) the utterance introduced by *clar* echoes the previous intervention:

(15) PPP (... 2.71) hauré: de demanar   I'll have to ask for a holiday, shit, I
festa\ (. 0.24) punyeta\ (... 2.02) haig   have to, huh?
de demanar festa no/

CME (. 0.27) *clar* \ haurà de dema-   *clar* 'of course', she'll have to ask for a
nar [festa\] (COC07, 1913–1917)   holiday

---

16. The marker has two main forms: the fuller one, *és clar*, and the shortened one, *clar*. The former is sometimes written as *esclar*, a form that shows the phonological reduction typically associated with fossilization processes.

In (16), *clar* prefaces MMM's intervention, which continues the argumentation by posing a question:

(16) PPP [4 i què] et penses que a can
Cabero no no pleguen perquè de
què viurien\

??? [4 xx]

PPP (.. 0.46) clar\ [xx]

MMM [*clar* \ per]què vo- -- q- --
qui vols que ho [llogui\] (COC07,
1130–1137)

And [why] do you think that at
Can Cabero [a firm] they do not
close? Because how would they live

clar 'of course',

clar 'of course', because who do you
think would rent it?

As turn introducer, the marker can filter the possible negative effects of turn taking or maintaining by presenting the action as in line with the addressee's previous intervention, as we can see in the previous example and also in (17), where *clar* introduces an agreement that turns into a partial contrast (*clar però*) that, nonetheless, is co-oriented with EUU's intervention and qualifies it:

(17) EUU que altres carnavals és només
anar disfressats_ lluir la disfressa i
tornar cap a casa\

MJJ *clar* \ p(e)rò Sitges_

EUU que no--

MJJ [p(e)rò Sitges_]

EUU [el carnaval no és] això\

MJJ jo crec que Sitges guarda això
p(e)rò_ (COC05: 534–541)

that other carnivals is just going
there in fancy dress, showing off and
going back home

clar 'of course', but Sitges

that no

but Sitges

Carnival is not that

I think that Sitges is still like that
but...

Inside a turn, it serves as a reorientation marker that indicates that what follows is in line with what has been already said or introduces a side comment.

(18) NAT [encara no he vist] mai el
principi jo d'ET eh\

MER (. 0.22) i arribem_ ens as-
seiem_ i aquest\ (. 0.26) (a)nava
aquest-- *esclar* allà fo:sc i així_
(. 0.27) assegut aixís a la punta de la
cadira_ (COC03, 890–896)

I've never seen the beginning of ET,
huh?

and we get there and sit down, and
this, and this... was going... *esclar* 'of
course' it's dark and everything, we
were sitting like this on the edge of
the chair

In (18), *és clar* 'repairs' an interrupted segment and introduces a reorientation in the speaker's discourse.

(És) clar usually combines with basic conjunctions to qualify a cause (*perquè clar*), a consequence (*i clar*) or an antithesis (*però clar*), as already shown in (13).

(19) VIE [2 pot- potser no hi ha la riquesa] [3 que hi ha a França {(??) per (ai)xò eh\}]	Maybe there's not so much wealth as in France, though, huh?
MAG [3 el turisme\]	tourism
VIE (.. 0.36) *perquè clar*\ allà és molt Pi- --- és molt Pirineu allò_ (.. 0.44) i potser no:_ (. 0.23) està una mica_ m:hm_ està una mica deixat\ (COC10: 142–150)	*perquè clar* 'because of course', over there it's very much in the Py_ it's deep in the Pyrenees and maybe no... it's a little bit... neglected

In (19), *perquè clar* introduces a qualified cause, a cause that is considered as certain and generally acceptable. In fact, whenever *clar* follows a conjunction or another discourse marker, it reinforces the propositional meaning of the upcoming segment adding a modal sense of certainty. It is an upgrading device that presents a cause, a consequence or an antithesis as obvious, i.e. as part of the shared knowledge.

In conclusion, the marker *(és) clar* blends modal functions (as epistemic marker of certainty) and structural functions (as turn or move introducer) (see Fuentes 1993). It exhibits the main features that Waltereit (2001) identifies as distinctive of MPs: it operates at a speech-act level modifying the speech-act conditions and has a non-modal counterpart – the adjective *clar* –, to which it is related metonymically. The adjectival meaning (something that is clear is easier to grasp, either perceptually or intellectually) was the basis for the inference that something which is clear intellectually is something that most people would agree on.

However, it also introduces turns and utterances, as conjunctions, parenthetical connectives and pragmatic connectives do, and it is parenthetical and combines with conjunctions, just like parenthetical and pragmatic connectives. It can be thus considered a form occupying the fuzzy space between pragmatic connectives and modal particles.

5.   Case study 3. The marker *és que*

There are two basic syntactic configurations in which the copula *és* ('is') plus the complementizer *que* ('that') can co-occur (for an extended analysis, see Cuenca & Marín, 2012). The basic configuration is a copular structure where B is a clause introduced by *que*: "A *és* [*que* B]". But in oral texts the most frequent configuration is a different one. The copula and the complementizer become a fixed complex unit that introduces an utterance: "*És que* B".

a. copular structure: SN + $\acute{e}s_{verb}$ + que_{conj} + Clausal attribute
b. *és que* (marker):   *és que*$_{modal\ particle}$ + Utterance/Sentence

As a marker *és que* introduces an utterance that expresses an inferred causal relationship.

(20) MEC es veu que eren incompatibles   It seems that they were incompat-
      a casa seva amb ell\   ible at home

      MAT hi\   ha

      MEC (.. 0.41) bueno\ *és que* la [mare   well, *és que* '(it) is just that' his
      és] de jutjat eh\ (COC04: 1506–1509)   mother is very difficult to deal with

In (20) MEC justifies the assertion "it seems that they were incompatible" by adding an information "his mother is very difficult to deal with", that by the use of *és que* becomes a qualified or subjective cause ('the fact that his mother is very difficult to deal with is the reason why they were incompatible') that cancels other inferences that the hearer could derive from it.

A pseudo-cleft copular structure ("general noun/clause *és que* B", e.g. *the reason why they were imcompatible is that his mother is very difficult to deal with*) turns into "a finite clause embedded as the complement of an expletive copular matrix clause" (Delahunty & Watzkiewicz 2000, 301). The next step implies that *és que* is frozen as an introductory modal particle presupposing a previous utterance to which it is a response or a reaction.

5.1   Formal features

a. Morphosyntactically, *és que* has become a fixed particle, regardless of its formal structure (a copula, *és* 'is', plus the subordinating conjunction *que* 'that'). The verb *és* has lost its basic properties (it cannot license a subject and it is fixed in the 3rd person singular and present tense) and *que* is no longer integrated with the following clause but is lexicalized with *és*.
b. As a marker, *és que* becomes utterance initial and alternates with other markers (Fuentes 1997; Porroche Ballesteros 1998).
c. Its frequency of use in oral texts increases (151 cases of marker use, 81.6%, in contrast with its 34 cases as a copular structure, 18.3%).

5.2   Functional features

És que as a marker is used to express modal values related to the speaker's intention of justifying his or her response to what has just been said, often in order to avoid a face-threatening act (Delahunty 2001, Porroche Ballesteros, 1998,

Pusch 2007).[17] It is thus a mitigation marker in most cases (Pusch 2006, 2007, Sancho 2010).

És que usually introduces a justification of a previous content, as in (20) above and in (21):

(21) NIA (.. 0.58) què t'anava a di:r\   What was I about to say? I am sorry
       (. 0.27) que em sap greu de no   I didn't tell you I was coming here in
       haver-te avisat al final de que venia   the end. *És que* '(it) is that' I thought
       aquí\ (. 0.17) *és que* em pensava que   that I already had
       t'ho havia dit\ (COC06: 383–385)

In accordance with the paraphrase "The reason for/why A is that B", NIA's last intervention roughly means: 'The reason why I didn't tell you that I was coming here is that I thought I already had'. But, in contrast with the same sequence without *és que*, it also implies that the speaker feels guilty (or supposes that the hearer might think she is) and wants to justify her behavior. On the other hand, as observed by Sancho (2010, 115), when *és que* introduces a justification, it is similar to *perquè* ('because') but they are not interchangeable either on semanticopragmatic or syntactic grounds: *perquè* is a linking word (a conjunction) introducing a 'neutral' cause, whereas *és que* is a modal particle introducing a subjective cause and presupposing a previous content, whether explicit or implicit, to which the following utterance is a justification or excuse. In fact, *és que* cannot be generally replaced by *perquè*, which clearly indicates that it cannot be considered a conjunction. The marker has scope over the next utterance and modifies its illocutionary value but does not connect it with a previous linguistic unit, as conjunctions or other connectives do.

Although justification and mitigation are the key fetaures of *és que*, it is an emphasis marker in some contexts.

(22) NAA p(e)rò quanta gent hi cap a   But how many people can get into
       dins l'ermita El Puig\   the chapel of El Puig
       HIL [1 mira\]   look
       NAA [1 xx\]
       SUS [1 no arri]ben a cent\ (.. 0.66)   Not even a hundred, no way, *és que*
       què va\ *és que* ni ni cinquanta no hi   '(it) is that' not even fifty can get in
       caben\ (COC02: 9–14)   there.

---

17. *És que* constructions have been identified as a key element in conversation in several languages and have been generally described as inferential constructions introducing an explanation or justification (cf. (Berenguer & Salvador 1998, Declerck 1992, Delahunty 2001, Delahunty & Gatzkiewicz 2000, Fernández Leborans 1992, Fuentes 1997, Porroche Ballesteros 1998, Pusch 2006, Sancho 2010).

The paraphrase "The reason why not even 100 people can get in the chapel is that not even 50 people can" does not correspond to the meaning of the intervention: "if 50 people cannot get in the chapel, let alone 100".

In these cases, *és que* generally indicates emphasis. It introduces an argument that is co-oriented with the previous one and is presented as argumentatively stronger. In the previous example, the argument is that the chapel is small.

A similar effect is activated when *és que* is turn initial, as in (23):

(23) NAA amb la despedida de soltera que vem (a)nar al Mercashow_

At the hen party when we went to Mercashow

HIL (... 1.49) *és que* totes les despedides de soltera acaben així_ al Mercashow_ (COC02: 696–698)

és que '(it) is that' all the hen parties end up the same, in the Mercashow

In (23) HIL echoes what NAA has just said and generalizes the idea while upgrading it. Emphatic uses are very frequent when the addressor echoes the addresee's previous turn.

És que expresses complaint in some contexts, especially when it combines with some discourse markers such as *però* ('but') or *home* (literally, 'man'):

(24) PEI (. 0.20) i de vegades també trobes_ que els atres no deixen jugar\

And sometimes you also find that others don't let you play

RRR (.. 0.48) [1 sí\ és que és això\]

Yes, that's it

PEI [1 que es queden allà::] en_ [2 tapant la porteria_ i no deixen {(??) ni} jugar\]

They stay there in... blocking the goal and they don't let anybody play

RRR [2 esclar\ guanyen_ guanyen_ p(e)rò és] que no han deixat que els demés fessin_ (COC08: 339–349)

of course, they win, they win, *però és que* 'but (it) is that' they haven't let anyone else do anything

The last utterance can be paraphrased as: 'I complain that they win because they haven't let anyone else do anything'.

In summary, *és que* is a former copular construction reanalyzed as a marker. *És que* expresses a pragmatic meaning related to modality (i.e., justification, excuse, emphasis, complaint), modifies the illocutionary content of the following utterance and is always reactive. It introduces an utterance that is a presented as a justification or reaction to something that has been said before or to an extralinguistic situation. The previous event triggers a presupposition that links the speaker's and the hearer's stance and assumptions.

6. Discussion

All the units analyzed in the previous case study sections exhibit a hybrid nature and some have developed more than one function even as particles. They are "sequentially dependent units that bracket units of talk ([Schiffrin] 1987[a], 31), i.e. nonobligatory utterance-initial elements that function in relation to ongoing talk and text" (Schiffrin 2001, 57) and, at least in some uses, they can be considered connectives since they "express certain meanings which presuppose the presence of other components in the discourse" (Halliday & Hasan 1976, 236). They also carry pragmatic meanings related with the attitude, knowledge or stance of the speaker in the interaction, although they are generally located at the left periphery (or pre-field position) in contrast with German MPs, syntactically attached to the verb (middle field). In fact, Catalan is included among the languages not having MPs or at least not having prototypical ones.[18]

Since there does not seem to be a clear-cut boundary between modal and discourse marking, I propose a cline from prototypically modal to prototypically structural marking, the intermediate area being occupied by particles as those analyzed (cf. Cuenca & Marín 2012).

The idea of different but intersected zones for invariable words used as modal and discourse markers is diagrammed in Figure 1, where the relative position of the units described here in their use as markers, is indicated.

The intersection is occupied by items belonging to three different classes, namely interjections, modal particles and pragmatic connectives.

The features that characterize the classes are summarized in Table 1.[19]

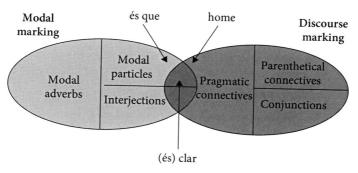

Figure 1. The modal-discourse marking space

---

18. About modal particles in Catalan, see Ferrer Mora (2001a, 2001b), González (2005); Torrent-Letzen (2009, 2011).

19. For a similar approach to the analysis of a polyfunctional marker in German and Swedish (*also* and *alltså*), see Fischer and Alm (this volume).

Table 1. Discourse and modal marking: Word classes[20]

Word class	Function	Position	Combined (+conjunction)	Type of marker	Basic type of meaning
Conjunction	Linking word	Left-periphery of the following content unit	No	Connective (two position operator)	Propositional
Parenthetical connective	Appositional adjunct	Variable (typically left periphery or following a conjunction)	Yes	Connective (two position operator)	Propositional (addition, disjunction, contrast, consequence) and Structural
Pragmatic connective	Appositional adjunct	Left periphery	Yes	Connective/ Modal	Structural and Modal
Interjection	Sentence/ utterance equivalent	Isolated or juxtaposed	No	Modal (one position operator)	Modal
Modal **particle**	Verb modifier	Internal (modifier)	No	Modal (one position operator)	Modal
Modal **adverb**	Verb complement or adjunct	Internal (complementor adjunct position)	No	Modal (one position operator)	Modal

If we put together the defining features of the three markers described in this presentation, it will be possible to differentiate characteristics that are common to all markers as grammaticalized items, characteristics that are typical of DMs (in *italics*) and those typical of MPs (**bold**).

The analysis of the three markers can be summarized as follows:

Home/dona is a particle whose counterpart is a very basic noun ('man', 'woman'). As a marker, it is almost completely fixed and admits no specifiers or complements. It shows a strong tendency to invariability: no plural forms can be used as markers, the alternation of the masculine and the feminine is limited, and the masculine form is also used to address women. If it occurs isolated, it is an expressive interjection. In final position, it is an emphasis marker and its modal nature is still foregrounded. In initial position, however, the connective nature is more prominent and the marker, generally *home*, is more similar to a contrastive connective.

---

20. As already said in Section 2, conjunctions and modal adverbs can be considered outside the space of marking if a narrow definition is assumed or included (or at least some cases) in a broader perspective.

Table 2. Defining features of the markers

Markers	home/dona	(és) clar	és que
Counterpart	Noun ('man', 'woman')	Adjective, attributive construction ('(it) is clear')	Copular verb ('is') + complementizer ('that')
Other functions	Interjection	Interjection, Adverb	
Morphology	Tendency to morphological invariability	Invariable fixed form	Invariable, fixed in 3rd person singular, present tense
Syntax	*Detached from the predicative structure (parenthetical)*	*Parenthetical constituent that prefaces utterances, sometimes following a conjunction*	**Integrated particle**
Position	*Tendency to be utterance initial,* although, like vocatives, *home/dona* can occur in final position	*Utterance initial*	*Utterance initial*
Frequency	Increased (134 cases as a marker vs 29 instances as a noun)	Increased (54 cases as a marker vs 13 instances as an adjective)	Increased (151 cases as a marker vs 34 as a copular construction)
Basic meaning(s)	**Attenuation, emphasis**	**Certainty and shared knowledge (emphasis)**	**Justification, emphasis**
Interactive value	**Solidarity marker**	**Agreement marker (co-oriented)**	**Reactive inferential marker**

(És) clar has also experienced a process (or several processes) of semantic and syntactic change. The literal referential meaning ('fair', 'clear') of the source form has changed to pragmatic meanings related to the hearer's involvement in the interaction and to conversation management, activating presuppositions and modifying the illocution. Syntactically, it has developed behaviors that can be identified with those of interjections and markers that blend modal and connective functions.[21] From a contrastive point of view, the marker *(és) clar* is similar to English *you know*, characterized by Fitzmaurice (2004: 438) as "the ubiquitous interactive discourse marker, used to keep things going in a conversation". More specifically, *(és) clar* as a marker would lie somewhere between English *you know* and German *ja*.

Finally, the use of *és que* in conversation as utterance introducer shows the development of modal meanings in discourse deriving from implicatures of a

---

21. On the polysemy of Spanish *claro*, see Pons (2003), Freites Barros (2006) and Maldonado (2010).

pseudo-cleft construction. It can be considered one of the discourse or pragmatic markers "evolving out of subordinating constructions" (Pusch 2006: 173). The increase of the modal meaning and a process of syntactic reanalysis make *és que* functionally similar to a discourse marker, since it introduces a reactive speech-act. It functions either as a mitigator of a face-threatening act or an emphasizer. Although it introduces utterances like DMs do, *és que* is not a linking word (it does not connect two linguistic units) but a modal particle that frames the utterance as a plausible or necessary cause from the point of view of the speaker, though (s)he assumes that the hearer may not agree.

7.   Conclusions

Modal and discourse marking are general functions that invariable words or phrases can express. Some elements are clearly modal or connective but it is often the case that an item is ambiguous or intermediate:

a.   Most DMs and MPs, and other MMs such as secondary interjections, are grammaticalized words. If the process of structural fixation and pragmaticization of meaning has been completed, then the particle and its lexical counterpart can be clearly distinguished. Otherwise, ambiguous contexts can be found and the category adscription is not always straightforward.

b.   Many DMs and MMs are polyfunctional not only as the result of a grammaticalization process from lexical words or phrases but even as particles. In the case of the markers analyzed:

  b.1.   *home/dona* can be an interjection, when it can stand on its own, and also a marker that acts as a pragmatic connective introducing an utterance; in this case, it blends structural and modal functions as a discourse marker that prefaces and qualifies what comes next.

  b.2.   *(és) clar* can also function as an interjection and as a marker that is functionally a modal particle but it is parenthetical like DMs, so that it can be located between modal particles and pragmatic connectives.

c.   As markers, their behavior is often intermediate because they exhibit features typically associated with DMs (initial position, parenthetical character) and others typically associated with MPs (subjective and intersubjective meanings):

  c.1.   *home* can be considered a peripheral pragmatic connective. In initial position, its connective character (generally related to contrast) is enhanced, whereas the modal nuance is prominent in final position (where it is an emphasis marker);

c.2. *(és) clar* is functionally a modal particle but it is parenthetical as DMs, so that it can be located between modal particles and pragmatic connectives;

c.3. *és que* can be considered a modal particle because of its contribution to the utterance and the fact that it is not syntactically or prosodically detached; however, it is utterance initial and can be associated with the function of the causal marker *perquè* 'because'.

In this paper, I have tried to show that by describing focal category behaviors in a cline from discourse to modal marking and checking the defining features of a marker or a group of markers in a specific language it is possible to account for 'anomalous' items that challenge any attempt of classification.

In conclusion, the analysis of the distinctive features of particles helps identifying category boundaries and hence defining discourse and modal marking, from a category perspective,[22] assuming a dynamic and fuzzy model of categorization.

Acknowledgements

This research is part of the project *Cohargument* (reference FFI2011-25236) supported by the Spanish Ministry of Education and Science and of the research group GEV, Grup d'Estudi de la Variació (reference 2009-SGR 521) supported by Generalitat de Catalunya. I want to thank the anonymous reviewers for their contribution to the final version of this paper.

References

Aijmer, Karin, and Simon-Vandenbergen, Anne-Marie. 2004. "A Model and a Methodology for the Study of Pragmatic Markers: The Semantic Field of Expectation." *Journal of Pragmatics* 36 (10): 1781–1805.

Aijmer, Karin, and Simon-Vandenbergen, Anne-Marie. 2006. *Pragmatic Markers in Contrast*. Amsterdam: Elsevier.

Berenguer, Josefa, and Salvador, Vicent. 1998. "Análisis de algunos marcadores discursivos en un corpus conversacional bilingüe español-catalán." In *Atti del XXI congresso internazionale di linguistica e filologia romanza*, ed. by Giovanni Ruffino, vol. 4, 41–50. Tübingen: Niemeyer.

---

22. The perspective presented here should be complemented by an approach departing from the meanings that DMs and MMs express. The identification of the forms indicating these meanings and the differences introduced by the selection of a specific marker would lead to a complete description of what the two types of markers are. However, as a preliminary step, the meanings should be identified, which is by no means an easy task in the case of modal markers.

Chafe, Wallace. 1986. "Evidentiality in English Conversation and Academic Writing." In *Evidentiality: The Linguistic Coding of Epistemology*, ed. by Wallace Chafe, and Johanna Nichols, 261–72. Nordwood, N. J.: Ablex,

Cuenca, Maria-Josep. 2000. "Defining the Indefinable? Interjections." *Syntaxis* 3: 29–44.

Cuenca, Maria-Josep. 2006. *La connexió i els connectors: perspectiva oracional i textual*. Vic: Eumo.

Cuenca, Maria-Josep. 2008. "Pragmatic Markers in Contrast: The Case of *well.*" *Journal of Pragmatics* 40 (8): 1373–1391.

Cuenca, Maria Josep. 2011. "Catalan Interjections." In *The Pragmatics of Catalan*, ed. by Lluís Payrató, and Josep Maria Cots, 173–211. Berlin/Boston: Mouton de Gruyter.

Cuenca, Maria Josep. (ed), 2007, *Catalan Journal of Lingüistics* 6. Monographic volume on "Contrastive perspectives on Pragmatic Markers."

Cuenca, Maria Josep, and Maria Josep Marín. 2001. "Verbos de percepción gramaticalizados como conectores. Análisis contrastivo español-catalán." In *Estudios cognoscitivos del español*, ed. by Ricardo Maldonado, 215–238. Logroño: Revista Española de Lingüística Aplicada (RESLA).

Cuenca, Maria Josep, and Maria Josep Marín. 2012. "Discourse markers and Modality in Spoken Catalan: The Case of *(és) clar.*" *Journal of Pragmatics* 44 (15): 2211–2225.

Cuenca, Maria Josep, and Marta Torres. 2008. "Usos de *hombre/home* y *mujer/dona* como marcadores del discurso." *Verba* 35: 235–256.

Declerck, Renaat. 1992. "The Inferential *it is that*-Construction and its Congeners." *Lingua* 87: 203–230.

Delahunty, Gerald. 2001. "Discourse Functions of Inferential Sentences." *Linguistics* 39: 517–545.

Delahunty, Gerald, and Laura Gatzkiewicz. 2000. "On the Spanish Inferential Construction *ser que.*" *Pragmatics* 10(3): 301–322.

Detges, Ulrich, and Richard Waltereit. 2007. "Different Functions, Different Histories. Modal Particles and Discourse Markers from a Diachronic Point of View." *Catalan Journal of Linguistics* 6: 61–81.

Diewald, Gabriele. [this volume]. "'*Same same but different*' – Modal Particles, Discourse Markers and the Art (and Purpose) of Categorization"

Fernández Leborans, Mª Jesús, 1992. "La oración del tipo: *es que.*" *Verba* 19: 223–239.

Ferrer Mora, Hang. 2001a. "Les partícules modals alemanyes i els seus equivalents en català des d'una perspectiva contrastiva." *Caplletra* 30: 95–110.

Ferrer Mora, Hang. 2001b. "De las partículas modals alemanas a los conectores pragmáticos en español: un puente." In *Quaderns de Filologia. Estudis lingüístics VI, La pragmática de los conectores y las partículas modales*, ed. by Hang Ferrer, and Salvador Pons, 93–114. València: Facultat de Filologia, Universitat de València.

Fitzmaurice, Susan. 2004. "Subjectivity, Intersubjectivity and the Historical Construction of Interlocutor Stance: From Stance Marker to Discourse Markers." *Discourse Studies* 6 (4): 427–448.

Fischer, Kerstin. (ed) 2006. *Approaches to Discourse Particles*, [Studies in Pragmatics 1]. Bingley, UK: Emerald Group Publishing.

Fischer, Kerstin, and Maria Alm. [this volume]. "A Radical Construction Grammar Perspective on the Modal Particle-Discourse Particle Distinction".

Fraser, Bruce. 1990. "An Approach to Discourse Markers." *Journal of Pragmatics* 14: 383–395.

Fraser, Bruce. 1999. "What are Discourse Markers? *Journal of Pragmatics* 31 (7): 931–952.

Fraser, Bruce. 2009. "Topic Orientation Markers." *Journal of Pragmatics* 41 (5): 892–989.

Freites Barros, Francisco. 2006. "El marcador de discurso *claro*: funcionamiento pragmático, metadiscursivo y organizador de la estructura temàtica." *Verba* 33: 261–279.

Fuentes Rodríguez, Catalina. 1993. "*Claro*: modalización y conexión." In *Sociolingüística Andaluza 8. Estudios sobre el enunciado oral*, 99–126. Sevilla: Servicio de Publicaciones de la Universidad de Sevilla.

Fuentes Rodríguez, Catalina. 1997. "Los conectores en la lengua oral: *es que* como introductor de enunciado."*Verba* 24: 237–263.

Fuentes Rodríguez, Catalina, 2003. "Operador/ conector, un criterio para la sintaxis discursiva." *Rilce* 19 (1): 61–85.

Fuentes Rodríguez, Catalina. 2009. *Diccionario de conectores y operadores del español*, Madrid: Arco/Libros.

Gerdes, Kim, and Sylvain Kahane. 2007. "Prasing it Differently." In *Selected Lexical and Grammatical Issues in the Meaning-Text Theory*, 297–335. Amsterdam: John Benjamins.

González, Montserrat. 2004. *Pragmatic Markers in Oral Narrative: The Case of English and Catalan*. Philadelphia/Amsterdam: John Benjamins.

González, Montserrat. 2005. "An Approach to Catalan Evidentiality." *Intercultural Pragmatics* 2 (4): 515–540.

Halliday, Michael A. K., and Ruqaiya Hasan. 1976. *Cohesion in English*. London: Longman.

Jacobs, Joachim. 1991. "On the Semantics of Modal Particles." In *Discourse Particles: Descriptive and Theoretical Investigations on the Logical, Syntactic and Pragmatic Properties of Discourse Particles in German*, ed. by Werner Abraham, 141–162. Amsterdam: John Benjamins.

Lamiroy, Béatrice, and Pierre Swiggers. 1993. "Patterns of Mobilization. A Study of Interaction Signals in Romance." In *Conceptualizations and Mental Processing in Language*, ed. by Richard A. Geiger, and Brygida Rudzka-Ostyn, 649–678. Berlin: Mouton de Gruyter.

Maldonado, Ricardo. 2010. "*Claro*: de objeto perceptible a refuerzo pragmático." In *Adjetivos en discurso. Sobre emociones, posibilidades, certezas y evidencias*, ed. by M. José Rodríguez Espinería, 61–113. Santiago de Compostela: Universidad de Santiago de Compostela.

Marín, Maria-Josep. 2005. *Marcadors discursius procedents de verbs de percepció. Argumentació implícita en el debat electoral* [Quaderns de Filologia, Annex 59]. València: Servei de Publicacions de la Universitat de València.

Marín, Maria-Josep. 2007. "Political (im)politeness. Discourse Power and Political Power in Electoral Debates." *Catalan Review* 21: 43–68.

Norrick, Neal R. 2007. "Discussion article: Pragmatic Markers, Interjections and Discourse." *Catalan Journal of Linguistics* 6: 159–168.

Norrick, Neal R. 2009. "Interjections as Pragmatic Markers." *Journal of Pragmatics* 41 (5): 866–891.

Payrató, Lluís, and Alturo, Núria. 2002. *Corpus oral de conversa col·loquial. Materials de treball*. Barcelona: Publicacions de la Universitat de Barcelona. http: www.ub.edu/cccub. (COC)

Pons, Salvador. 2003. "From Agreement to Stressing and Hedging: Spanish *Bueno* and *Claro*." In *Partikeln und Höflichkeit*, ed. by Gudrun Held, 219–236. Frankfurt: Peter Lang.

Porroche Ballesteros, Margarita. 1998. "Sobre algunos usos de *que, si* y *es que* como marcadores discursivos." In *Los marcadores del discurso. Teoría y análisis*, ed by Mª Antonia Martín Zorraquino, and Estrella Montolío, 229–242. Madrid: Arco Libros.

Portolés, José, and Vázquez Orta, Ignacio. 2000. "Mitigating or Compensatory Strategies in the Expression of Politeness in Spanish and English? "Hombre"/"Mujer" as Politeness Discourse Markers Revisited." In *Transcultural Communication: Pragmalinguistics Aspects*, ed. by M. Pilar Navarro Errasti *et al.*, 219–226. Zaragoza: Ambar.

Pusch, Claus D. 2006. "Marqueurs discursifs et subordination syntaxique: La construction inférentielle en français et dans d'autres langues romanes." In *Les marqueurs discursifs dans les langues romanes. Approches théoriques et méthodologiques,* ed. by Martina Drescher, and Barbara Frank-Job, 173–188. Frankfurt: Peter Lang.

Pusch, Claus D. 2007. "Pragmatic Markers Involving Subordination in Romance: Do They Structure Discourse or Comment on It?." *10th International Pragmatics Conference,* Göteborg, Sweden, July 2007.

Rouchota, Villy. 1998. "Procedural Meaning and Parenthetical Discourse Markers." In *Discourse Markers. Descriptions and Theory,* ed. by Andreas H. Jucker, and Yael Ziv, 97–126. Amsterdam/Philadelphia: John Benjamins.

Sancho, Pelegrí. 2010. "Anàlisi de les unitats fraseològiques amb funció connectiva en un fragment de conversa col·loquial." *Caplletra* 48: 93–125.

Schiffrin, Deborah. 1987. *Discourse Markers.* Cambridge: Cambridge University Press.

Schiffrin, Deborah. 2001. "Discourse Markers, Meaning, and Context." In *The Handbook of Discourse Analysis* (Blackwell Handbooks in Linguistics). ed. by Deborah Schiffrin, Deborah Tannen, and Heidi E. Hamilton, 54–75. Oxford/Maldon, MA: Blackwell.

Torrent-Letzen, Aina. 2009. "Polifonía de las emociones. Estudio pragmático sobre la función emotiva de las partículas modales en castellano, catalán y rumano." *Estudis Romànics* 31: 7–34.

Torrent-Letzen, Aina. 2011. "Catalan Modal Particles." In *The Pragmatics of Catalan,* ed. by Lluís Payrató, and Josep Maria Cots, 81–114. Berlin/Boston: Mouton de Gruyter.

Traugott, Elizabeth Closs, 2007. "Discourse Markers, Modal Particles, and Contrastive Analysis, Synchronic and Diachronic." *Catalan Journal of Linguistics* 6: 139–157.

Traugott, Elizabeth C., and Richard B. Dasher. 2002. *Regularity in Semantic Change.* Cambridge: Cambridge University Press.

Waltereit, Richard. 2001. "Modal Particles and their Functional Equivalents: A Speech-Act Theoretic Approach." *Journal of Pragmatics* 33: 1391–1417.

Appendix 1. Transcription conventions (cfr. Payrató 1995 and Bladas 2009)

1. *Prosodic aspects*
    Intonation unit (one line for each intonation unit)
    Boundary tone/Closure
        falling   \
        rising   /
        continuative   –
    Truncated intonation unit   --
    Manner/Quality
        high   {(A) text}
        low   {(B) text}
    Voice of another   {(EV) text}
    Tempo
        accelerated speech   {(AC) text}
        piano, attenuated speech   {(DC) text}

Lenghtening (short, medium and long)   :   ::   :::

2. *Vocal aspects*
   Laughing text   {(@) text}
   Laugh
      One symbol per pulse   @
      Long fragment, timed   @R(time)R@
   Inhalation and exhalation   (INH) (EXH)

3. *Pauses and overlaps*
   Pause, timed
      very short (0.1 < p < 0.3)   (. time)
      short (p < 1)   (.. time)
      medium (1 ≤ p < 3)   (... time)
      long (p ≥ 3)   (.... time)
   Overlaps   [text]

4. *Regularizations and comments*
   Deletion   use of brackets to mark the
                                          deleted sound

   Transcriptor's comments
      concrete   (comment)
      general   ((comment))

5. *Difficult fragments*
   Uncertain words   {(??) text}
   Unintelligible
      One sign per syllable   x
      Long fragment, timed   xX(time)Xx

6. *Other aspects*
   Code-switch   {(L2) text}
   Truncated/cut-off word   *wor-*

From discourse markers to modal/final particles

What the position reveals about the continuum

Katsunobu Izutsu and Mitsuko Narita Izutsu
Hokkaido University of Education and Fuji Women's University

The present article investigates a cross-linguistic correlation between the meaning/function and the position of modal/final particles. It argues that some of the modal particles and their analogs in German, French, and Japanese derive from discourse markers that have come to express some (inter)subjective meanings in a limited sentential position, and it elucidates that the position that directly follows the tensed verb group can serve to motivate the development of modal particles with (inter)subjective meanings. Referring also to English data, it further demonstrates that the utterance-final position is another site of marking intersubjective meanings.

1. Introduction

"Modal particle" was chiefly a language-specific notion in the early stages of its investigation (Weydt 1969; Abraham 1991, *inter alia*). Nevertheless, there have been an increasing number of studies that deal with French modal particles (e.g., Hansen 1997, 1998; Waltereit 2001; Waltereit and Detges 2007). Some inquiries have noticed semantic and functional similarities between German modal particles and Japanese sentence-final particles (e.g., Kawashima 1987).

It is a clear fact that such particles exhibit language specific differences in syntactic behavior. German modal particles are restricted to a certain sentence-internal position (see Section 2.1). In contrast, French modal particles are not strictly limited to one specific sentential position (see Section 2.2), and Japanese counterparts manifest themselves as final rather than modal particles (see Section 3). To treat the apparently heterogeneous particles in different languages as comparable linguistic forms with similar pragmatic meanings and functions, we need to devise a broader perspective of modal particles and a cross-linguistic framework or model for their analysis.

Despite the observed discrepancy, some German modal particles and their comparables in French and Japanese manifest striking similarities. Some modal particles in German and French derive from discourse markers that have developed (inter)subjective meanings along with their occurrence becoming restricted to a specific sentential position: the middle field in German and the final or internal position in French. Interestingly, some Japanese discourse markers express similar (inter)subjective meanings in the final position, thus best characterized as modal as well as final particles. Moreover, some "turn-final" discourse markers in German (Diewald 2006) occur exclusively in the utterance-final position just like some French and most Japanese modal particles do.

Building on these facts, the present article argues that there are two sentential positions available for the development of modal particles. One is the position that directly follows a tensed verb group, while the other is the utterance-final position. Some discourse markers have come to express (inter)subjective meanings in such a restricted sentential position. As far as such functional and notional changes hold for different languages, they deserve to be taken seriously as a cross-linguistically applicable developmental path of modal/final particles.[1]

---

1.   Discourse markers and modal particles are both subsumable under a broader category of pragmatic markers (cf. Brinton 1996, 336 n.3). However, they are distinguished in functional, notional, and structural terms (Diewald 2006; Fischer 2007; Waltereit and Detges 2007, among others). Discourse markers "concern the structure or *form* of discourse" while "modal particles are highly content-dependent and have a scope which is conventionally fixed" and "they are subject to heavy syntactic restrictions" (Waltereit and Detges 2007, 63). Comparing the Spanish discourse particle *bien* and its French cognate modal particle *bien*, Waltereit and Detges argue that their functional difference derives from different diachronic pathways and characteristic pragmatic strategies. They tabulate German and English as well as French and Spanish patterns of the adverb 'well' and its derived discourse marker and modal particle as below:

	adverb	discourse marker	modal particle
French	*bien*	*bien*	*bien*
Spanish	*bien*	*bien*	–
German	*gut*	*gut*	–
English	*well*	*well*	–

(Waltereit and Detges 2007, 64)

The observed distribution strongly suggests the possibility that the adverb acquired a discourse-marker use, which, in French alone, further developed into a modal-particle use. It points to a certain developmental pathway: from adverb through discourse marker to modal particle. This is fully compatible with the grammaticalization path of modal particles discussed in this article.

2. Modal particles in German and French

2.1 Modal particles in German

There has been a large literature written in German on modal particles since Weydt (1969). To the best of our knowledge, Abraham (1991) is the first work written in English to discuss the grammaticalization of German modal particles extensively. He claims that "the modal particle function can be derived from its counterpart with full categorial status either synchronically or diachronically" (Abraham 1991, 332). Such counterparts include "sentential connectors" (e.g., *aber* 'but' and *schon* 'already'), "adjuncts" (e.g., *halt* 'to be sure' and *wohl* 'well'), "scalar particles" (e.g., *nur* 'only' and *auch* 'also'), adjectives (e.g., *eigentlich* 'real' and *eben* 'flat'), and interjections (e.g., *ja* 'yes'), most of which can or could serve as discourse markers as well. The modal particles differ from their "non-modal" counterparts in that their linear position is restricted to the "middle field" in German (and Dutch) and that they "usually cannot carry stress" (Abraham 1991, 333).[2]

The middle as well as "initial" and "final" fields are characterized as in the generalized sentential structure of (1a). The middle field is described as "the linear and structural domain between V-second (...) and V-final," which corresponds to "what traditionally has been called the "verbal bracket" in German" (Abraham 1991, 340). Modal particles (MP) fall within that field, not outside it, as *ja* and *wohl* do in (1b).[3] The same holds for *denn* and *doch* in (2) (emphasis added). While *doch* simply expresses contradiction or opposition in its sentence-connecting adverbial function as in (3), it can express types of attitudes like "[i]mpatience, annoyance, disapproval, indignation, blame and anger" (Abraham 1991, 358) in its modal particle use such as (2c-d).

(1) a. {INITIAL FIELD} [V-second]{MIDDLE FIELD} [V-final]({FINAL FIELD}).

    b. {*Er*}   [*hat*] {*ja den Mann **wohl***} [*gesehen*] {*heute*}
        he   has MP the man   MP   seen   today
                                    (cf. Abraham 1991, 347)

(2) a. *Was$_i$ hat er (**denn**) dem Koch*   *(**denn**) [e$_i$] getan?*
     What has he then   the cook.DAT then   done
                               (Abraham 1991, 356)

    b. *Hat (**denn**) der Mann (**denn**) dem Koch*   *(**denn**) einen*
     Has then   the man then   the cook.DAT then   a

---

2.   Abraham (1991, 348) further points out that the "nexus field" in Mainland Scandinavian languages like Danish, Norwegian, and Swedish is comparable to the German middle field and that those languages also restrict the occurrence of modal particles to the nexus field.

3.   See Fischer and Alm (this volume) for further details.

   Hieb (*denn) versetzt?
   blow then given   (Abraham 1991, 356)

  c. *Das hat **doch** wohl schon Geniecharakter (schon=scalar)*
    this has MP MP already properties.of.a.genius
                     (Abraham 1991, 354)

  d. *Denk **doch**!* 'Do think! Use your brain!'   (Abraham 1991, 358)

(3) *Er ist klein. **Doch** kann er [er kann] hoch springen.*
  'He is little. Nevertheless, he can jump very high.' (Abraham 1991, 358)

Abraham (1991, 336) emphasizes that the sentential middle field (MF) plays a crucial role in the emergence or grammaticalization of German modal particles. Departing from different grammatical categories, sentential functions, and semantic meanings, the original, pre-modal-particle lexemes "abandoned their distinct and different syntactic properties and aligned with the single MF-restriction"; they thereby constitute "a unique and easily identifiable formal paradigm," which helps them to form a single category of modal particles (Abraham 1991, 372–373).

  Moreover, Abraham (1991, 373) states that the emergence of German modal particles involves the stages: "LOCALISTIC > TEMPORAL > LOGICAL > ILLOCUTIVE/ DISCOURSE FUNCTIONAL." Full lexical and/or functional meanings of the original, pre-modal-particle lexemes "have been replaced by pragmatic meanings of an illocutive and of a rhematic type" (Abraham 1991, 357) along with attitudinal or (inter)subjective meanings like impatience, annoyance, disapproval, and so forth. Waltereit (2001, 1397) attempts to characterize the illocutive meaning as a means of modifying the "preparatory conditions of the speech act."

2.2 Modal particles in French

Unlike German, French is assumed to have "no grammatical category akin to German modal particle" (Abraham 1991, 331) or "only very few modal particles" (Waltereit 2001, 1392). However, Hansen, analyzing French *alors* and *donc* as discourse markers, argues that *donc* in its 'discursive' use as in (4) should be treated "as a modal particle, rather than as a discourse marker" (1997, 168) and that the "utterance-final *alors*" as in (5) "may be a candidate for a grammaticalization as a modal particle" (1997, 182). She also points out that *donc* in the relevant use "does not occur as an independent tone unit at the beginning of the host utterance" (1997, 168). This characteristic comes closer to that of German modal particles, which are restricted to the middle field and usually do not carry stress.

(4) a. *Que ta maison est **donc** jolie!* 'Your house is wonderful!'
   b. *Donne-le-lui **donc**!* (as said by a mother to her son who is fighting with his younger sister over a toy) 'Give it to her!'
   c. *Pourquoi **donc?*** 'Why on earth?'

   (Hansen 1997, 168; our English translations)

(5) A. *mais Estier c'est peut-être de la mauvaise tactique électorale, car deux listes, une du RPR et une de/ de l'UDF peuvent faire, 53 ou 54%, 55% tandis qu'une liste unique, qui va susciter à côté: des listes petit/ mai/ maigre importance/ de faible importance qui peut faire que 48 ou 49 ça serait donc, une mauvaise tactique & électorale &&*
   B. *& vous êtes pour && deux listes **alors** (VS2: 16)*
   A. but Estier it may be bad election tactics, because two rolls, one for the RPR and one for the UDF may get 53 or 54%, 55%, whereas a single roll, which may give rise to smaller rolls on the side which may not get more than 48 or 49 that would DM be bad election & tactics &&
   B. & you're for && two rolls DM

   (Hansen 1998, 351; cf. Hansen 1997, 182; our emphasis)[4]

Hansen (1997, 168) further notes that the discursive use of *donc* has "the additional 'emphatic' function of reinforcing the illocutionary force of the utterance" as in (4), which is comparable to the "illocutive" meaning of German modal particles (Abraham 1991, 373). She reports that the utterance-final *alors* as in (5) "is often found with statements made on the basis of inference from prior discourse by the interlocutor, and which therefore usually function pragmatically as requests for confirmation" (Hansen 1997, 182), again comparable to a pragmatic meaning of German modal particles.

Degand and Fagard (2011) deal with the French discourse marker *alors* and substantiate the relationship between its different meanings and the position it occupies in each meaning. They define the position of *alors* as below, postulating that clause-internal medial *alors* typically expresses "temporal concomitance," that initial *alors* can function as a connective that expresses "temporal succession, causal or conditional relations, or a metadiscursive meaning, especially topic shift," and that final *alors* expresses "a metadiscursive meaning of intersubjectivity" (2011, 45).

---

4. The symbols & and && indicate the beginning and end of overlap (Hansen 1998, xi). This example is excerpted from "a collection of recording and (in a few cases only partially) transcribed corpora, obtained from the archives of the UFR de linguistique française of the Université de Paris III," where *VS2* represents Corpus number 6: *Vendredi soir* ('Friday evening') 2 (Hansen 1998, 201–202).

- initial *alors* is located in the left periphery of the sentence/utterance, that is, outside the argument structure of the verb; occurrences of *et alors*, *puis alors*, *mais alors*, etc. are counted as initial;
- medial *alors* is internal to the argument structure, mostly after the finite verb and before the non-finite verb, if present;
- final *alors* is located in the right periphery, after the non-finite verb, if present.

(Degand and Fagard 2011, 38)

According to Degand and Fagard (2011, 37), *alors* in the final position is "exclamative" (Hybertie 1996) or "intersubjective" (Franckel 1989); it denotes "the urgency of the invitation" in *Tu viens, alors?!* 'Are you coming, [alors]?' (Franckel 1989). This exclamative or intersubjective meaning, unlike the temporal, causal, or conditional meanings, overlaps much more with the illocutive meaning of German modal particles. This use of *alors* largely corresponds to what Hansen (1997) proposes to treat as a modal particle.

Degand and Fagard's statistical research on historical data reveals that *alors* first occupied the internal position dominantly with the temporal meaning, then extended into "a new predominant initial position" to develop the causal meaning and eventually innovated the metadiscursive meaning in the final as well as initial position "with a decrease of temporal uses and an increase of causal and metadiscursive uses" (2011, 49).

This evolution of the syntactic position and meaning of *alors* is parallel to the emergence or grammaticalization of German modal particles (Abraham 1991, 336, 357, 363). Degand and Fagard's remarks that "syntactic change is a prerequisite for semantic change" (2011, 49) and that "the appearance of new syntactic positions precedes the occurrences of new meanings" (2011, 51–52) are comparable in spirit with Abraham's observation that "the development of the syntactic MF triggered the rise of the pragmatic properties characteristic of the MPs in German" (1991, 357).

As with German modal particles, French modal particles are confined to a "fixed syntactic position" (Waltereit and Detges 2007): the final or internal position. In Degand and Fagard's definition cited above, each sentential position in French is identifiable in a structure like (6). As modal particles, *donc* occupies the internal or final position as in (4) and *alors* occurs in the final position as in (5). Likewise, *quand même* (Waltereit 2001) and *bien* (Waltereit and Detges 2007) serve as modal particles in the internal position. They are all "subject to heavy syntactic restrictions" (Waltereit and Detges 2007, 63)

(6) {INITIAL POSITION}[finite V]{INTERNAL POSITION}(non-finite V){FINAL POSITION}.

3. Modal/final-particle use of Japanese discourse markers

Japanese differs both syntactically and morphologically from languages like German and French. However, it manifests a striking similarity in the developmental path from discourse markers to modal (more specifically "final") particles. Discourse markers can occur more or less freely in either the sentence-initial, internal, or final position when they serve to combine two discourse units (Watts 2003; Hagiwara 2012, for example). When they assume certain emotive and (inter) subjective meanings, however, they tend to be subject to syntactic restrictions. In some dialects, such discourse markers become fixed in the sentence-final position and develop into final particles, i.e., analogues of German and French modal particles. Both synchronic and diachronic data corroborate this tendency.

Present-day colloquial Japanese has a number of discourse markers, each of which is known to have developed from various lexical and morphological sources. One example is *dakara* as illustrated in (7) and (8).[5] In its discourse-connective use, with the meaning 'so/therefore', it can be used in either the sentence-initial, internal, or final position, as represented by the parentheses in (7).[6]

(7) A: *Ame   huru-kamosirenai-yo.*
     rain   fall-may-FP
     'I'm afraid it may rain.'

   B: *Un.   (**Dakara**) kyoo (**dakara**) kasa   (**dakara**)*
       yeah so   today so   umbrella   so
       *mottekoo-tte   (**dakara**) omotte (**dakara**).*
       will:take-that so   think   so
       'Yeah. So I think I'll take an umbrella with me today.'

(8) A: *Ame   huru-kamosirenai-kara kasa-motteki-nasai.*
     rain   fall-may-because   umbrella-take-IMP
     'Take an umbrella with you, because it may rain.'

   B: *(**Dakara**) yohoo-de-wa   (ʔ**dakara**) kyoo   (ʔ**dakara**)*
       told:you   forecast-at-TOP   told:you   today   told:you
       *huranai-tte   (ʔ**dakara**) itten-no   (**dakara**).*
       don't:rain-that told:you   be:saying-FN   told:you
       'I've told you the weatherman says it won't rain today!'

---

5. (7) and (8) are constructed examples, in which *dakara* is originally located in the sentence-initial position. Four native speakers of the Tokyo and Kanagawa dialects (two each) were asked if the discourse marker was acceptable in different positions when used in conversations like (7) and (8). The naturalness (unmarked) and slight unnaturalness (marked with a question mark) are grounded on their judgment.

6. Hagiwara (2012, 140) also makes the same point for the *dakara* used in speech.

As illustrated in (8), this same discourse marker is used to express some emotive senses like the speaker's impatience, annoyance, and disapproval, which are comparable to the (inter)subjective senses of German modal particles. The discourse marker in such an emotive use does not convey the connective sense 'so/therefore' but serves to emphasize that the speaker has already informed the addressee about the intent of the current utterance, as shown by the gloss 'told you.' In this use, the discourse marker is less acceptable in the internal position, which suggests that the (inter)subjective meaning and function are more or less incompatible with the sentence-internal position in Japanese. This (inter)subjective *dakara* favors the initial and final positions because they correspond to what Shinzato (2006) describes as the sites for expressing (inter)subjective meanings.

As such discourse markers develop one step further into markers for emotive and (inter)subjective meanings, they come to be fixed in the sentence-final position. This will be demonstrated by some more data from dialectal research of discourse markers. We have demonstrated elsewhere (2010) that some discourse markers in the Hokkaido, Hiroshima, and Osaka dialects are used nearly exclusively in the sentence/utterance-final position to convey (inter)subjective meanings like surprise, anger, impatience, disapproval, blame, and complaint, as illustrated in (9) to (11). A remarkable characteristic of this particular usage is that the sentence ends with a falling intonation that signals the end of an utterance and does not leave any implication unstated. The discourse markers occupy the final position, logically, as a result of "backshift" from the initial position, not "truncation" of a longer sentence (Izutsu and Izutsu, forthcoming a). Discourse markers like those used in (9) to (11) approximate to German and French modal particles in that they have largely been fixed in a position and serve as final particles of emotive and (inter)subjective meanings rather than as connectives.[7]

(9) Hokkaido Dialect
  a. (About a restaurant serving good sausage at reasonable prices)
      Zawaakurauto-toka tuitekuru-wake sosite?
      sauerkraut-etc.   come:with-FN   DM
      'And does it come with sauerkraut as well?'

  b. (Interrupted by a child while doing some work)
      Iyaa hontoni bundan bundan-de sigoto-ga   susuma-nai.
      shit   really   chop   chop-with work-NOM proceed-not

---

7. (10a), (11a), and (11b) are cited from the following websites, respectively. The English glosses and translations are ours.

  (10) a. http://qb5.2ch.net/test/read.cgi/sakud/1095421468/
  (11) a. http://blog.livedoor.jp/h8739/archives/cat_ 10007870.html
  (11) b. http://jerrylove.jugem.jp/?cid=17

> *Kore simatte-kite*   ***sosite.***
> this   put:aside:and-come   DM
> 'Oh, no! I can't concentrate on my work because of your interruption!
> Go and put this aside, anyway.'   (Izutsu and Izutsu 2010, 79)

(10)   Hiroshima dialect

     a.   *Omae dare-nimukatte kabati*   *tare-toru-n-nara-**hoidee.***
         you   who-towards   complaint flow-PERF-FN-COP-DM
         'Who are you complaining to?'

     b.   *Nantyuu*   *kotoo yuu-n-nara-**hoitee.***
         what:sort:of thing say-FN-COP-DM
         'What a stupid thing you say!'
                   (Fujiwara 1993, 182; our glosses and translation)

(11)   Osaka dialect

     a.   *Unagi buattu! Tee   hurue-te   kireeni   toren-gana*   ***sikasi.***
         eel   thick   hand shiver-and properly cannot:take-FP   DM
         'The eel is thick! I cannot photograph it properly!'

     b.   *Nani asi kun-de   tabako   suuton-nen!   Tabako   nan-ya?*
         what leg fold-and tobacco breathe:in-FP tobacco what-COP
         Mine-ka!? Dare-mo   siran-tyuu-nen   ***sikasi!***
         Mine-FP   who-either not:know-(I):say-FP   DM
         'Why're you smoking with your legs crossed? What's the cigarette?
         Mine!? Nobody cares about it!'

When used as ordinary connectives or discourse markers, *sosite* 'and' in Hokkaido, *hoide* 'and' in Hiroshima, and *sikasi* 'but' in Osaka occur canonically in the initial position and optionally in the final and internal positions, as illustrated in (12a). In their emotive and (inter)subjective use instantiated in (9) through (11), however, they do not tolerate the initial position, let alone the internal position, as shown in (12b), (12c), and (12d).[8]

(12)   Hokkaido dialect

     a.   *Mado   simete.* **(*Sosite*)** *kore* **(*sosite*)** *simatte-kite*   **(*sosite*)**.
         window close   and   this   and   put:aside:and-come   and
         'Close the window. And go and put this aside.'

---

8.   The sentences in (12) are elicited from native speakers of each dialect. (12b-d) are constructed out of (9a), (10b), and (11a), respectively. We asked some of the native speakers of the respective dialect if each discourse marker was acceptable in different positions when used in the context of (9a), (10b), and (11a). The acceptability of the examples is based on those speakers' judgment.

b. (Informed that a restaurant serves good sausage at reasonable prices)
   (#*Sosite*) *zawaakurauto-toka* (ʾ*sosite*) *tuitekuru-wake* (*sosite*)?[9]
   DM   sauerkraut-etc.   DM   come:with-FN   DM
   'And does it come with sauerkraut as well?'

Hiroshima dialect

c. (??*Hoidee*) *nantyuu*   *kotoo* (??*hoidee*) *yuu-n-nara*(-*hodee*).
   DM   what:sort:of thing   DM   say-FN-COP- DM
   'What a stupid thing you say!'

Osaka dialect

d. (??*Sikasi*) *tee*   *hurue-te*   (??*sikasi*) *kireeni*   (??*sikasi*)
   DM   hand shiver-and   DM   properly   DM
   toren-gana   (*sikasi*).
   cannot:take-FP   DM
   'I cannot photograph it properly!'

The final particle use of *sosite*, *hoide*, and *sikasi* in (9) to (11) can be identified as modal particles on the same grounds that some German and French discourse markers are regarded as such. Their occurrence is restricted to a fixed sentential position: the sentence/utterance-final position. They carry no stress or emphasis, conveying (inter)subjective meanings. No prosodic break is allowed before the discourse markers; moreover, one of them, *hoide*, is phonologically and morphologically bound to the preceding element (Izutsu and Izutsu, forthcoming a). *Sosite* in (9) and *hoide* in (10) express the speaker's surprise, irritation, dissatisfaction, or complaint rather than the sequentiality or additionality sense of 'and'. *Sikasi* in (11) has nearly lost the original sense 'but', and it is more like an intensifier, expressing the speaker's surprise, irritation, or pleasure.[10] Its occurrence is possible even where a causal rather than concessive relation is inferred as in (11a).

Japanese has a canonical sentence structure that ends with a main verb, optionally followed by auxiliaries as well as final particles in the final position, as diagramed in (13). The internal position is not clearly separated from the initial position, but it can be largely defined as the position between the topic phrase and the main verb.

(13) {INITIAL POSITION}[topic]{INTERNAL POSITION}[main V](aux){FINAL POSITION}.

9. "#" indicates that the ordinary connective use is, but the (inter)subjective use is not, possible in the initial position.

10. An online dictionary gives an explanation on the usage of the Osaka dialect *sikasi*: "It means 'nevertheless' in the sentence-initial position and 'indeed' in the sentence-final position" (www.weblio.jp/content/しかし).

In grammatical terms, the main verb and the following auxiliaries form a complex predicate, which is followed by final particles that occupy the sentence-final position. As noted above, modal particles *sosite*, *hoide*, and *sikasi* as in (9)-(11) are confined to the sentence-final position. Therefore, they also count as final particles.

Japanese sentence-final particles (*shuujoshi*) are expressions of (inter)subjective meanings (Sakuma 1952; Matsumura 1969; Suzuki 1976; Shinzato 2006). It could be that various discourse or sentential units, which originally occupy different positions in utterances, result in the sentence-final position through a process of "truncation" or "backshift" (Izutsu and Izutsu, forthcoming a) and gradually develop into final/modal particles. Major final particles in Classical Japanese (*fa*, *mo*, *zo/so*, *ya*, and *ka*) derive from non-sentence-final lexemes or particles that came to be used in the sentence-final position (Matsumura 1969). A number of final particles in Present-day Japanese (*kara*, *node*, *kedo*, *noni*, and *ga*) develop from conjunctive particles that end up in the sentence-final position with their following main clause suspended (Ohori 1996; Izutsu and Izutsu forthcoming b). The sentence--final position itself has thus been the site of linguistically coding (inter)subjective meanings and functions since Classical Japanese (cf. Shinzato 2006). When used in the final position of an utterance, some discourse markers lose their combining function and come to acquire the meaning and function of the sentence-final position or of the sentence-final particles unique to that position. In other words, this function of the sentence-final position can plausibly be identified as a synchronic and diachronic motivation for the development of modal/final particles.

4.   Development from discourse markers into modal/final particles

4.1   (Inter)subjectivity marking in a restricted sentential position

Based on the review of the earlier works and the observation of language data, Sections 2 and 3 have argued that some discourse markers in German, French, and Japanese have come to serve as modal particles by developing (inter)subjective meanings and functions in a limited sentential position: the middle field in German, the final or internal position in French, and the final position in Japanese. Although those modal particle positions in the languages appear to differ, they are all analyzable as the one that directly follows a "tensed verb group" which consists of one tensed verbal in its simplest form or of one tensed and (an)other nonfinite verbal(s) in its more complex forms, as is represented in (14).[11]

---

11.   Note that the verb group differs from the verb phrase or VP, which ordinarily refers to a complex structure that consists of a verb and its complement(s). The underscore indicates a relevant "tensed verb group" in (14) and (15) below.

(14)   …[tensed verb group]{   **MP**   }(…).

In French, the first and the following verbal(s) can compose a verb group as illustrated in (15a). In German, in contrast, they do not, as in (15b); the tensed element in the "V-second" counts as the relevant verb group. In Japanese, the main verb (*miwake*) invariably combines with the auxiliary (*rare*) to form a verb group as in (15c).

(15)   a.   *Je <u>savais reconnaître</u>, du premier coup d'œil, la Chine de l'Arizona.*
>
> (Antoine de Saint Exupéry, *Le Petit Prince*, §1)

   b.   *Ich <u>konnte</u> auf den ersten Blick China von Arizona unterscheiden.*
>
> (Grete und Leitgeb, *Der Kleine Prinz*)

   c.   *Hitomede   Chuugoku-to Arizona-o   miwake-rare-ta.*
        at:a:glance China-with   Arizona-ACC distinguish-can-PAST
        'I could distinguish China from Arizona at a glance.'
>
> (Our Japanese and English glosses and translations)

A majority of modal particles have their non-modal counterparts (adverbials, conjunctions, or discourse markers) synchronically or diachronically (Abraham 1991; Hansen 1997; Waltereit 2001; Diewald 2006; Degand and Fagard 2011). As discussed in the previous sections, their development is characterizable as a change or grammaticalization in which such adverbials, conjunctions, or discourse markers come to express (inter)subjective meanings in a limited sentential position that directly follows the tensed verb group. Insofar as a significant number of modal particles in German, French, and Japanese can be viewed as following this similar grammaticalization path, we may see it as a possible cross-linguistic model for the development of modal particles.

The (inter)subjective meanings expressed in modal particles might appear to vary from one language to another, but in fact fall within a speech act conception: the speaker's reference to, or 'consultation' of, an assumption. Waltereit (2001, 1399) argues that the German modal particle *ja* refers to the presupposition that "speaker and addressee agree about the propositional content of the assertion containing the particle." He argues that the French modal particle *quand même* expresses a "counter-expectation" or "the speaker's doubts as to whether or not the addressee shares assumptions that are required for compliance with the preparatory condition of the speech act in question" (2001, 1403). Diewald (2006, 417) claims that modal particles "refer back to a proposition that has not been linguistically expressed before but is nevertheless treated as pragmatically given."[12] As these characterizations reveal, modal particles indicate that the speaker not only

---

12.   See also Diewald (this volume).

utters the sentential content but also refers to or 'consults' his assumption (recognition and expectation) related to that content. In this sense, modal particles are regarded as (inter)subjective markers.

The speaker usually views the assumption in positive or negative mental attitudes, which account for emotive or affective meanings accompanying modal particles. If the situation mentioned conflicts or the addressee disagrees with his assumption (recognition and expectation), he will feel and exhibit "[i]mpatience, annoyance, disapproval, indignation, blame and anger" (Abraham 1991, 358). In order to negotiate agreement with his assumption, he may activate "the additional 'emphatic' function of reinforcing the illocutionary force of the utterance" (Hansen 1997, 168); therefore, his utterance may sound like "exclamative" (Hybertie 1996) or an emphasis on "the urgency of the invitation" (Franckel 1989). Exclamative sentences are a kind of "mirative" expression, the prototypical values of which are "beyond or against the speaker's expectation" (Izutsu and Izutsu 2008).

4.2   Intersubjectivity marking in the utterance-final position

Section 4.1 has proposed a possible cross-linguistic model for the development of modal/final particles from discourse markers. In short, some discourse markers that occur more or less freely in either the initial, internal, or final position come to express (inter)subjective meanings in a restricted sentential position that directly follows the tensed verb group. It should be noted, however, that there is another possible position of modal/final particles or discourse markers of intersubjectivity. German utterance-final particles like *ja* and *oder* in (16) are not ordinarily regarded as modal particles but are similar to some uses of the French modal particles *donc* and *alors* in evoking intersubjective meanings like request for confirmation (Hansen 1997, 183) or urgency of the invitation (Franckel 1989).[13]

(16)   a.   *und dann kommt der Querflügel, ja?*
            and then, the crossbeam comes next, JA?

       b.   K: *und das wird dann da so seitlich draufgeschraubt oder?*
            and that's going to be screwed there to the side this way, isn't it?
            (Sagerer et al. 1994, quoted from Diewald 2006, 406; our emphasis)

The understanding that the utterance-final position is largely specialized for expressing the intersubjective meanings agrees with the observations made by earlier studies. Traugott (2011) reports that "right periphery (RP)," roughly

---

13.   French *n'est-ce pas*, German *nicht wahr*, and Japanese *daro* and *desyo* also serve a similar function in the sentence-final position.

identifiable with the utterance-final position, is likely to be "intersubjective" in French and English, and it is usable for "exclamations (subjective)" and "tags (intersubjective)" in Japanese.

The utterance-final position can be included in the possible cross-linguistic model as in (17). Central members of modal particles occupy the position that directly follows the tensed verb group. In contrast, discourse markers of inter-subjective meanings (or peripheral members of modal particles) occur more frequently in the utterance-final position, namely the underlined part in (17).

(17) ...[tensed verb group]{   **MP**   }(...){__**MP**__}.

Some language-specific differences should also be noted here, however. In German, the position directly following the tensed verb group is usually separated from the utterance-final position by some other phrases like complement, modifier, and/or V-final. In French, the two positions overlap more frequently, because pronominal complements in their weak form do not intervene between the positions. In Japanese, the two positions almost invariably overlap and sometimes merge together.

As far as German, French, and Japanese are concerned, central members of modal particles are restricted to the position that directly follows the tensed verb group. However, peripheral members (or intersubjective discourse markers) like German *ja* and *oder* are placed in the utterance-final position. A similar perspective seems applicable to English comparable expressions. Even though "English has no grammatical category akin to the German modal particle" (Abraham 1991, 331), it does have intersubjective discourse markers identifiable as peripheral members of modal particles in our perspective.

Traugott and Dasher (2002, 22) argue that the discourse marker *actually* has an intersubjective meaning in the expression *Actually, I will take you to school.* They further point out that *actually* "may be used in spoken language to serve as hedges or softeners" (2002, 173) and to "create contact with the listener" (Aijmer 1986, 128). In this intersubjective use, "it often occurs clause-finally" (Traugott and Dasher 2002) as in (18), and it could thus be regarded as a kind of modal particle.

(18) a. *No, I was determined to get married **actually**.*
      b. *I enjoyed it, **actually**.* (Excerpted from Traugott and Dasher 2002, 173)

Discourse markers like *right* and *innit* also convey intersubjective meanings like *ja* and *oder*. They occur in the utterance-final position as in (19a-b) but do not tolerate the initial position, much less the internal position, as in (19c-f). This implies that the internal and initial positions in English could hardly serve as a site of intersubjective marking and neither establishes itself as the one that motivates the development of modal particles.

(19) a. *You went to see Angie on Monday, **right**?*
     b. *It's the easiest way, **innit**?*
     c. *??**Right**, you went to see Angie on Monday?*
     d. *??You **right** went to see Angie on Monday?*
     e. *??**Innit**, it's the easiest way?*
     f. *??It's **innit** the easiest way?*   (cf. *Oxford Dictionary of English*)

The observation that English has no or only very few modal particles (Abraham 1991, 331; Waltereit 2001, 1392) may correlate with the fact that English has not established a clearly defined (sentence-internal) position as the one that directly follows a tensed verb group. What can be regarded as the internal position in English may be the "medial position" (Quirk et al. 1985, 491–494), which is described as that between the subject and the verb. However, its structural definition is indeterminate; it is typically located before the tensed verb, if there is no auxiliary as in (20a), or after the first auxiliary if there is one as in (20b), but it is situated before the negated auxiliary as in (20c).

(20) a. {INITIAL POSITION}S{MEDIAL POSITION}[tensed V](...){FINAL POSITION}
     b. {INITIAL POSITION}S[aux]{MEDIAL POSITION}[V](...){FINAL POSITION}
     c. {INITIAL POSITION}S{MEDIAL POSITION}[aux(neg)](...)[V](...){FINAL POSITION}

Though much closer to French than to German and Japanese, English is still marked by the structural indeterminacy of the internal position, as shown by a comparison of (21) with (22). Yet the utterance-final position is definite; accordingly, it is more or less exploited as illustrated in (19a-b). So-called final *but* (Mulder and Thompson 2008), as illustrated in (23), is another example of utterance-final exploitation.[14]

(21) a. *They can **probably** find their way here.*
     b. *(?)They **probably** can find their way here.*
     c. **They can't **probably** find their way here.*
     d. *They **probably** can't find their way here.*
     e. *He was **probably** unhappy.*
     f. *He **probably** wasn't unhappy.*   (Quirk et al. 1985, 494)

---

14. In its meaning and function, however, this final *but* is more akin to the Japanese backshifted conjunctions *sosite* 'and', *hoide* 'and', and *sikasi* 'but' in their dialectal use (Izutsu and Izutsu forthcoming a).

(22) a. *Ils   ne   viendront **peut-être** pas.*
     they NEG will:come maybe   NEG
     'They probably won't come.'

   b. *Il   n'est   **peut-être** pas intelligent, mais il   est consciencieux.*
     he NEG:is probably NEG intelligent but   he is   conscientious
     'He probably isn't intelligent, but he is conscientious.'
     (*Shogakukan Dictionnaire français-japonais*; our glosses and translations)

(23) a. *It's a hot day, **but?***
   b. *I didn't do it **but**.*   (Richards 2005, 35; our emphasis)

The generalization in (17) may apply to different languages to different degrees: it is more applicable to the languages that have a more definite position that directly follows the tensed verb group, whereas languages not equipped with such a definite post-tensed-verb-group position are not apt to develop (central members of) modal/final particles.[15] Instead, the utterance-final position may be somehow exploitable for (peripheral) intersubjectivity marking in most languages. The position that directly follows the tensed verb group in the sentence is structurally definite in German and Japanese with a marked development of modal/final particles. In French, with a relative underdevelopment of modal particles, the position is somewhat ambiguous to the extent that it mostly corresponds to the final, but sometimes to the internal position. In English, the internal position (medial position) itself is indefinite, fluctuating between the position directly preceding the negated auxiliary or tensed verb and that directly following the first auxiliary. Except for the utterance-final position, English seems to lack a sentential position structurally definite enough for modal particle development.

5.   Conclusion

The present article has proposed a possible cross-linguistic model for the development of modal/final particles from discourse markers. Some discourse markers in German, French, and Japanese have come to serve as modal particles by developing (inter)subjective meanings in a limited sentential position: the middle field in German and the final or internal position in French, and the final position in Japanese. Although those modal particle positions appear to differ, they are all describable as the one that directly follows a "tensed verb group" which consists of either one tensed verbal in its simplest form or one tensed and (an)other verbal(s) in its more complex forms. The meanings of those modal particles may be viewed

---

15.   See Valdmets (this volume) for a related discussion.

as having developed in later stages of semantic change through "subjectification" and/or "intersubjectification" (Traugott 2003) along with a restriction in sentential position.

The article has also demonstrated that there is another possible position of modal particles: utterance-final position. It is occupied by utterance-final discourse markers, or what can be termed peripheral members of modal particles such as German *ja* and *oder* and English *right* and *innit*. They can also serve to express intersubjective meanings like request for confirmation, urgency of the invitation, and so forth.

The two positions for modal particles, the one directly following the tensed verb group and the utterance-final position, merge together in languages like Japanese, split into the middle and final fields in languages like German, and overlap more frequently but are more or less separable from each other in languages like French. In any case, the languages coincide in utilizing the two syntactically restricted positions for marking certain (inter)subjective meanings. Yet, it is not clear what accounts for those common features, what it signifies in notional and functional terms for a discourse marker to directly follow the tensed verb group, and what cognitive status a discourse marker achieves by being an utterance-final element. An elucidation of the possible notional, functional, and cognitive motivations must be one of the key topics of further research.

Abbreviations

ACC	accusative	IMP	imperative
COP	copula	MP	modal particle
DAT	dative	NOM	nominative
DM	discourse marker	PAST	past tense
FN	formal noun	PERF	perfect
FP	final particle	TOP	topic

References

Abraham, Werner. 1991. "The Grammaticization of the German Modal Particles." In *Approaches to Grammaticalization, vol. II*, ed. by Elizabeth Closs Traugott and Bernd Heine, 331–380. Amsterdam/Philadelphia: John Benjamins.

Aijmer, Karin. 1986. "Why is *actually* so popular in spoken English?" In *English in Speech and Writing: a Symposium*, ed. by Gunnel Tottie and Ingegard Bäcklund, 119–129. Uppsala: Almqvist and Wiksell.

Brinton, Laurel J. 1996. *Pragmatic Markers in English: Grammaticalization and Discourse Functions*. Berlin and New York: Mouton de Gruyter.

Degand, Liesbeth and Benjamin Fagard. 2011. "*Alors* between Discourse and Grammar: The Role of Syntactic Position." *Functions of Language* 18: 29–56.

Diewald, Gabriele. 2006. "Discourse Particles and Modal Particles as Grammatical Elements." In *Approaches to Discourse Particles*, ed. by Kerstin Fischer, 403–425. Amsterdam: Elsevier.

Fischer, Kerstin. 2007. "Grounding and common ground: Modal particles and their translation equivalents." In *Lexical Markers of Common Grounds*, ed. by Anita Fetzer and Kerstin Fischer, 47–66. Amsterdam: Elsevier.

Franckel, Jean-Jacques. 1989. "*Etude de quelques marqueurs aspectuels du français*." Langue et cultures 21. Genève: Librairie Droz.

Fujiwara, Yoichi. 1993. "Nihongo bunkoozoo (koobun) joo no bunmatsushi [Final particles in Japanese sentential structures (constructions)]." In *Gengo Ruikeiron to Bunmatsushi* [Linguistic typology and final particles], ed. by Yoichi Fujiwara, 171–187. Tokyo: Miyaishoten.

Hagiwara, Takae. 2012. *"Dakara" no Goyooron: Tekusuto Kooseiteki Kinoo kara Taijin Kankeiteki Kinoo e* [The pragmatics of "dakara": from textual function to interpersonal function]. Tokyo: Koko Shuppan.

Hansen, Maj-Britt Mosegaard. 1997. "*Alors* and *Donc* in Spoken French: A Reanalysis." *Journal of Pragmatics* 28, 153–187.

Hansen, Maj-Britt Mosegaard. 1998. *The Function of Discourse Particles: A Study with Special Reference to Spoken Standard French*. Amsterdam/Philadelphia: John Benjamins.

Hybertie, Charlotte. 1996. *La conséquence en français*. Paris: Ophrys.

Izutsu, Katsunobu and Mitsuko Narita Izutsu. 2008. "A Cognitive Mechanism of Mirative Connectives." *Lingua Posnaniensis* 50: 127–142.

Izutsu, Mitsuko Narita and Katsunobu Izutsu. 2010. "*Okashii sho soshite*: Hokkaidoo no hanashi kotoba de mochiirareru *soshite* no imi kinoo teki hoogen tokusei [*Strange, and*: dialectal characteristics of *soshite* used in the Hokkaido speech]." *Proceedings of the 25th Japanese Association of Sociolinguistic Sciences*, 78–81.

Izutsu, Mitsuko Narita and Katsunobu Izutsu. Forthcoming a. "Truncation and Backshift: Two Pathways to Sentence-Final Coordinating Conjunctions." *Journal of Historical Pragmatics* 15.1.

Izutsu, Mitsuko Narita and Katsunobu Izutsu. Forthcoming b. "'Leap' or 'Continuum'?: Grammaticalization Pathways from Conjunctions to Sentence-final Particles." *Language and the Creative Mind: Selected Papers from the 11th Conceptual Structure, Discourse, and Language Conference*.

Kawashima, Atsuo. 1987. "Japanische Satzschlußpartikeln und ihre Entsprechungen im Deutschen." In *Deutsch und Japanisch im Kontrast, Band 4: Syntaktisch-semantische Kontraste*, ed. by Tohru Kaneko and Gerhard Stickel, 415–452. Heidelberg: Groos.

Matsumura, Akira (ed.). 1969. *Kotengo Gendaigo Joshi Jodooshi Shoosetsu* [A detailed explanation of particles and auxiliaries]. Tokyo: Gakutosha.

Mulder, Jean, and Sandra A. Thompson. 2008. "The Grammaticization of *But* as a Final Particle in English Conversation." In *Crosslinguistic Studies of Clause Combining: The Multifunctionality of Conjunction*, ed. by Ritva Laury, 179–204. Amsterdam/Philadelphia: John Benjamins.

Ohori, Toshio. 1996. "Remarks on Suspended Clauses: A Contribution to Japanese Phraseology." In *Essays in Semantics and Pragmatics: In Honor of Charles J. Fillmore*, ed. by Masayoshi Shibatani and Sandra A. Thompson, 201–218. Amsterdam/Philadelphia: John Benjamins.

Quirk, Randolph, Sidney Greenbaum, Geoffrey Leech, and Jan Svartvik. 1985. *A Comprehensive Grammar of the English Language*. London: Longman.

Richards, Kel. 2005. *Word Map: What Words are Used Where in Australia*. Sydney: ABC Books.

Sagerer, Gerhard, Hans-Jürgen Eikmeyer, and Gert Rickheit. 1994 "Wir Bauen Jetzt ein Flugzeug. Konstruieren im Dialog. Arbeitsmaterialien." Technical Report, SFB 360 Situierte künstliche Kommunikatoren, University of Bielefeld.

Sakuma, Kanae. 1952. *Gendai Nihongohoo no Kenkyuu* [A study of present-day Japanese grammar]. Tokyo: Koseikaku.

Shinzato, Rumiko. 2006. "Subjectivity, Intersubjectivity, and Grammaticalization." In *Emotive Communication in Japanese*, ed. by Satoko Suzuki, 15–33. Amsterdam/Philadelphia: John Benjamins.

Suzuki, Hideo. 1976. "Gendai nihongo niokeru shuujoshi no hataraki to sono soogo shoosetsu nitsuite [The function and ordering of sentence-final particles in present-day Japanese]." *Kokugo to Kokubungaku*, November volume: 58–70.

Traugott, Elizabeth Closs. 2003. "From Subjectification to Intersubjectification." In *Motives for Language Change*, ed. by Raymond Hickey, 124–139. Cambridge: Cambridge University Press.

Traugott, Elizabeth Closs. 2011. "*He...withdrew, disconcerted and offended, no doubt; but surely it was not my fault*. On the Function of Adverbs of Certainty at the Left and Right Peripheries of the Clause." Special Lecture, Japan Pragmatic Association, Kyoto, March 6.

Traugott, Elizabeth Closs and Richard B. Dasher. 2002. *Regularity in Semantic Change*. Cambridge: Cambridge University Press.

Waltereit, Richard. 2001. "Modal Particles and their Functional Equivalents: A Speech-Act-Theoretic Approaches." *Journal of Pragmatics* 33, 1391–1417.

Waltereit, Richard, and Ulrick Detges. 2007. "Different Functions, Different Histories: Modal Particles and Discourse Markers from a Diachronic Point of View." *Catalan Journal of Linguistics* 6: 61–80.

Watts, Richard. J. 2003. *Politeness*. Cambridge: Cambridge University Press.

Weydt, Harald. 1969. *Abtönungspartikel*. Bad Homburg: Gehlen.

Index

A

aber 16, 24, 25, 27, 29, 31, 34, 37, 43, 56, 70, 76, 84, 140
Abtönungspartikel 18, 27, 28, 32, 43, 45, 159–161, 169, 173, 235
adverbial 5, 11, 22, 23, 37–39, 41, 53, 54, 65–66, 90, 91, 105, 109, 113–119, 121, 122, 124–127, 143, 151, 156, 190, 193, 200, 219 *see also* conjunctional adverb, manner adverb, modal adverb, temporal-aspectual adverb
adversativity 96, 111, 122
alltså 10, 47, 51–74, 77–79, 81, 82, 84, 86, 208
alors 188, 220–222, 229, 234
also 10, 25, 47, 51, 52–75, 78, 79, 81, 84, 85

B

backchecking 12, 13, 163, 165, 170–172, 183, 185–188
backgrounding 98–100, 102
backshift 224, 227, 231, 234

C

Catalan 3, 4, 9, 13, 14, 18, 27, 154, 156, 187, 190–193, 197, 200, 208, 213–215
categorization 1–4, 7, 9, 12–14, 16–21, 26, 40–42, 104, 108, 161, 212, 213
change
    semantic change 13, 113, 114, 131, 190, 198, 215, 222, 233, 235
    syntactic change 115, 210, 222
(és) clar 14, 200–202, 204, 210–213
collocation 73, 74, 92, 102
communication
    dialogic communication 6, 23, 26, 166, 177, 180

emotive communication 14, 16, 223–225, 229, 235
communicative domain 26, 32, 41, 112
communicative function 10, 33, 81,
complementizer 170, 204, 210
conceptualization 12, 133, 134, 141, 149–151, 156–158, 160
conceptual space 47, 79–82
concession 11, 23, 90, 96, 192, 196, 201
conjunction 6, 9, 11, 29, 30, 32, 34, 35, 37, 38, 64, 69, 70, 76, 81, 96, 141, 152, 192–194, 196, 201, 204–206, 209, 210, 228, 231, 234
conjunctional adverb 9, 52-54, 56, 63–66,
connective 5, 6, 9, 11, 14, 19, 22–24, 26, 27, 34, 36, 38, 52, 54, 94, 103, 105, 127, 192, 195, 197, 202, 209–211, 221, 223, 224, 226
    parenthetical connective 13, 193, 194, 196, 208, 209
    pragmatic connective 14, 196, 197, 202, 204, 209, 211
construction 3, 6, 7, 10, 16–18, 26, 40, 41, 44, 47–52, 58, 65, 70, 73–75, 77–80, 82, 84, 85, 106, 160, 190, 200, 206, 207, 210, 211, 213, 215, 234
    (radical) construction grammar 10, 16, 17, 44, 47–52, 73, 74, 79, 80, 82, 84, 85, 160, 213
context
    bridging context 114, 180
    context-adjusting 102
    switch context 114, 115
corpus data 4, 11, 128
cross-linguistic comparison 14, 15, 47, 49, 58–63, 78–82, 101, 154–156, 219–227

D

dakara 223, 224, 234
dialogic structure 34, 40 *see also* dialogic communication
direct questions 165, 187
doch 16, 27, 31, 37, 43, 66, 84, 136, 139, 140, 155, 156, 161, 219, 220
donc 155, 156, 220–222, 229, 234

E

emphatic uses 11, 94, 95, 111, 123, 125, 187, 200, 207, 221, 229
English 4, 7, 16–18, 22, 35–37, 41, 44, 45, 50, 53, 62, 80, 84, 86, 89, 91–93, 102–107, 110, 112, 116, 124, 129–131, 137, 154, 156, 159, 171, 177, 193, 195, 210, 213, 214, 217–219, 221, 224, 228, 230–235
Erinnerungsfrage 171
és que 14, 192, 201, 204–207, 210–212
Estonian 3, 4, 9, 11, 12, 18, 45, 107–109, 111–113, 115, 116, 121, 124–126, 128, 130, 131

F

position
    final position 14, 52, 54, 68–70, 72, 80, 198, 200, 209–211, 217, 218, 222–224, 226, 227, 229–233
    fixed position 23, 35, 115, 222, 224, 226
    non-initial position 34, 67, 78, 101, 171, 187, 200 *see also* middle field
    sentence-internal position 3, 14, 89, 217, 218, 222, 224–227, 230–232 *see also* middle field

fixed expression 73, 80, 119, 200, 204, 205, 209, 210, 218, 223
foregrounding 93, 98,
form-meaning pairs 47, 74, 82
French 3, 4, 9, 12–14, 27, 44, 80, 91, 103, 133, 134, 154–158, 163–169, 171, 174, 182, 184–189, 217–224, 226–234
functional approach 3, 6, 8–11, 20, 24–26, 28, 35, 39, 41, 42, 77–79, 86, 89–82, 109, 110, 164, 169, 183–185, 187, 198, 205, 212

G
German 3, 4, 7–10, 12, 14–17, 19–23, 25, 27–30, 32–37, 39–41, 43–45, 47, 51–59, 61–66, 68–71, 73, 74, 78–84, 89, 99, 102, 103, 129, 133, 134, 136, 138, 139, 141, 142, 154–161, 168, 169, 171, 173, 189, 193, 195, 208, 210, 214, 217–224, 226–233
grammatical category 3, 8, 21, 32, 36, 41, 183, 220, 230
grammaticalization 14, 16, 17, 21, 27, 28, 39–44, 84, 86, 87, 90, 91, 102, 107, 113, 114, 128–130, 143, 156, 159, 189, 192, 196, 198, 211, 218–220, 222, 228, 233–235
granularity 9, 12, 133, 134, 141, 145–149, 151–153, 156–158

H
heterosemy 20, 39, 144 see also polysemy
hoide 225–227, 231
home/dona 14, 192, 197–199, 209–211

I
idiomaticity 73, 74, 84
illocutionary domain 3, 31, 34, 186–188
illocutionary force 25, 43, 135, 155, 186, 221, 229
illocutionary functions 7, 33, 187, 202, 206
illocutionary type 31, 195
indexical function 2, 10, 14, 15, 24, 26, 34–36, 110,
information status 12, 22, 49, 76, 80, 93, 96, 98–100, 102, 103, 116, 118, 161, 163–165, 169, 171–178, 183–188

intercategoriality 21, 28, 36, 37, 39–41
interjection 5, 12–14, 22, 25, 48, 77, 163, 165, 166, 172–184, 192, 194, 196, 200, 201, 208–211, 213, 214, 219,
intonation (prosody) 5, 13, 42, 54, 58–52, 64, 67, 72, 73, 76, 82, 83, 90, 112, 135, 160, 161, 170, 179, 193, 196, 212, 215, 224, 226
Italian (North-Western) 163–190

J
ja 16, 20, 21, 25, 27, 28, 30, 31, 34, 35, 37, 43, 75–78, 84, 135–140, 153, 160, 161, 173, 174, 195, 210, 219, 228–230, 233
Japanese 3, 4, 9, 14, 112, 217, 218, 223, 224, 226–235

L
language-specific category 7, 19–21, 26, 35, 40–42, 79, 82, 154, 155,
left periphery 35, 198, 208, 209, 222
linguistic classification 2, 4–15, 19–32, 34, 35, 38, 40–42

M
manner adverb 113, 121, 124, 200, 202
marker
    conclusive marker 13
    confirmative marker 173, 174, 183
    discourse marker 5, 10, 17, 19, 20, 22, 23, 37, 38, 44, 45, 54, 84–86, 89, 90, 92–96, 101–103, 108, 113, 163, 196, 204, 210, 211, 218, 220, 221, 223–225, 230, 233
    hesitation marker 5, 6, 9, 25, 35, 56, 62, 70, 71, 73, 76–78, 153
    meta-discursive marker 166
    pragmatic marker 5, 11, 15, 23, 24, 26, 34, 83, 85, 91, 105, 107–122, 124, 126–128, 163, 164, 169, 178, 189–191, 211–215
    reformulation marker 56
    repair marker 56, 62, 71
    text-connective marker 19

middle field 7, 11, 14, 15, 30, 31, 35, 39, 40, 52–54, 56, 63, 65–69, 71, 76, 128, 135–137, 142, 144, 150, 155, 157, 208, 218–220, 227, 232
modality
    epistemic modality 7, 81, 89, 91, 110, 111, 119, 120, 122, 128, 129, 131, 188, 204
    modal adverb 11, 13, 30, 89–91, 104, 142, 143, 146, 147, 192, 196, 208, 209
    see also particle (modal)
multifunctionality 1, 4, 13, 35, 41, 81, 91, 92, 102, 113, 234 see also polyfunctionality

O
of course 11, 22, 89–103, 105–108, 111, 116–118, 128, 154, 200–204, 207

P
parenthetical 13, 100, 170, 193–197, 202, 204, 209–212, 215
particle
    final particle 14, 226, 233, 234
    modal particle 3, 10, 17, 19–21, 29, 31, 33, 34, 37–39, 44, 47, 49, 51, 56, 67, 68, 78, 80–82, 89–93, 96, 97, 100–103, 105, 108, 113, 129, 133, 134, 141, 148–150, 157, 205, 206, 211–213, 217–220, 222, 227, 228, 230, 232, 233
    scalar particle 27, 29, 31, 152, 219
    situative particle 137, 140, 146, 148, 152, 153
polyfunctionality 20, 21, 50, 192, 196, 197, 199, 200, 211 see also multifunctionality
polysemy 16, 44, 84, 85, 113, 144, 189, 191, 210 see also heterosemy
pragmatic pretext 33,
prefield 53–56, 58, 59, 61, 69, 71, 76, 77
propositional meaning 6, 110, 112, 127, 152, 192, 195, 196, 204
    propositional content 3, 6, 33, 66, 93, 113, 127, 165, 174, 176, 177, 180, 181, 183, 186, 228

propositional domain 22–24,
    26, 34, 35,
prosodic break 83, 226 *see also*
    intonation
prototypicality 12–14, 28, 40,
    133–135, 141–146, 148, 149, 151,
    156–158
prototype 2, 3, 12, 139, 142–146,
    150, 157–159

R
reactive turn 34
relational function 24
right periphery 11, 112, 128, 170,
    222, 229

S
semantic space 79
sentence
    integration into the sen-
        tence 11, 12, 20, 22, 23, 26,
        30, 31, 35, 52–54, 56, 58,
        61–65, 67, 68, 70–72, 76,
        78, 80, 101, 135, 150, 170,
        195, 205

cleft sentence 170
    sentence type 31
sikasi 225–227, 231
sosite 224–227, 231
Spanish 7, 13, 18, 98, 164, 166,
    179, 182, 184, 187, 189, 190, 193,
    199, 200, 210, 212–214, 218
Swedish 3, 4, 10, 16, 27, 47, 51–55,
    57–59, 61–72, 74, 77–80, 82–84,
    86, 89, 92, 93, 95, 102–106, 115,
    116, 208, 219

T
TAM 12, 45, 163, 167, 174, 175,
    178, 183, 184
temporal-aspectual adverb 163,
    165
tensed verb group 217, 218,
    227–233
topic continuity 58
topological integration 22, 135,
    170–172, 195
translation 7, 11, 16, 28, 32, 53, 54,
    83–85, 92, 93, 95, 98, 102, 105,
    133, 134, 161, 225, 234

truncation 224, 227, 234

U
unintegrated 22, 56, 58, 68,
    71, 74
universal category 4, 20, 35, 36,
    79, 80, 103
uptake 56, 78

V
V-final 219, 230
V-second 219, 228

W
word order 108, 112, 115, 122, 128

Y
yeah 50, 51, 200, 201, 223